D0850691

THE APPLICATION
OF SOCIAL PSYCHOLOGY
TO CLINICAL PRACTICE

THE SERIES IN CLINICAL AND COMMUNITY PSYCHOLOGY

CONSULTING EDITORS:

CHARLES D. SPIELBERGER and IRWIN G. SARASON

Becker	• Depression: Theory and Research
Brehm	• The Application of Social Psychology to Clinical Practice
Endler and Magnusson	• Interactional Psychology and Personality
Friedman and Katz	• The Psychology of Depression: Contemporary Theory and Research
Klopfer and Reed	• Problems in Psychotherapy: An Eclectic Approach
Reitan and Davison	• Clinical Neuropsychology: Current Status and Applications
Spielberger and Sarason	• Stress and Anxiety, volume 1
Sarason and Spielberger	• Stress and Anxiety, volume 2
Ulmer	• On the Development of a Token Economy Mental Hospital Treatment Program

IN PREPARATION

Averill	• Patterns in Psychological Thought: Readings in Historical and Contemporary Texts
Bermant, Kelman, and Warwick	• The Ethics of Social Intervention
Cattell and Dreger	• Handbook of Modern Personality Theory
Cohen and Mirsky	• Biology and Psychopathology
Janisse	• A Psychological Survey of Pupillometry
Kissen	• From Group Dynamics to Group Psychoanalysis: Therapeutic Application of Group Dynamic Understanding
London	• Strategies of Personality Research
Olweus	• Aggression in the Schools
Sarason and Spielberger	• Stress and Anxiety, volume 3
Spielberger and Sarason	• Stress and Anxiety, volume 4
Spielberger and Diaz-Guerrero	• Crosscultural Research on Anxiety

THE APPLICATION OF SOCIAL PSYCHOLOGY TO CLINICAL PRACTICE

SHARON S. BREHM

The University of Kansas

HEMISPHERE PUBLISHING CORPORATION
Washington   London

A HALSTED PRESS BOOK

JOHN WILEY & SONS

New York   London   Sydney   Toronto

Hemisphere Publishing Corporation
1025 Vermont Ave., N.W., Washington, D.C. 20005

Distributed solely by Halsted Press, a Division of John Wiley & Sons, Inc.,
New York.

1 2 3 4 5 6 7 8 9 0   MAMA   7 8 4 3 2 1 0 9 8 7 6

Library of Congress Cataloging in Publication Data
Brehm, Sharon S
    The application of social psychology to clinical
practice.

    (The Series in clinical psychology)
    Includes bibliographies and indexes.
    1. Psychotherapy. 2. Social psychology.
3. Personality. I. Title. [DNLM: 1. Psychology,
Social. 2. Psychology, Clinical. WM100 B834a]
RC480.B68   616.8'914   75-38684
ISBN 0-470-15215-X

Printed in the United States of America

"Faith" is a fine invention
When Gentlemen can *see*—
But *Microscopes* are prudent
In an Emergency.

Emily Dickinson

CONTENTS

ACKNOWLEDGMENTS

In many ways, I have been living with and working on this book for the last eight years. Through a particular combination of circumstances, some personal, some professional, I have been constantly exposed to the possibility of applying social psychology to clinical practice. My husband, Jack Brehm, bears a large share of the responsibility for this exposure. It was impossible not to begin to apply social psychological principles to clinical endeavors when virtually every night at home there would be descriptions of clinical episodes (from me) intermingled with social psychological interpretations (from him). Both of us have learned from these discussions, and this book can be considered the logical outcome of our conversations.

In support of this personal factor, a tremendously stimulating professional context has been available to me. My introduction to graduate level psychology occurred in the clinical program of the Department of Social Relations at Harvard, where the atmosphere welcomed cross-disciplinary thinking. My later experiences as a graduate student at Duke greatly amplified this initial orientation. The two professors who had the most impact on me during graduate school were both highly sympathetic to social psychology's usefulness to clinical work. Philip Costanzo, a member of the Duke clinical faculty, received his training from Marvin Shaw, a social psychologist, and with Shaw has written a book on theories in social psychology. Robert Carson, as will be noted later in this text, had already begun the process of integrating social and clinical approaches in his book *Interaction Concepts of Personality*. It was very easy to discuss clinical matters in social terms with both of these men, and, again, it was almost impossible not to. This book stands as an example of the impact that their teaching has had on me.

I have thus been very fortunate in having such congenial personal and professional influences. I have also been very fortunate to have had a great deal of day-to-day help and support during the time I was writing this book. The vast majority of the writing took place during my year at Virginia Polytechnic Institute and State University, and I wish to thank Charles Noblin, Chairman of the Department of Psychology, for his encouragement and provision of facilities. In addition, I am very grateful to those—Judith Conger, Edward E. Jones, Robert Wicklund, and Philip Worchel—who were kind enough to read and comment on various chapters.

Finally, I wish to indicate my special appreciation of the assistance given me by my husband. He did not darn my socks, nor type my manuscript; he did read many of the chapters, give me invaluable comments, and tolerate my obsession. I thank him for all of this.

Sharon S. Brehm

THE APPLICATION
OF SOCIAL PSYCHOLOGY
TO CLINICAL PRACTICE

CHAPTER ONE

INTRODUCTION

Perusal of the current state of affairs in clinical psychology suggests a predicament not unlike that of Ulysses being caught between the perils of Scylla and Charybdis. Clinical psychologists are torn between two opposing models of understanding and analyzing human functioning, neither one of which adequately meets their professional, intellectual, and personal needs. The oldest and perhaps still predominant model is that of psychoanalysis, either in its classical expression by Freud or in its more modern version as propounded by "ego psychologists" such as Erik Erikson. The psychoanalytic model has vast intellectual appeal with its virtuoso complexity and universalistic claims to complete understanding of personality structure. It lacks, however, the rigorous experimental validation that graduates of doctoral programs come to expect, and it has a certain professional drawback, given its domination, in the applied field, by psychiatrists and their control of analytic institutes and training programs. If clinical psychology could bring nothing more to clinical practice than psychoanalytic methods and the psychoanalytic view of human functioning, then as a profession it would be at worst second-rate and at best redundant.

Some of these difficulties with psychoanalysis may account for the enthusiasm that clinical strategies based on learning theories have aroused among some clinical psychologists. Behavior modification as a clinical approach has the distinct advantages of having more adequate experimental validation and of representing a clear-cut psychological, as opposed to psychiatric, speciality. However, many psychologists are less than happy about adopting a view of human functioning that in its most coherent theoretical form, i.e.,

1

Skinnerian operant conditioning, rejects the very complexity and richness of personality that probably first attracted a large number of psychologists to clinical work.

This description of the shipwrecked state of clinical psychology should, of course, not be overdrawn. Experimental validation of psychoanalytic principles is certainly possible and would seem especially amenable to the research training and interests of clinical psychologists (see, for example, Sarnoff, 1971). Behavior modification is no doubt still in its infancy, and the thinking of some leading figures (e.g., Bandura, 1969; Lazarus, 1971) portends the possibility of an increasingly complex view of human functioning. In addition, behavior modifiers are becoming less and less theoretically dogmatic (London, 1972), and their techniques may become more and more compatible with a variety of theoretical perspectives.

Be that as it may, it still seems that for a great many clinicians the time is propitious for the development of an alternative model of human functioning, a model that would avoid the dilemma of Scylla and Charybdis by being in itself scientifically respectable, intellectually stimulating, personally satisfying, and given to specific expertise by psychologists. The purpose of this book is to elucidate such an alternative model.

SOCIAL PSYCHOLOGY AS AN ALTERNATIVE MODEL

The primary thesis of this undertaking is quite simple: that a viable alternative model exists in the literature of social psychology and that a significant number of clinicians would find this model helpful if they were familiar with the theories and findings of social psychology. There have been others who have shared this idea, most notably Jerome Frank (1961/1973) in *Persuasion and Healing,* Goldstein, Heller, and Sechrest (1966) in *Psychotherapy and the Psychology of Behavior Change,* and Robert Carson (1969) in *Interaction Concepts of Personality.* This book differs from these previous works in that somewhat different theories of social psychology will be focused on and a more inclusive utilization of these theories will be advocated. Anyone interested in the content of the present book should, however, also consult these other sources.

Simple as the idea behind this book is, it could stand some clarification. What, for instance, is meant by that grand and nicely ambiguous phrase "model of human functioning"? Skinner and Freud purport to have all-encompassing understandings of human functioning; does social psychology claim such an all-inclusive understanding? These are important questions to be answered prior to working with the material presented here.

"Model of human functioning" is taken to mean one's general perspective when approaching another human being. In such an endeavor, we are all blind men trying to decipher an elephant. Our perspectives guide and determine the nature of our understanding. Someone whose perspective is geared to psychoanalytic ways of thinking will see "ego deficiencies" and "eruptions of primary process." Upon viewing the same person with the same behavior, the behavior modifier of a Skinnerian bent will see reinforcement of "sick behavior" and lack of reinforcement of "well behavior." If a clinician adopts the model proposed in this book, he might see "attribution problems" and "an arousal of reactance." All of this, of course, might be purely an academic exercise, if not for the fact that the problems clinicians see determine their interventions to modify these problems. And, needless to say, our interventions, are rather crucial to our clients.

It should be understood, however, that while social psychology does have a general model, a general perspective, to offer, it does not have the universal inclusiveness claimed by Freud and Skinner. Social psychology, as the following pages will show, is made up of a number of mini-theories, each with its particular province in human functioning. Some of these mini-theories will be useful with some clients, while others will be useful for other clients.

A further clarification is needed for readers who are already familiar with some elements of social psychology. Social psychology is at present more a designation of professional identification than a specific area of scientific endeavor. Psychologists with interests varying from group processes to mathematical models identify themselves as social psychologists. This book does not attempt to cover all of social psychology (a review of the entire field is best found in the five-volume *Handbook of Social Psychology*, Lindzey & Aronson, 1968). The present book will explicate and apply to clinical practice only those theories that (1) the author has knowledge of and preference for, (2) seem most relevant to clinical practice, and (3) deal with intrapsychic functioning as a process.

The last criterion means in practical terms that the extensive social psychological research on group processes that would be highly applicable to group therapy will not be discussed. Only social psychological theories concerning processes that occur within the individual (although these processes may typically be stimulated by events occuring external to the individual, especially social events) will be examined. This focus on intrapsychic functioning as process denotes a theoretical and methodological perspective that is critical to the present writings.

PERSONALITY AS PROCESS

The distinction and controversy between state and trait models of personality have a lengthy if not always illuminating history. A trait approach to personality is exemplified by a long line of psychologists who assessed personality through the measurement of various traits believed to be characteristic of a person (e.g., Taylor, Murray, McClelland, Rotter). Closely associated with the measurement of traits has been an interest in individual differences. Roughly, this approach to personality seeks to determine what type of person the individual under consideration is and then to compare the individual to other individuals. Every student of psychology has surely been inundated with studies of high anxious people versus low anxious people, high need achievers versus low need achievers, and, more recently, internals ("I's") versus externals ("E's"). Within the trait approach to personality, a study, for example, of high versus low anxious *people* is undertaken to understand how a type of person behaves. By definition, the experimenter does not induce this anxiety; it is a characteristic of the person entering the experimental setting.

A state or situational approach to personality reflects considerable differences in perspective and methodology. In a study of high versus low anxiety *states,* the experimenter arranges certain elements of the person's environment in order to elicit the desired level of anxiety. Through the utilization of random assignment to experimental conditions, all subjects are treated alike and individual differences existing prior to the experiment are ignored. This type of investigation is undertaken to understand the *process* of anxiety, a process that is deemed to be applicable to all people and distinct, at least theoretically, from the unique characteristics of the individual.

The areas of social psychology discussed in this book may best be thought of as constituting a state or process approach to personality. This approach seeks not to ascertain personality traits, or types, or structures, but to understand the operation of certain intrapsychic processes. The processes are intrapsychic because they occur within the individual. They may be stimulated by environmental events, especially events in the person's social environment, but their locus of operation is within the individual.

It should thus be noted that while the theories and findings of social psychology to be explicated here deal with intrapsychic processes, they are not based on individual differences. Consistent with a process approach to personality, the social psychologist manipulates the experimental environment in such a fashion as to induce the operation of certain psychological processes. Individuals are not measured according to traits they possess prior to the experiment and are not compared to other individuals on such traits. Rather, individuals are exposed to certain environmental stimuli to induce psychological processes in them and then compared to other indivudals in whom other psychological processes are induced. It is a fundamental principle of social psychology that such manipulations of the environment and measurement of the resultant behavior establish a theoretical understanding of cause and effect that can be applied to all individuals.

At first, this approach to personality may seem somewhat strange to the clinician. Clinicians typically are very concerned with and sensitive to individual differences. They may be tempted to exclaim, "But you can't treat Mrs. X the same way as Mrs. Y." In fact, a sophisticated understanding of the clinical application of the principles of social psychology does not lead to homogeneous clinical treatment.

On this issue, the current model is much like the older models of psychoanalysis and behavior modification. Experimental social psychology, psychoanalysis, and behavior modification all offer statements of process:

1. People tend to reduce dissonance.
2. Reaction formation can serve as a defense against ego-alien impulses.
3. Behavior that is reinforced will tend to occur more frequently than behavior that is not reinforced.

In each case, the general principle then becomes modified by events specific to the individual.

1. Coming to therapy for Mrs. X is dissonant with drinking heavily at home. Coming to therapy for Mrs. Y is dissonant with fighting with her husband but not with drinking heavily at home.
2. Mrs. X finds anger unacceptable. Mrs. Y finds sexuality unacceptable.
3. Social attention is a potent reinforcer for Mrs. X. Food is a potent reinforcer for Mrs. Y.

Such individual differences modify application of the general principle, and it is precisely this modification that offers an opportunity for the exercise of clinical skills. Basic theory and research can establish general principles, but clinical skill will always be needed to provide the individual tailoring. Throughout this book, it will be advocated that this tailoring be based on the clinician's knowledge of the individual client rather than on the client's score on some individual difference measure. Individual difference research that has been conducted on the theories to be examined will be discussed, but, as will be seen, this research does not have much to offer in the way of clinical application.

METHODOLOGICAL ISSUES

The Issue of Deception

Those who are already committed to a general perspective in psychotherapy will probably find the theories and therapeutic strategies explicated in this book less compelling than those therapists not so committed. However, every therapist regardless of his theoretical orientation should be aware of certain methodological issues that can and should be raised concerning the empirical evidence that has been generated by the social psychologists whose work will be considered here.

Because social psychology deals with processes induced in individuals, instead of examining inherent traits, much of social psychological research involves deception. That is, subjects in experiments are misled about the purposes of the experiment and frequently are not told the truth about what is really occurring in the experiment.

For example, subjects in a classic experiment (Festinger & Carlsmith, 1959) generated from principles of the theory of cognitive dissonance (Festinger, 1957) were first induced to perform a boring task. They were requested to misinform the "next subject" (actually a confederate of the experimenters) about the nature of the task they had completed and the "next subject" was due to perform. They were asked to inform the "next subject" that the task was enjoyable (instead of honestly saying how boring it was). Some subjects were offered $1.00 to do this, while other subjects were offered $20.00 to do this (and to agree to be on call to do it in the future). Now, the deceptions in this experiment were several: subjects were told that the experimental confederate was another subject; subjects were promised $1.00 or $20.00 to do something when, in fact, at the end of the experiment all subjects returned the money; and subjects were not told that the concern of the experimenters was how the varied incentives to lie about the actual nature of the task would affect the subject's attitude toward that task after he had lied. (Details concerning the theoretical significance of this and other dissonance experiments can be found in Chapters Five through Seven.)

This use of deception is distasteful to many people, who consider it unethical to misinform subjects this way, although, interestingly enough, researchers seem to find it more distasteful than their potential subjects (Sullivan & Deiker, 1973). In any case, the issue of deception is not easily resolved. The value of the specific research question must be weighed against the specific type of deception that is to be used. These matters have to be weighed by individual researchers as well as by ethics committees on which both researchers and laymen are often represented. The dilemma is not unique to psychological research. In medical research, the discomfort of the subject must be weighed against the importance of the research. In medical research, however, one is generally concerned only about the physiological welfare of the subject (perhaps too narrow a concern); in psychological research utilizing deception, one is concerned about the subject's psychological welfare.

However the issue of deception is resolved by an individual researcher for an individual experiment, the general purposes of deception should be clear. First, there is the problem of helpful subjects. Subjects tend to want to help the experimenter. If they know the purpose of the experiment, they may, wittingly or unwittingly, act in such a way as to confirm the hypothesis of the experimenter. It is thus very important for subjects not to know the experimenter's hypothesis, and one way to reduce the likelihood that subjects will figure out the hypothesis is to use deception. After the experiment is over, it is equally important that the subject be told in full about the experimenter's hypothesis and about what was really happening in the experiment. During this "debriefing," the nature of and need for any deceptions used should be explained to the subject.

Second, there is the necessity for subjects in an experiment to act as "naturally" as possible in a situation that seems as "real" as possible. Of course, subjects are aware that they are in an experiment and this realization never goes away completely, but through the use of skillful experimental presentations, usually involving deception, subjects can be presented with a situation that seems so real, is so full of impact, that they make responses not unlike the responses they would make to such situations in the real world.

Some psychologists, disturbed by the use of deception, have suggested role-playing as an alternative to deception. For example, in the Festinger and Carlsmith study (1959) role-playing instructions would have been, "Act as though you were lying to someone about the task they are to perform." The problem with role-playing is that role-playing is just that, role-playing. Our behavior may well be different when we pretend we are in a certain situation than when we believe we are really in that situation. The nature of role-playing behavior itself is a most interesting area for psychological research, but if one is interested in how people really behave, rather than in how they think they would or should behave, the creation of a convincingly real situation is imperative.

The Statistical Question

Another aspect of the typical experiment in social psychology that may be of issue to the clinician is that of statistical treatment of the subject's responses. Subjects are conducted through an experiment individually or in groups. Regardless of how they went through the experiment, subjects' responses are treated statistically by group methods. That is, subjects who were given one experimental treatment are compared to subjects who experienced another type of treatment (another experimental treatment or a control situation). Thus the results of the study are not based on what any one individual did, but on the average behavior of a group of people.

This method of analysis guarantees that a certain amount of slippage (or, more technically, error, or uncontrolled variance) will occur. Given a statistically significant difference between groups, most of the subjects will have behaved in the predicted fashion, but some individuals may not have so behaved. What this means for clinical practice is simply that a blind, mechanical application of experimental procedures to a specific client will not necessarily induce the desired psychological process in him. This translates into the aspect of clinical work noted earlier: the necessity to resolve general principles into individually tailored programs.

A final aspect of the specifics of social psychological research of interest to the clinician is the issue of the magnitude of statistically significant results. In using group analysis, the magnitude of difference needed for the results to be significant can be rather small. In the Festinger and Carlsmith experiment, for example, the difference between the $1.00 group and the $20.00 group in their evaluation of the experimental task after they had misled the "next subject" was only 1.4 points on an 11-point scale, and yet this difference was statistically significant ($p < .03$).

In clinical practice, of course, one is generally interested in effecting changes of considerably greater magnitude. Does this mean, then, that the theories of social psychology, while extensively validated, are not capable of producing the range of effects that a clinician desires? That argument can be made, and until clinicians put social psychology into practice, it will not be possible to resolve the point, either way, to anyone's complete satisfaction.

It is likely, however, that the magnitude of effect is related to the power of the conditions designed to induce that effect.

Experimenters are severely limited in the power of their inducing conditions. No matter how realistic the experimental procedure, no matter how involved the subject, the subject is aware that he is a subject in an experiment and that the experiment is not his "real life." The skillful experimenter tries to reduce the saliency of this knowledge, to make the subject's experience as "real" to him as possible. The experimenter may, as noted, utilize deception in order to achieve this "reality," but, also as noted, it is impossible to totally remove awareness of the artificial nature of behavior in an experiment. In addition, the experimenter typically sees a subject for one session only, a session frequently lasting only one-half hour, and such a session is quite irrelevant to the rest of the subject's life.

In contrast, psychotherapy is very "real" to most clients. It represents a considerable financial and emotional investment. The client has a relationship with the therapist over time, seeing the therapist, for example, once or twice a week for fifty minutes a session over several months. And, perhaps most important, most clients choose to come to therapy. They come unhappy and distressed and are very involved with their problems and their therapy.

Thus it seems a reasonable assumption that the therapist has a great deal more power in his relationship with the client than the experimenter has in his relationship with the subject, power in the sense that the therapist's behavior has significantly more effect on the client than the experimenter's behavior has on the subject. We would expect, then, that the therapist would be able to create much more powerful inducing conditions than the experimenter. With sufficiently powerful inducing conditions, the resultant effects should be of the magnitude that the clinician and the client desire.

CLINICAL COMPLEXITY

Although the theories to be explored here differ considerably from the theoretical principles on which behavior modifiers base their work, the applications derived from social psychology will surely be subject to an objection frequently raised to behavior modification. This objection concerns the use of apparently simple principles in the immensely complex undertaking of clinical practice. On behalf of social psychological applications, there are two major responses to such objections.

First, the social psychological theories and findings explicated in this book are far from simple. The upcoming presentation has not been simplified for clinical utility. An effort has been made to present for each theory the most recent and most elaborated version of that theory and its related findings. Modifications in the theories have been noted as well as currently unresolved issues. Social psychology cannot usually claim to be as complex as the chesslike intricacy of Freudian theory, but it sometimes borders on such complexity.

Second, and more important, the issue of clinical complexity has to be scrutinized. Clinical work is complex; there can be no question of this. This very complexity, however, underlines the need for a coherent theoretical approach to clinical activity. To refer to our earlier example, spontaneous exploration of the elephant may not be very productive. As clinicians we desperately need some perspective, some model, some theory to guide us.

This does not mean, of course, that whatever theory one relies on is necessarily totally accurate. Psychological theories represent the best approximation that one currently has of psychological functioning. They constantly need to be modified, refined, and elaborated. Furthermore, every theory is at some level of simplification of "truth." "Truth" about human psychology is no doubt so complex that we human psychologists may never be able to formulate it. But if we forsake theory, any theory, because it is not the "truth," then we go back to spontaneous exploration of the elephant.

The perspective of this book is that one has to utilize theoretical principles in clinical work. From this perspective, the issue is not theory versus no theory, but, rather, which theory to adopt. This book will present a number of social psychological theories, the empirical evidence obtained in their support, and their applications to the clinical setting. Each reader is then free to decide whether the adoption of social psychological principles can enhance his effectiveness in clinical practice.

PLAN OF THE BOOK

The major emphasis of this book will be on three theoretical perspectives in social psychology: reactance theory, dissonance theory, and theories of attribution (Chapters Two through Ten). In addition, three more recent, less extensively documented, social psychological theories will be examined: commitment, objective self-awareness, and self-expressive decision making (Chapter Eleven). An overview of each of these theories will be provided, followed by application of the theory to clinical activities. The concluding chapter discusses a variety of implications underlying the suggested applications, including an examination of ethical issues and suggestions about the training of clinicians.

An effort has been made throughout to minimize the amount of jargon and detailed data analysis incorporated into reports of various experimental findings. This effort derives from the author's belief that one reason many clinicians know little about social psychology is that without a preexisting interest in a specific topic, reading experimental reports in journals is a boring and tedious enterprise. Thus most references to relevant journal articles are short and to the point. Complete source information on the original publications is provided in the References at the back of the book. In addition to these specific references, books or papers of more general interest are listed at the conclusion of the discussion of each theoretical area.

In applying social psychology to clinical practice, several alternative approaches would seem viable, and this book has been written so as to facilitate them. One could take a problem-oriented approach. This orientation would focus on a specific problem and try to work out (from one or several theories) the set of principles that would apply to that problem and that if applied could create beneficial change. The chapters on clinical applications are primarily problem-oriented in order to facilitate use of this procedure.

A somewhat different approach would be theory-oriented. Here the clinician would seek to understand relevant theoretical perspectives and to become familiar with experimental work bearing on these theories. These theories could then be applied to a variety of clinical problems. The chapters on theory have been provided to facilitate this approach.

A combination approach is also possible and, indeed may be most appropriate. It can be argued that understanding theory is simply the first step to an adequate problem-oriented approach. In the absence of mastery of theory, problem-oriented approaches may suffer from a lack of knowledge about what strategies would, in fact, be applicable to the problem at hand. On the other hand, a theoretical understanding that is not disciplined by a focus on specific problems runs the risk of being diffuse, obscure, and irrelevant to successful clinical intervention. The notion of theory-orientation leading into problem-orientation is carried out here by having the theory chapters precede, but be directly related to, the chapters on clinical application.

PART ONE

REACTANCE THEORY

CHAPTER TWO

REACTANCE THEORY

Karen Horney (1939) on resistance:

Much work has been done in studying the ways in which the patient defends his positions, how he struggles, retreats, evades the issue. (p. 34)

David Shapiro (1965) on the paranoid style:

While the normal person feels not only competent, but also free to exercise his will, and, in that sense as well, self-directing, in charge of his own life, and, master of himself, the paranoid person is continuously occupied and concerned with the threat of being subjected to some external control or some external infringement of his will. (p. 82)

Austin DesLauriers and Carole Carlson (1969) on the treatment of autistic children:

The most general strategy used here is neither uncommon, nor is it unknown to most mothers confronted with the *No, No* phase of their young child. It consists, essentially, either of demanding of the child the exact opposite of what one might actually want him to do, or of pretending convincingly that one doesn't really care one way or the other whether the child does what he is asked. (p. 156)

These examples represent a selection of the behaviors that clinicians have variously labeled resistance, paranoia, negativism, or oppositionalism. Striking in their diversity, these behaviors are remarkable for their similarity. All of them denote the individual's concern with his freedom to behave as he wishes and his desire to avoid being subject to another person's directives.

This chapter examines a social psychological theory that focuses specifically on people's responses to threats to their behavioral freedoms. The theory of psychological reactance offers the clinician a chance to reexamine client behaviors such as those mentioned above, but in a more rigorous theoretical and empirical form than has been possible previously. This first chapter on psychological reactance will concentrate on an exposition of the theory, an exploration of related theories and techniques that have been proposed by clinicians, and an example of how one translates from the experimental literature into clinical applications. Chapters Three and Four detail various clinical strategies that can be derived from the theory of psychological reactance.

THE THEORY

In his original presentation of reactance theory, J. W. Brehm (1966) stressed a critical assumption of the theory.

> It is assumed that for a given person at a given time, there is a set of behaviors any one of which he could engage in either at the moment or at some time in the future. This set may be called the individual's "free behaviors." (p. 3)

According to Brehm, these "free behaviors" may be any specific behaviors (e.g., thoughts, acts, decisions). It is important to note the specificity of the designation; Brehm is not talking about freedom in general, but rather about specified behaviors that the individual both knows he may engage in and possesses the ability to do so.

Based on this assumption, the central tenet of reactance theory is that a person will experience psychological reactance whenever any of his free behaviors is eliminated or threatened with elimination. The possible sources of such freedom eliminations or threats are varied. There can be *personal* threats to or eliminations of freedom, such as when an adult demands obedience from a child. There can be *impersonal* reducers of freedom, for instance, the proverbial wiping out of the planned picnic by unexpected rain. Finally, there can be *self-imposed* threats to or eliminations of freedom.

Self-imposed threats to and eliminations of freedom are perhaps best illustrated by what may happen to a person as he approaches and then makes a decision. In most instances, as he approaches the decision, he will experience a preference for one alternative over another. This preference threatens his freedom to *have* the other, *less preferred* alternative and also his freedom to *reject* the *preferred* alternative. After the person has made his decision, he has by his own actions eliminated the freedom to choose the rejected alternative and also the freedom to reject the chosen alternative. Thus, the potential sources of threats to freedom are multiple. Such threats (or eliminations) can come from other people who indicate their direct intention to influence our behavior, from social or asocial events that are not directed at us but affect our behavior anyway, and even from our own behavior.

Determinants of Reactance

Brehm (1966) has specified that the magnitude of the reactance experienced by a person for whom a specific freedom is threatened or eliminated is determined by three factors. The first is the importance of the freedom.

> The importance of a given behavior is a direct function of the unique instrumental value which that behavior has for the satisfaction of needs, multiplied by the actual or potential maximum magnitude of those needs. (pp. 4-5)

These two aspects of the importance of a freedom may be clarified by considering each in turn. "Unique instrumental value" is a significant aspect because if a need can be satisfied by a thousand possible behaviors, the loss of one of the thousand is of no great moment. The person has numerous available alternatives to obtain satisfaction. But if a behavior is unique in its ability to satisfy a need, considerably more importance becomes attached to the freedom to engage in that behavior.

The second aspect of the importance of a freedom simply states a psychological truism; if a need is trivial, the loss of a behavior that satisfies that need is equally trivial, but if the need is important, so too is the freedom to behave in the way that satisfies the need. Brehm sees these two aspects of importance as interacting, although he makes no precise statement of the mathematical properties of this interaction. The interaction stipulation holds that with an important need *and* with unique instrumental value, one can obtain a magnitude of reactance exceeding what would be expected from a mere addition of these psychological elements.

There is one further determinant of the importance of a behavioral freedom: its relation to other freedoms. If we consider one behavioral freedom and then place it in relation to other freedoms, the relative importance of the freedom we are focusing on increases as the absolute importance of the other freedoms decreases. For example, if a person has to choose among four types of 50-cent cigars, the importance of the loss of the freedom to choose any one (say Brand A) will be less than if he lost the freedom to choose Brand A over three 10-cent cigars. This postulate resembles the unique instrumental value stipulation, but is in fact theoretically distinct. Presumably, all the cigars fulfill the need to smoke, and the importance of this need remains constant. The importance of the freedom in the case of Brand A is determined not by its instrumental value, nor by the importance of the need it satisfies, but by comparing it to the importance of the other available alternatives.

The second factor that can affect the magnitude of reactance is the proportion of freedoms eliminated or threatened with elimination. Holding instrumental value constant among six alternatives, consider a person's response to the loss of two of these alternatives versus his response to the loss of four of these alternatives. Reactance theory postulates that the magnitude of reactance will be greater in the latter case than in the former; the greater the proportion of freedoms eliminated, or threatened with elimination, the greater will be the reactance aroused. One can, of course, obtain the same effect by reducing the size of the original array. A person who loses the freedom to engage in one out of three possible behaviors should experience more reactance than a person who loses the freedom to engage in one out of eight alternatives.

In cases where there is no elimination of freedom but only the threat of elimination of a freedom, the final factor affecting the magnitude of reactance that will be aroused is the magnitude of the threat. The relationship is as one would expect: the greater the threat, the greater the reactance. Maximum reactance arousal is produced, by definition, when a freedom is eliminated. Up to that point the magnitude of the threat to a freedom is a direct and significant determinant of the magnitude of the reactance that will be aroused.

Although this statement of the relationship between magnitude of threat to freedom and reactance aroused is simple and straightforward, there are two derivations from this relationship that may, in real life at least, considerably complicate the effects of reactance. Both of these derivations are based on the common-sense assumption that people perceive continuity in their lives and generalize from one situation to another. Thus a threat directed toward one freedom may *by implication* threaten other freedoms. Such implications can be elicited by similarity of behavioral freedoms (if my right to smoke is threatened, then my right to drink may soon be under attack), by situational similarity (if X freedom of mine is threatened in this situation, then the next time I'm here, Y freedom may be threatened), or by similarity of the threatening agent (if I obey my employer about this, then he may expect me to obey him on that other issue). One would expect that the more freedoms that are implicated by one threat, the more reactance would be aroused.

Thus, what may look to the observer like a mild threat directed at what appears to be an insignificant freedom (on other grounds such as importance and proportion of freedoms) may to the person appear a threat of considerable magnitude because other freedoms are implicated.

To complicate the situation even more, Brehm (1966) proposed that a person can experience reactance when he is not directly threatened with freedom reduction but observes someone else threatened. Again, one would expect principles of generalization to operate. A threat to another implicates our behavioral freedom insofar as those others are similar to us, are in similar circumstances, or are threatened in regard to behavior similar to that which we have engaged in, are engaging in, or may want to engage in in the future. It should be obvious that these implication hypotheses vastly extend the possible realm of the arousal of reactance.

The Effects of Reactance

Essentially, reactance arousal is a motivational state that will be directed toward the restoration of the threatened or eliminated freedom. There are several ways in which this motivation may be expressed. The most effective way is, of course, to act directly to restore the threatened freedom. The person choosing between an apple and an orange is told to take the apple. By taking instead the orange, the person has directly restored his freedom. This mode of direct restoration is obviously not possible for those for whom a freedom has been eliminated.

A second method of restoration, applying either to threatened or eliminated freedoms, is that of indirect action. As has been noted in the discussion of the determinants of reactance, the principle of implication is an important element in reactance theory. Implication can operate on the effect side of reactance as well as on the determinant side. A person can act indirectly to restore his freedom by engaging in acts that reestablish freedom by implication. If one freedom in a class of behaviors is threatened or eliminated, a person could engage in another behavior in the same class. If an individual has been successfully influenced by another person to act in some way, the individual could disobey the other person's next request. Furthermore, Brehm (1966) states that the observation of someone who directly or indirectly restores his own freedom can serve, by implication, to restore our freedom.

There will, however, be some situations where freedom restoration through action, direct or indirect, is impossible and where observing another restore his freedom does not occur. In this third case, the person has little alternative, but to "sit on" his reactance and, presumably, as with other motivational states, it will dissipate over time. This does not mean though that the existence of reactance is then undetectable. The person should still desire to engage in the behaviors that would reestablish his freedom and, in most circumstances, should be willing to verbalize this heightened desire. Thus even if no restoration actions are possible, the threatened or eliminated behavioral freedoms should increase in attractiveness. This increase in attractiveness provides a means to examine the effects of reactance even in behaviorally restricted situations.

There is a fourth and final effect of reactance that deserves consideration in presenting the general outline of the theory. Reactance may be accompanied by aggression toward any social agent who threatens a person's behavioral freedoms. These aggressive tendencies may reflect either one or both of two possible processes. First, aggression may simply be a form of direct reassertion of the threatened freedom. In its most extreme degree, if one murders the person who threatens a freedom, the threat to freedom is removed. Lesser degrees of aggression may, by intimidating the threatener, also remove the threat to freedom. An aggressive process of greater theoretical interest has been shown recently in an experiment by Worchel (1974) that demonstrated that reactance arousal was accompanied by arousal of aggressive tendencies even when such tendencies served no restorative purpose. The details of how and why this process occurs are still unclear, but it seems that threatening or eliminating a person's freedom can be viewed by the person as a provocative act and that retaliatory aggressive acts can ensue.

Areas of Empirical Investigation

In his book detailing the empirical investigations relevant to reactance theory, Wicklund (1974) describes three major areas of psychological functioning that have been addressed by the theory: social influence, barriers, and self-imposed threats to freedom. Since most of the experiments that will be cited later are classified by Wicklund as involving social influence or self-imposed threats to freedom, a brief description of reactance effects resulting from barriers will be given here.

A barrier can be defined as any asocial entity that makes engaging in a behavioral freedom more difficult or impossible. In most respects, barriers function as impersonal threats to or eliminations of freedom. As indicated earlier, it is theoretically possible for social stimuli to represent impersonal threats or eliminations, since the definition of "impersonal" is only that such actions not be intentionally directed at the person receiving the threat or elimination. In practice, however, impersonal threats are virtually synonomous with asocial entities and thus with barriers. It is difficult for a person to have a freedom threatened or eliminated by another person without perceiving such threats or eliminations as intentional and directed.

In the experimental research on reactance theory that has involved barriers, the impersonal threat or elimination has been implemented by such devices as convincing subjects that an item failed to arrive due to a shipping error or, more directly, by erecting physical constraints, such as distance to the object, against obtaining a decision alternative. Experiments conducted within these methodological paradigms have supported basic hypotheses of reactance theory such as: (1) if a person believes he is free to choose among several alternatives and one becomes unavailable, the unavailable item increases in attractiveness and the available items decrease in attractiveness (J. W. Brehm, Stires, Sensenig, & Shaban, 1966); (2) reactance arousal is maximal when the number of available alternatives, from which some are eliminated, is small (Brehm, McQuown, & Shaban, in Brehm, 1966); and (3) making something more difficult to obtain increases the likelihood of its being chosen (Brehm & Hammock, in Brehm, 1966).

While these studies may not have the degree of interest for clinicians that other studies in the reactance literature have, they do illustrate very common behavior that is seen both in everyday life and in clinical practice. Indeed, the second finding noted above may be especially prevalent in clinical settings. As clinicians we often see people whose behavioral repertoires are quite limited. There are a lot of things clients feel they cannot do and, especially for those in institutional settings, there are many things they may not do. It would not be surprising then if reactance arousal occurred quite frequently for such people, perhaps more frequently than for the general population who have a greater number of behavioral freedoms available.

This increased vulnerability to reactance arousal may also throw some light on the generalized anger and hostility that one often observes in clinical populations. Given the potential accompaniment of reactance by both instrumental (i.e., freedom-restoring) and noninstrumental (i.e., nonrestorative) aggression, it would seem likely that as a person's proclivity toward experiencing reactance increases, so would that person's anger. The more people who pose threats to the person's freedoms, and the more situations in which such threats can occur, the more generalized and diffuse would be the person's anger.

Reactance versus Frustration

This discussion of anger and reactance brings up a question that may have already occurred to many readers: One may ask, why use the term "reactance"? Isn't it all just "frustration"? In fact, it isn't just frustration, and it is critical to realize that reactance is conceptually separate and distinct from frustration.

Frustration is usually defined as not obtaining what one desires. In most experiments on reactance, care is taken that the freedom threatened is not the freedom to have the *most* desirable alternative, but the freedom to have a *less* desirable alternative. The reactance that occurs under such conditions (such as in the Brehm, Stires, Sensenig, & Shaban experiment) manifests itself by a relative increase in attractiveness of the threatened or eliminated alternative and a relative decrease in the attractiveness of the other alternatives. At no time is the person's freedom to have the most desirable alternative interfered with; therefore, such effects are clearly due to reactance and not frustration. In addition, reactance theory would postulate that forcing the most desirable alternative on a person would arouse reactance. This, of course, would be a totally nonfrustrating situation.

While reactance experiments have attempted to rule out frustration effects, experiments on frustration have not controlled for reactance effects. It is possible that some psychological effects that have been deemed to result from frustration are in fact created by reactance. In Worchel's experiment (1974), aggression was examined in relation to frustration, disconfirmation of expectancy (an alternative view of frustration), and reactance. Each subject in this experiment was led to believe that one of three events would occur: the experimenter would give him one of three rewards; the experimenter would give him the reward he (the subject) had rated most attractive; or the experimenter would let the subject select the reward he wanted. Regardless of what the subject had been led to expect, however, the experimenter decided which of three rewards each person received. Aggression toward the experimenter was examined by means of the subject's rating of the experimenter's performance, an evaluation the subject was told would be used in considering the experimenter for future employment.

Worchel's data showed that aggression from pure frustration (i.e., receiving the second or third most attractive alternative instead of the most attractive one in the no-choice and no-expectancy condition) was minimal. Furthermore, for subjects who had expected to receive the most attractive alternative (i.e., the one they had rated as most attractive), little aggression was evidenced when they received the second most attractive alternative, but there was significant aggression displayed when they received the least attractive alternative. Thus for aggression to result from disconfirmation of expectancy, there must be a sizable disconfirmation. Finally, subjects who had expected free choice of alternatives showed some aggression when they were forced to take the most attractive alternative, more aggression when they were given the second most attractive item, and most aggression when they received the least attractive alternative. Clearly, reactance in this experiment was the most powerful determinant of aggression. It is possible, then, that when "frustration" leads to aggression under free-choice conditions, the major cause of the aggression is not frustration at all, but reactance. Apparently, people are not necessarily angered by receiving a less than totally desirable outcome, but Worchel's data suggest that people do act in a clearly aggressive fashion when they see their behavioral freedoms being usurped.

RELATED THEORIES

As indicated by the quotations opening this chapter, reactance-like effects have not gone unnoticed by clinicians and clinically oriented theorists. In addition to general designations of "resistant," "paranoid," or "oppositional" behavior, a number of more formal presentations of reactance effects have been made in a therapeutic context. Interestingly, many of these presentations have focused not on the difficulty caused by such effects, but on how these effects can be utilized by the therapist to help the client achieve therapeutic goals.

Psychoanalysis: Resistance

There has been, in fact, only one major theoretical consideration of the difficulties caused by reactancelike effects in therapy. Psychoanalytic theory indicates that resistance is an important and expected occurrence during analysis. Theoretically, this resistance has been taken to reflect the defenses erected intrapsychically against the expression of forbidden and feared impulses. Operationally, however, resistance typically occurs in response to the therapist's interpretation. That is, the therapist suggests that the client may, for example, harbor some less than positive feelings toward his father. If the client denies this, this denial may be viewed as contributing to other evidence suggesting that indeed the client does have negative feelings toward his father. Stepping outside the psychoanalytic context, it is possible to view the client's denial as having nothing to do with the true state of his feelings toward his father, but rather as reflecting his attempts to maintain his freedom to feel any way he wants about his father. Thus, therapeutic interpretations can be seen as attempts to influence the client. As will be discussed later in this volume, it has been shown that where there are pressures to conform to social influence, there are also pressures to preserve one's freedom of thought and opinion and not conform.

Haley: Paradoxical Injunctions

In directing our attention to theories of therapy that have focused on possible beneficial results to be obtained from reactancelike effects, we should first consider the most elaborated, and perhaps most compelling, of these theories. Jay Haley (1963) has written at some length and with great ingenuity about "paradoxical injunctions" and "taking control of the patient's symptoms." Haley suggests that the therapist is able to take control of the client's symptoms by emitting a paradoxical injunction. This would operate in the following way. A client comes into the therapeutic setting with a symptom, for example, excessive hand-wringing, insommia, obsessive thoughts. Once the therapist and the client have identified the troublesome behavior, the therapist can issue a paradoxical injunction instructing the client to engage in this symptomatic behavior. Typically the therapist sets the level of the client's involvement with the symptom higher than it presently is. Thus, a client who wrings his hands twelve times a day might be instructed to wring his hands twenty-four times a day. The client is also expected to keep track of how often he performs the symptom and to report this to the therapist.

Haley argues that this is a foolproof therapeutic technique. For, after all, what can happen? The client can obey the therapist, in which case the therapist now has control of the client's symptoms and presumably can instruct the client to engage in lower as well as higher levels of symptomatic behavior. Or the client can disobey the therapist's instructions and reduce the symptomatic behavior, thus contributing to the elimination of the problems that brought him into therapy in the first place.

Now, of course, life and clinical practice aren't always so simple. Any clinician can envision numerous difficulties that might occur in the utilization of such a therapeutic strategy. For our purposes, however, it is sufficient to note that Haley reports that this strategy has been successful for at least some clients and to indicate the relationship of Haley's proposals to reactance theory. While specific predictions would vary depending on some aspects of the therapeutic relationship and its members' characteristics (e.g., the strength of the therapist's influence, the magnitude of the client's need to engage in the symptomatic behavior), in general, reactance theory would predict a significant tendency for the client to disobey the therapist.

One critical and somewhat difficult assumption is necessary for this prediction. A paradoxical injunction threatens the client's freedom *not* to engage in his symptomatic behavior. In order for this threat to create reactance, the freedom *not* to engage in his symptom must exist for the client. It is the latter stipulation that creates difficulties. Clearly, the client knows that he *can* engage in the symptomatic behavior, and while it may cause him numerous social problems, he knows that he *may* engage in the symptoms, simply because the fact that he currently acts symptomatically indicates that the social environment will tolerate his behavior at least to some degree. However, it is not clear that he feels free *not* to engage in these behaviors. Presumably if he did, he would have quit on his own. No doubt, in fact, if one asked such a client if he felt free not to behave symptomatically, he would say that he did not have this freedom.

Clients and other individuals may not, however, always be able to articulate their psychological freedoms. Sometimes the best way to discover what they feel free to do or to not do is to try out some injunctions, paradoxical or otherwise. One thing is certain: telling the client to stop engaging in his symptom is unlikely to be successful. We know the client thinks he can't quit and thus he probably won't in response to a direct command. We also know that he feels free to engage in the symptom and that direct commands to stop behaving symptomatically threaten this freedom. Haley's paradoxical injunction is intriguing because it may, by tapping unrealized freedoms, help control the client's symptom without triggering an unproductive power struggle between the therapist and the client. The therapist who issues a paradoxical injunction wants to be disobeyed, wants to create reactance, and seeks to utilize these forces to his client's benefit.

Behavior Modification

The process of creating productive reactance may be relevant to a clinical occurrence that is familiar to behavior modifiers. Behavior modifiers (e.g., Thoresen & Mahoney, 1974) have noticed that when a client begins to count target behaviors during the establishment of a baseline (i.e., before any reinforcement contingencies have been instituted), there may occur temporarily (although sometimes permanently), a reduction in target behaviors. In this case, no paradoxical injunctions have been issued, but it may be that as the client attends more carefully to the target behaviors, the increased awareness and saliency of these behaviors constitute a threat to his freedom not to engage in them *or* to his freedom to engage in alternative behaviors. By counting and thus becoming aware of the frequency and duration of the target behaviors, the client may begin to feel as though he's spending his entire life performing the target behaviors.

This focus on the threat to other behavioral freedoms that engaging in the symptomatic behavior can represent provides an alternative and, perhaps, more acceptable analysis of Haley's paradoxical injunction. Even though the client may not have the freedom not to engage in the symptomatic behavior, he does have the freedom to engage in other, nonsymptomatic behaviors. When he is instructed to engage in the symptom excessively, or when he becomes aware through counting that he is engaging in the symptom at an excessive rate, this may present a threat to his freedom to engage in other behaviors. Such a threat should create reactance and lead, at least temporarily, to a reduction of the symptomatic behavior as the client directly restores his freedom by engaging in those other behaviors.

The temporary nature typical of "baseline cures," and possibly of the effects of paradoxical injunctions as well, suggests that reactance effects need to be augmented by other procedures. In general terms, these other procedures might consist of strengthening the more socially and personally acceptable behaviors that result from a reduction in symptomatic behavior. A reactance manipulation along the lines of Haley's paradoxical injunction or of simply having the client attend to symptomatic behavior may, however, be an effective way to generate initial disengagement from the symptomatic behavior.

Frankl: Paradoxical Intent

Two other clinicians have described clinical strategies that may reflect reactance effects. Victor Frankl (1967) has suggested a technique of "paradoxical intent." This is a kind of *reductio ad absurdum* in reverse. Instead of reducing the client's symptoms, they are exaggerated to an absurd degree. For example, a client who obsesses over the possibility of being contaminated by handling bathroom doorknobs might be instructed also to worry about all other doorknobs, and sinks, and glasses, and . . . *ad infinitum.* Writing from an existentialist point of view, Frankl believes that by making the symptomatic behavior absurd, the client can distance himself from that behavior, laught at it, and relinquish it. Frankl's technique may actually consist of the same types of threats to the client's freedom (either not to engage in the symptom or to engage in alternative behaviors) that were described above.

Lindner: Accepting a Delusion

Lindner (1954) reported a case study that seems to utilize Haley-like, Frankl-like, and, in terms of the present discussion, reactance-like effects with a client who manifested extensive psychotic delusions. Lindner's approach was to accept his client's delusion and take it to its logical conclusion. The client, Kirk, spent a great deal of his time writing the autobiography of his fantasy self, a self that lived on another planet and roamed the galaxy engaging in exciting adventures. Complementing the text of this autobiography, Kirk, a research physicist in his "real" life, had composed an enormous set of astronomical charts and star maps. Lindner took the unusual therapeutic tack of studying this apparatus of his client's delusion and going over it in detail with Kirk as though he (Lindner) believed it to be real and important. Lindner pointed out any errors or inadequacies he found in the record and charts and asked Kirk to correct them.

Although at first Kirk was quite gratified by his therapist's interest in his autobiography, after a while he appeared to resent the therapist's desire for constant correction of the autobiography. Lindner reports that Kirk finally states that their poring over the records together was absurd, since his text and maps were all "nonsense" and "made up." Lindner stated that his technique was predicated on the client's being "forced to take up a critical position on his behavior." However, the relationship of this technique to reactance theory should be obvious. By his support of Kirk's delusion, Lindner increased the demands of this delusion on Kirk's time and energy and may have threatened both his freedom not to engage in the delusion and his freedoms to engage in other, nondelusional behaviors.

This section has illustrated several ways in which therapists have taken advantage of what seem to be reactance effects. By presenting these therapeutic techniques and discussing them in reactance theory terms, it should be clear that while a general idea is held in common, the therapeutic techniques lack the theoretical rigor and empirical support that are integral aspects of reactance theory. In essence, Haley Frankl, and Lindner are saying: "Tell, urge, or force the client to do what you don't want him to do and he won't do it." Reactance theory can generate a much wider variety of possible therapeutic techniques, some of which will be considered in detail in the chapters on clinical application.

THE TRANSLATION FROM EXPERIMENTAL INVESTIGATION TO CLINICAL APPLICATION: AN EXAMPLE

The basic premise of this book is that the theories and findings of experimental social psychology are relevant to the problems and goals of clinical practice. In order to support this premise, translations will be made from experimental evidence to clinical application. There are, of course, numerous pitfalls associated with such translations. They are not backed by research evaluating their effectiveness in clinical work, but are derived from common sense, logic, and the clinical intuition of the author. Thus the translations might not be reliable, that is, other workers might make different translations, and they might not be valid, that is, they might not work. The redeeming feature in this enterprise is that no specific application is being "sold" to the reader, but rather a general framework is being provided for the consideration of therapeutic endeavors. The goal of these translations is to stimulate practicing clinicians to utilize social psychology to engineer their own translated strategies for effecting therapeutic change.

To aid in achieving this goal, one experiment and the applications derived from it will be described in detail. Shorter versions of experiments and applications that will be found in the clinical application chapters throughout the book reflect the same kinds of processes. These versions are intended to serve only as sketches of the possible. The clinician interested in a particular theoretical point or clinical application is urged to consult the original theoretical paper or experimental report.

The Experiment

In a study entitled "Effect of a favor which reduces freedom," J. W. Brehm and A. H. Cole (1966) reasoned that the typical effect of a favor is to increase the probability of that favor being reciprocated—we tend to help out those who have helped us out. This would certainly be the case when it is of minimal importance to be free of obligation to another person. However, Brehm and Cole hypothesized that when the importance to be free of obligation to another person is high, receiving a favor may create reactance and may lead to restoration of freedom by not returning the favor. The following experiment was conducted in order to examine this hypothesis.

A subject arrived for an experiment supposedly on "projective testing," and was told, by a note, to wait outside the laboratory. There he was joined by a person who presented himself as another subject, but who was actually the experimenter's confederate. When the experimenter appeared, the confederate asked if there was time for him to be excused for a moment. The experimenter said there was, and the confederate left. At this point, the experimenter discussed the upcoming experiment with the subject and delivered the Importance manipulation. The experimenter told the subject that, in addition to her research on projective testing, she had agreed to gather some data for a friend. These data would consist of first-impression ratings that the two subjects in each experimental session would make of each other. In the High Importance condition, the friend was described as a professor, who had received a large grant for his research. The experimenter further indicated that careful and accurate first-impression ratings were very important since accuracy on such ratings was predictive of success in life. In the Low Importance condition, the friend was described as a student, and the experimenter said the ratings were for a class project and therefore of no great moment.

Soon after this discussion, the confederate returned. In the No Favor condition, he simply returned to the waiting area and the group of three proceeded into the laboratory. In the Favor condition, he brought a soft drink with him, gave it to the subject, and refused to take any money for it if any was offered; the group of three then went into the lab.

In the laboratory, the experimenter told the confederate what she had told the subject. She asked that the first-impression ratings be made prior to her own research. After these ratings were completed by the subjects, the experimenter asked the confederate to stack some papers for her. The dependent measure in this experiment was the number of subjects in each condition who helped the confederate stack papers. After the stacking was done, the experimenter talked with the subject and explained the actual topic under investigation.

The results provided strong support for the original reasoning by Brehm and Cole (1966). When subjects had received no favor, the importance variable did not affect their helping behavior. Approximately 50 percent of these subjects helped the confederate stack the papers. For subjects who received a favor and for whom the importance of the first-impression ratings was low, over 90 percent helped the confederate. However, for subjects who received a favor and for whom the importance of accurate ratings was high, only 13 percent helped. It should be noted that the first-impression ratings were essentially unaffected by experimental conditions. Only on the ratings on the dimension of "friendly-unfriendly" did the favor have an effect: receiving a favor increased the subjects' perception of the confederate's friendliness in the Low Importance condition and had no effect in the High Importance condition.

Thus while subjects showed little effect of having received or not received a favor in terms of their impressions of the confederate, their willingness to help the confederate was dramatically affected. Compared to a baseline helping rate of about 50 percent, receiving a favor when the freedom to not be obligated was low significantly increased helping, whereas receiving a favor when the freedom to not be obligated was high significantly decreased helping.

The Translation

What might the results of this experiment mean for clinical practice? First, we have to translate "favor" into activities more indigenous to the clinical setting. Therapists may or may not think of themselves as performing favors for their clients. They do, however, have many opportunities to do things that would be helpful—such as, aiding in getting the client a job, getting the client out of academic obligations, assisting him in coping with bureaucratic systems such as welfare and the courts. On the other side of the therapeutic coin, clients probably don't think of themselves as doing favors for their therapist, but they probably do often think of themselves as doing other things *for* the therapist. The comment, "Well, all right, I'll give it a try, but just because you asked me to," is not uncommon in many therapeutic endeavors. Indeed, it is often this willingness of the client to go along with the therapist's suggestions that provides the most powerful inducement to initial behavior change. For the purposes of this translation, then, both the therapist's helping the client and the client's trying things "for the therapist" will be considered "favors."

Second, we have to translate the importance variable into clinically meaningful characteristics. In general, it would certainly seem that therapy can be a high-importance, real-life condition. The therapy itself, in terms of money and effort, is important. More specifically, it may be very important for some clients, particularly in the initial stages of therapy, to not be obligated to the therapist. Many clients come into psychotherapy with a wary and indeed suspicious attitude. "What is this person going to do to me or make me do?" Under these circumstances it can be very important to the client that he maintain operating freedom from the therapist, at least until he sees whether or not he can trust "the shrink."

The Application

In order to apply Brehm and Cole's findings to clinical practice, the therapist must first assess the client's desire to remain free of obligation to the therapist. Typically this desire is most intense during the early stages of therapy and/or with clients who are particularly sensitive about their personal autonomy. This sensitivity can arise as part of a psychological disturbance such as paranoia, or as an aspect of a developmental period such as adolescence, or as simply a characteristic of the individual client. Second, the therapist must assess whether it is, or might be, desirable for the client to give things a try "for the therapist." While therapists in general may prefer clients to engage in new behaviors because they want to, initially the only way to get the client to engage in novel behaviors may be through the client's doing the therapist this kind of favor.

If the therapist concludes that he wants to keep the possibility of the client's doing him "a favor" a viable alternative and that the client places a high value on his freedom to not be obligated to the therapist, the therapist should refrain from helping the client with his (the client's) everyday affairs. He should refrain not because he is heartless and cruel, nor because of any general principles concerning doing favors for clients, but because if he helps, he will make it more difficult for this client to be willing to give things a try just because the therapist asked him to.

If, on the other hand, the therapist perceives that the client does not place much importance on his freedom to not be obligated to the therapist and if the therapist wishes to increase the probability of the client's trying out new behaviors in which he asks the client to engage, the therapist would be well advised to help the client in some extratherapeutic activity and to make it clear to the client that he (the therapist) is doing him a favor. Again, this help would not be predicated on personal characteristics of the therapist nor on general principles about favor-doing in therapy, but on the reactance theory relationship demonstrated by Brehm and Cole, indicating that helping the client out under these conditions should increase his willingness to try something "for the therapist."

It is hoped that this explication of the experiment by Brehm and Cole illustrates how the experimental literature may be translated into clinical application. This application is based on a synthesis of psychological science and clinical expertise. The principles of behavioral freedom, importance of the freedom, and threats to the freedom are based on reactance theory and are demonstrated empirically by the Brehm and Cole study. The successful application of these findings, however, depends greatly on the clinician's judgment and abilities. He must decide whether or not he wants the client to try things out for his (the therapist's) sake, and he must ascertain the psychological state of the client. Given the theory, the empirical evidence, and the clinician's expertise, it is possible to obtain a highly precise level of clinical intervention. The clinical strategies suggested do not represent simple, unidimensional prescriptions. Rather, one approach is suggested under one set of circumstances and another approach is advised when a different set of circumstances obtains. This precision allows the therapist to utilize the general psychological postulates of reactance theory in a highly specific manner for specific clients.

SUMMARY

This chapter has presented a detailed examination of the theory of psychological reactance. The theory can be briefly summarized as follows:

1. Individuals have free behaviors.
2. A person will experience psychological reactance whenever any of his free behaviors is eliminated or threatened with elimination.
3. The magnitude of reactance that a person experiences is determined by the importance of the freedom threatened or eliminated, the proportion of freedoms threatened or eliminated, and the magnitude of threats to freedom.
4. Effects of reactance arousal include direct restoration of freedom by engaging in the threatened behavior, indirect restoration, increased attractiveness of the threatened behavior, and aggression toward that which threatens the person's freedoms.

Relationships between reactance theory and other theories of therapeutic intervention have been explored. Parallels were presented between reactance theory and other concepts, such as psychoanalytic resistance, Haley's paradoxical injunctions, baseline cures during operant programs, Frankl's paradoxical intent, and Lindner's acceptance of a delusion.

As an examination of the process of translating from experimental material to clinical application, a study by Brehm and Cole (1966) on the effects of doing a favor was presented. It was shown how this experiment might apply to the therapist's being helpful to the client and to the client's trying out new behaviors "for the therapist." This type of translation process forms the basis for the extensive array of clinical applications to be surveyed in the following chapters.

CHAPTER
THREE

CLINICAL APPLICATIONS OF REACTANCE THEORY

*I   Persuading the client, social dependency,
and promoting prosocial behavior*

This chapter focuses on three major areas of clinical interest to which reactance theory can be applied: persuading the client, social dependency, and promoting prosocial behavior. For each area, empirical evidence is cited that documents the application to be derived from the theory. Some theoretical discussion is provided concerning each application, but a basic familiarity with the theory, which was detailed in the preceding chapter, is assumed. For the reader who desires to examine reactance theory in further detail, several sources that present both a theoretical and empirical overview are cited at the conclusion of Chapter Four.

PERSUADING THE CLIENT

In virtually every form of psychotherapy, there are occasions when the therapist attempts to influence the client through verbal (or nonverbal) persuasion. Behavior modifiers have to persuade people to use their techniques. Followers of Ellis's rational-emotive therapy have to convince the client that his worries are irrational. Interpersonally oriented therapists ask the client to accept their belief that interpersonal problems are the basis of his difficulty. Psychoanalysts make interpretations. Regardless of theoretical commitment, most practicing clinicians will acknowledge that verbal persuasion constitutes a major facet of their therapeutic repertoire. Indeed, Jerome Frank (1973) has argued strongly that persuasion is *the* fundamental basis of all psychotherapy. Given that verbal persuasion is, at least, an important element of psychotherapy, it is critical that therapists understand the variables that can lead to effective communications with the client and those that hinder such effectiveness.

Characteristics of the Communication

The general position of reactance theory in regard to any communication is simply that if it threatens the recipient's freedom, reactance will result, as well as any tendencies toward persuasion that might occur. This view postulates that two vectors of psychological pressure will be created, one leading toward resistance to conforming to the communication (reactance) and one leading toward conformity with the communication (persuasion). Whichever vector is the more powerful will determine whether the net result is a conforming or nonconforming belief or behavior.

From this theoretical position, one fact becomes apparent. The therapist's message is more likely to get across and to be adopted if the therapist phrases his communication in ways designed to reduce the likelihood of arousing reactance. Communications to clients should as much as possible avoid threatening their freedoms. Statements such as "But, of course, it's up to you," "It's your decision," "Think about it and see what you want to do" serve this function. On the other hand, words such as "must," "should," and "have to" may arouse reactance and reduce acceptance. M. L. Brehm (in J. W. Brehm, 1966) demonstrated this phenomenon in an early study on reactance when she gave college students two communications about an issue of interest to them. One was a persuasive communication; the other consisted of the same communication with the added statement, "You, as college students, must inevitably draw the same conclusion." The latter communication produced less positive attitude change toward the position advocated by the communication than the former.

Words, of course, are not the only means to convey strong social pressure. Looks, gestures, posture, and so on, can convey the same meaning, that is, "you must obey me." Such nonverbal signals can also act to reduce the likelihood of actual compliance. Therapists who are knowledgeable about what language they use, are aware of their nonverbal signals, and who can control these communicative elements are in the position to utilize whatever amount and/or form of social pressure they wish to, depending on the occasion. It is likely that such therapists can be more effective in helping their clients than therapists who either are not aware of their communication styles or who have little control over them.

One other reactance study is directly related to these considerations of the characteristics of the communication. R. A. Jones and J. W. Brehm (1970) found that if a person felt free to adopt either of two positions on an issue and received a one-sided communication, the effectiveness of that communication was reduced. Therapists may often be tempted to give one-sided messages, that is, to not discuss the other side of an issue with the client. Sometimes this is because the other side seems so obvious and so undesirable (to the therapist); sometimes it's because it's quicker to give a one-sided communication; sometimes it's because the therapist wants so strongly for the client to buy his (the therapist's) argument, that he (the therapist) doesn't want to take the chance of examining counterproposals. Whatever the reason, the Jones and Brehm experiment suggests that the therapist should proceed with caution. If a client is aware that there is another side to an issue and if he feels free to adopt this other side, should he so desire, then giving the client a one-sided communication runs the risk of arousing reactance and reducing the effectiveness of the communication. However, Jones and Brehm also found that when their subjects were unaware that there was another side to the issue, the one-sided argument was more effective than the two-sided one. Indeed, the one-sided message was somewhat more effective than the two-sided one even where the subjects were aware of the other side, but the reactance aroused in the aware condition greatly reduced its effectiveness. Thus, in general, the Jones and Brehm study actually supported the use of one-sided communications, but indicated that when such a communication threatens freedoms, it will lose considerable power.

Characteristics of the Therapist

It has been suggested that nonverbal characteristics of the therapist can threaten a client's freedom and reduce the effectiveness of a verbal persuasion. More specifically, J. W. Brehm and M. L. Brehm (in J. W. Brehm, 1966) found that when a threat to freedom (i.e., "you must agree") was given by an authority figure (a professor), college students were less likely to be persuaded than when this same threat to freedom was received from a high school student. When the professor's communication was without a threat to freedom, his message was as persuasive in convincing the college students as that of the high school student and both were quite persuasive. In this case, it appears that too much social pressure can boomerang. No doubt, authority figures, such as fatherly therapists, can be highly persuasive. However, the Brehm and Brehm study suggests that the more authoritative therapist should be especially cautious about those aspects of his verbal communication that pressure the client to comply.

Another characteristic of the therapist should be kept in mind. Sometimes therapists, perhaps especially those in training, become very involved personally in the success or failure of their therapeutic interventions. Clients of such therapists are likely to perceive two elements lurking behind any persuasive communication. First, the therapist can be very intent on persuading the client, believing that only if the client takes his advice can the therapy "work" and wanting very much for the therapy to work. Second, the client may sense, probably correctly, that this persuasive communication is not the last, but rather the first in a long series to come. A study by Brock (1965) suggests that the combination of these two elements can reduce the effectiveness of a persuasive communication.

When the client perceives the therapist's intent to persuade and anticipates future persuasion attempts, this may also amount to too much social pressure, and reactance will be created. If the intention to persuade is reducing the therapist's effectiveness, the therapist should work on changing, decreasing, or, at least, disguising his intentions. As for anticipated future attempts at persuasion there are numerous reasons (see p. 43) for the therapist to separate out a particular persuasion attempt from the implications it may have for future interaction. The therapist can tell the client that the present suggestions are "unusual," "unlikely to happen again," "just for this one time," and so forth. Any statement that helps to isolate one persuasion attempt so that future attempts are not anticipated will reduce the likelihood of reactance and increase the likelihood of persuasion.

Social influence by a peer. M. L. Brehm and J. W. Brehm (in J. W. Brehm, 1966) covaried both age and status. The authority figure was older and of higher status than the recipients of his communication; the high school student was younger and of lower status than the recipients of his communication. As was indicated, a strongly worded influence attempt by the authority figure created reactance, while the same message from the lower-status figure did not. No doubt most clinicians have found themselves in an authority relationship to most of their clients and in a non-authority relationship to some. But what about the clients with whom the therapist is a peer (i.e., of equal age and status)? In reactance studies that have involved the threatening of freedoms by a peer (e.g.,

Weiner, in Brehm, 1966; J. W. Brehm & Sensenig, 1966), it was found that when such threats were clear (e.g., "you must take that one"), reactance was created and there was the tendency for subjects to do the opposite of what had been suggested by the peer. Thus, we can conclude that unless a therapist is both younger and of lesser status than a client, there is good reason for the therapist to be concerned about and guard against crippling his persuasion attempts by the arousal of reactance.

Characteristics of the Client

Which clients are most likely to be subject to reactance arousal? Typically, to answer this question, we will look at interactions between characteristics of the client and characteristics of other elements of the situation. There is, however, one study that suggests what may be a general client characteristic. Wicklund and Brehm (1968) found that the more competent a person felt on an issue, the more likely that person was to experience reactance in response to a threat to freedom. This finding addresses the basic theoretical notion that for reactance to occur, the threatened freedom must be important to the individual. A person who feels incompetent regarding some behavior may simply not feel that his freedom to engage in this behavior is of any importance.

The application of the Wicklund and Brehm finding to the therapeutic situation is straightforward. When the client and therapist are discussing some behavior about which the client feels incompetent (never has done it, has no knowledge about it, etc.), the advice of the therapist may meet resistance (e.g., from fear of engaging in the behavior), but it is unlikely to create reactance. Under these circumstances, it is probably difficult to have too much social influence. If the therapist feels it is important for the client to engage in the behavior, he should strongly urge the client to take his advice. For the client who feels competent in regard to the behavior under discussion, however, too much social influence can occur and can create reactance. The therapist should thus monitor and control his own persuasive attempts accordingly.

Aside from the competence finding, most reactance studies that appear applicable to characteristics of the client involve an interaction of these characteristics with other elements in the communicative setting. Several of these studies involve an examination of the sequence of communicational events.

As reactance theory was originally formulated, Brehm (1966) hypothesized that reactance would be greater, the greater the degree of discrepancy between the attitude of the person and the attitude advocated by a persuader. Indeed, Brehm and Krasin (in Brehm,

1966) obtained evidence supporting this notion. Relatively soon thereafter, however, it became apparent that the problem was more complex than it had first appeared. Worchel and Brehm (1970) found that more reactance was induced by heavy-handed persuasion attempts that advocated the position initially held by the target subject than by persuasion attempts that advocated a position with which the target subjects disagreed. In other words, if subjects agreed with X and disagreed with Y, they showed more reactance when told they must agree with X than when they were told they must agree with Y. These findings, of course, directly contradicted the original hypothesis that the greater the discrepancy, the greater the reactance aroused.

Wicklund (1974) has examined this issue in detail. First, he notes that the Brehm and Krasin study was troubled with methodological difficulties that rendered it a less than adequate test of the original hypothesis. The Worchel and Brehm study, however, was free of such problems, and Wicklund adopts their conclusion that the original hypothesis was probably wrong. Wicklund then suggests that the important characteristic of the subjects who receive a communication strongly advocating a position they disagree with is that they, by disagreeing, have already demonstrated their freedom to hold the position opposite to the one being advocated as well as their freedom not to hold the position advocated. Such a prior demonstration of freedoms should, and apparently does, decrease reactance arousal. The situation is quite different for subjects who have endorsed the position that is subsequently advocated. They have not demonstrated their freedoms and thus when strongly urged to take the position they already hold, they respond with reactance arousal and, in order to reestablish their freedom, change their opinion away from the position they originally held. Thus reactance is greater for those subjects who originally agreed with the advocated position than for those who disagreed. Wicklund (1974) provides two studies (Ferris & Wicklund; Snyder & Wicklund) that support this reasoning.

But what if an opportunity is provided to subjects who agree with the advocated position to demonstrate their freedom prior to the influence attempt? Wouldn't this prior demonstration reduce their reactance arousal? Snyder and Wicklund examined these questions and showed that by assigning an essay on the merits of the side of the opinion with which they disagreed, subjects when confronted with a strong, freedom-threatening persuasive appeal to adopt the position they already believed in, showed little reactance and did not change toward the opinion with which they disagreed.

All of this is rather complicated and certainly is difficult to summarize intelligibly. Indeed, such a plethora of sides of the issue, agree or disagree with position advocated, etc., may account for why experimental social psychology is not particularly popular among clinicians. However, out of this mass of data, there are some practical ideas to be gained. The essential idea is really fairly simple and can be thought of in the following terms. When a therapist supports a position already held by the client—a belief the client holds that perhaps is not strong enough for him to act on without therapist support—the therapist will want to avoid reactance effects, which could cause the client to behave in a fashion opposite to that desired. These reactance effects can be avoided by giving the client an opportunity to take the other side of the issue prior to the therapist's supporting the client's original belief. The therapist then does not have to be very concerned about the possibilities of reactance. When the client is not given this opportunity, the possibilities for reactance remain, and if the therapist, wittingly or unwittingly, takes too strong a tack in his persuasive attempt, his efforts can bring about the opposite of the effect he wanted to achieve.

This issue may be fairly important. Therapists may well adopt, intuitively, the original reactance hypothesis. They may attempt to avoid persuasive communications that are widely discrepant from the client's position, feeling that such communications will not work and may even backfire. Psychoanalysts, for example, speak of not making the interpretation until the client is "ready for it," presumably, when the client is close to that interpretation himself. For a variety of reasons, widely discrepant communications may, indeed, not work, but the present evidence indicates that reactance is not what hinders their effectiveness.

On the other hand, probably very few therapists concern themselves with what can happen when they support a client's original belief. In fact, it may come as a relief to a therapist when he can be supportive of something the client already thinks. However, the literature cited above indicates that when the therapist is being supportive, there are possibilities for reactance to be aroused, greater possibilities than when the therapist is advocating a position discrepant with the client's belief. The literature also indicates that by providing the client with a chance to demonstrate his freedom to take the other side—prior to giving him the persuasive communication—undesired reactance effects can be avoided.

Such demonstrations of freedom are sequential in that they must take place before the persuasive communication in order for undesired reactance effects to be avoided. A study by Wicklund, Slattum, and Solomon (1970) indicates that a sequential aspect of therapist behavior can also affect reactance. Wicklund et al. obtained results indicating that, as already noted for barriers, the greater the proportion of freedoms that are threatened, the greater the reactance. This study differed from the barrier study on proportion of freedoms (Brehm, McQuown, & Shaban, in Brehm, 1966), however, by examining proportion as a function of behavioral sequence. They confirmed the hypothesis that a threat to freedom that is received early in a communicational sequence threatens, by implication, all of the remaining interchanges in that sequence and thus produces more reactance than a threat to freedom received toward the end of the sequence that threatens only the few remaining interchanges.

The relevance of this finding to therapy should be apparent and supports the clinical folklore that "you have to take it easy in the beginning." This particular "taking it easy" on social influence early in a therapeutic relationship is not, however, based on some implicit notion that as therapy progresses, the client will come closer to the therapist's understanding and thus make more powerful the therapist's interventions when they occur. Instead, the present suggestion of "taking it easy" in the early stages of therapy is based on the empirically supported hypothesis that there are more freedoms to be threatened early in a course of events than there are later. Thus, a clinician can probably arouse reactance more easily early in therapy than at a later time during therapy. If such reactance effects are undesirable, the therapist should make a special effort in the beginning stages of therapy not to threaten the client's freedoms.

It may be surprising that under the section Characteristics of the Client there has been no discussion of personality characteristics. This is not because such characteristics would not, in theory, affect reactance arousal, but because there has been only one study of the relationship between personality characteristics and reactance. Before describing this study and applying it to the clinical setting, I would like to indicate one of my beliefs about research on individual differences.

It would not be a very good research strategy for someone to administer every personality test known to man, and then to deliver a reactance manipulation, and then to correlate the findings. This sort of "shotgun" research is unlikely to be productive theoretically and may be difficult to apply to practical endeavors. Rather, individual research should focus on the personality characteristics that are postulated to be directly related to theoretical variables. Cherulnik and Citrin (1974) took this approach to relating personality characteristics to the reactance process. An examination of their reasoning will demonstrate how one can start with a consideration of the theory and relate this consideration to the appropriate personality dimension.

In examining reactance theory Cherulnik and Citrin noted that two types of external sources of threat were postulated. There were personal threats, where the threat was directed at the person (usually by other people), and impersonal threats where the threat affected the person but was not intentionally directed at him (e.g., the rain that cancels a picnic). They hypothesized that different types of people might be differentially affected by these different sources of threats. In particular, they reasoned that these sources of threats should be related to the beliefs about locus of control or causality under which the person usually operated.

Rotter (1966) has defined two types of people who differ on the locus of control dimension: "internals" ("I's"), who generally perceive the locus of causation to reside in themselves and who believe that they directly determine their outcomes in the world, and "externals" ("E's"), who perceive the locus of control to be in the external world and who believe that external sources control their outcomes. Synthesizing reactance theory with these differential personality types, Cherulnik and Citrin predicted that internals would experience more reactance in response to personal threats, and externals would experience more reactance in response to impersonal threats. The results of their experiment supported this prediction. It should be noted that Cherulnik and Citrin operationalized their threats such that the personal one was a social threat and the impersonal one was an asocial threat. One assumes, however, that Cherulnik and Citrin would predict the same results with two social threats, as long as one was personal and thus implicated the person's own behavior, and the other was impersonal and seemed unrelated to the person's behavior.

Having presented the only study thus far published relating reactance to an individual difference variable, there is little to expand on in its application to the clinical setting. Therapists don't usually administer the Rotter I-E scale to their clients, but the extreme types are probably easily recognized by therapists familiar with the I-E literature. The prescription for therapists who find themselves working with an extreme I or an extreme E is simply the direct application of the above findings. If the therapist wishes to avoid reactance arousal, he should avoid communications that constitute personal threats to I's and impersonal threats to E's. On the other hand, if the therapist wishes to arouse reactance adopting a therapeutic strategy à la Haley, he would suit the communication to the client, personal threats being administered to I's and impersonal ones to E's.

This discussion of the application of Cherulnik and Citrin's study illustrates some important problems in individual difference research. All we know from such a study is that given an extreme type of person (most individual difference research selects out the extremes of the population of interest), certain types of effects occur.

Personality variables are likely to be composed of many tendencies, and we don't know whether only one or a few of these tendencies account for the results obtained, or if all the tendencies have to be operative for the effect to result. An additional problem with the I-E dimension is that, as noted, it is not a personality variable that therapists commonly use in their assessments of a client.

Thus, instead of relying on individual difference studies such as Cherulnik and Citrin's, it may be a better procedure for clinicians to focus more on process variables, such as reactance, that apply to many individuals, or for clinicians to research the interfacing of those process variables with personality variables that are both directly related to the theory *and* clinically useful. Several such dimensions have been alluded to in the present discussion of reactance, including impoverishment of behavioral repertoires, suspiciousness, and competence in regard to behaviors. Others will be alluded to in the following pages, and practicing clinicians will no doubt be able to produce a host of their own.

SOCIAL DEPENDENCY AND ITS EFFECTS
ON THERAPEUTIC "FAVORS"

The translation section in Chapter One discussed an experiment by Brehm and Cole and applied the results of that experiment to a clinical setting. The application was based on the translation of the concept of "a favor" into therapeutic terms. It was suggested that the therapist has frequent opportunities to help the client out, usually in regard to the client's real-life situation, and that such help can be considered a favor. The client was considered to be doing the therapist a favor when he engaged in behavior or attitude change "for the therapist." (See pp. 27–31 for a more detailed discussion of this translation.)

There are other studies in the reactance literature that deal with favor-doing. These studies are especially relevant to clinical work because they include a consideration of social dependency. First the empirical findings will be described briefly; then the ways in which these findings might apply to the therapist and to the client will be discussed.

R. A. Jones (1970) conducted an elaborate study of the relationship between reactance and favor-doing. He varied three elements: choice versus no choice to do the favor, high versus low implication of the favor for future behavior, and high versus low dependence of the person who requested the favor. Dependence was defined as how much help was needed by the person requesting help: in the high dependence condition a great deal of help was needed; in the low dependence condition only a little was needed. Jones found two major effects. First, the greater the implication of doing the favor for future behavior, the less help was given. Second, if the person was free to choose whether or not to grant the favor, more dependency led to less help, but if the person could not choose (i.e., had to give some help), the more the dependency, the greater was the amount of help that was given.

Schwartz (1970) found results very similar to the ones cited above. He did not vary choice; all subjects had choice in all conditions. He found that if there was little chance that the favor would really occur (i.e., that the favor-requester would take the favor-doer up on his offer of help), the more help that was needed, the more help that occurred. On the other hand, if there was a good chance that the favor would really occur, a high level of need for help produced less help than a low or moderate level of need. Thus Schwartz found that implication for future behavior can interact with social dependency in the same way that Jones found for choice. Jones also found an effect for implication, but in his study this effect was not an interaction with social dependency, but rather a main effect such that the more implication, the less help. Thus, while there are some inconsistencies between the two studies (the main versus interactive effect for implication being the primary one), the results are quite similar.

In applying these studies to the clinical setting, let us first take the therapist's viewpoint. The therapist's goal will be assumed to be the same as it was in the discussion of Brehm and Cole in Chapter One: he wants the client to be willing to do things "for him" because in many cases this may be the only way to get the client to engage in novel and perhaps somewhat fear-provoking behaviors. When this "favor" is seen as likely to occur and the client has some choice about it, social dependency will create reactance and decrease the client's trying something "for the therapist."

There are, of course, many other reasons for the therapist not to be socially dependent on the client—it's considered "bad form" by the profession, may interfere generally with the therapist's interventions, and so forth—but here is a very specific one that documents the drawbacks that can be involved.

However, if such social dependency exists and the therapist knows that it exists and that the client perceives it (or if it doesn't exist, but the client thinks it does), the therapist still has some options to increase the probability that the client will try out behaviors "for him." One option is to reduce the implications for future behavior that the client might derive from one instance of favor-doing for the therapist. Jones's data suggest that this would be a good thing to do regardless of social dependency. The therapist can take care to isolate the one favor (or the one persuasion, discussed on p. 36) from other anticipated behaviors by stating that the present "doing it for him" is a rare event, is unlikely to happen again, and so forth. The therapist can also emphasize that future decisions to engage in new behaviors should be made on other grounds. This can act to reduce implications for future behavior and may also state the therapist's sincere feelings about the matter.

Another option, according to Jones's results, would be to reduce the perceived choice of the favor. The therapist would indicate that the client really has no choice but to do this for him. While this is theoretically tenable and might, indeed, reduce any reactance effects due to social dependency, it has serious practical drawbacks. First, such statements may be distasteful to many therapists, who prefer to emphasize the client's choice and responsibility rather than to command favors. Second, and perhaps more important, reducing choice in this situation may heighten the implication for future behaviors. "After all," the client may reason "if I obey his command in this case, what's he going to command me to do next session?" Thus any reduction of reactance that may take place by the therapist's decreasing the client's choice may be replaced by increased reactance due to the implicating of future behaviors. Theoretically, the sound strategy would be to decrease choice while simultaneously decreasing implications for future behaviors. The present author finds it impossible to envision how this could be done in practice; perhaps some readers may be able to devise a solution.

Since we are dealing with a dyadic interaction, these processes can also be considered from the client's point of view. For the sake of conceptual clarity, this was not done in the discussion of Brehm and Cole. Now, however, that a wide range of reactance effects and clinical applications have been presented, the reader has gained the freedom to "play with" the theory more easily, and it might be of interest to examine reactance and favor-doing from the perspective of the client.

First, let us reconsider the Brehm and Cole experiment (1966) from this perspective. Recall that Brehm and Cole found that the more important was the freedom to not be obligated to another person, the less likely it was that a favor would be reciprocated. It was pointed out that this freedom is likely to be most important to the client in the beginning stages of therapy and that the therapist should therefore refrain from doing favors for the client in such circumstances in order to increase the probability that the client will engage in new behaviors "for him" (the therapist). Interestingly enough, when considered from the client's point of view, the time sequence is reversed. The therapist probably places highest value on his freedom to be free from obligation to the client toward the end of therapy. Many therapists have a horror of the second part of Freud's "Analysis Terminable and Interminable" (1937) and want the therapeutic ties to end, or at least be drastically reduced, when therapy ends. This desire is quite reasonable and probably in the client's best interest. The typical therapeutic goal is independent functioning by the client and independent functioning is not achieved by the client who remains dependent on the therapist and/or to whom the therapist remains obligated. (The following discussion does not apply for clients for whom independent functioning is not the therapeutic goal.)

The client, then, who wishes to elicit favors from the therapist toward the end of therapy is generally well advised not to try to elicit them by doing favors for the therapist. Indeed, should the client employ favor-doing as a strategy, he may elicit fewer favors than would otherwise be the case. Favor-doing might, however, be effective early in therapy when the therapist does not place so much value on his freedom to not be obligated to the client.

What about the Jones and Schwartz studies? How do they apply from the client's point of view? The application is straightforward and simply reverses field from the previous discussion. Highly socially dependent clients are less likely to receive favors from the therapist than those who are not so dependent. If such social dependency exists or the therapist thinks it does, the client can increase the probability of eliciting favors by reducing implications for future behaviors ("just this one time") and/or by reducing choice. The latter approach has the same drawbacks as it did for the therapist and is probably even more difficult to carry out success-fully (or, at least, therapists like to believe it to be).

At this point some readers may be wondering why the coin of favor-doing was flipped. At one level, it is "playing with" the theory, and it is the author's firm belief that only when therapists begin to play with social psychological theories, by trying them out in their heads or on paper, will they be able use them successfully in their practice. There is another reason for looking at favor-doing from the point of view of the client. This is not meant to be a manual for client strategies, indeed relatively little attention will be paid to such procedures. But clients may act in such ways (being socially dependent, implicating future therapist behaviors, reducing the therapists' choices) for a multitude of reasons, and therapists should be aware of the effects these client behaviors can have on their (the therapists') behavior.

Therapists, presumably, should engage or not engage in favor-doing because of more objective reasons than the fact that the social dependency of the client produced reactance in the therapist. The therapist who is aware of the possibility of these effects may still not grant a favor to such a client because of other, more objective reasons, but this therapist is free to assess the situation with the client's benefit the primary concern instead of simply reacting to the client's dependency, denying the favor and using some "objective" reason to justify his (the therapist's) restoration of freedom. Therapists need to be good psychologists in order to help their clients. They also need to be good psychologists in order to understand their own behavior, be able to exert more control over it, and thus be more effective at helping their clients.

PROMOTING PROSOCIAL BEHAVIOR

A number of studies other than the ones already cited focus on help-giving as the dependent variable. These studies could be analyzed in terms of the therapist-client favor-doing paradigm discussed earlier. Rather than labor this point, however, and in the belief that the reader is by now well equipped to make this analysis himself, an alternative approach has been selected. The remaining studies of help-giving will be examined as illustrations of how current methods of promoting prosocial behavior may elicit reactance effects.

Instruction

Probably the easiest, although not necessarily the most frequently used, method of promoting prosocial behavior on the part of a client is for the therapist to instruct him to engage in such behavior. A variant of this approach is to emphasize the positive aspects of such behavior and to suggest that it will be rewarding to the client, the "Try it, you'll like it" approach to promoting prosocial behavior. Although we have relatively little empirical evidence on reactance effects occurring during the use of this approach, we would expect such injunctions to threaten the client's freedoms both to not try it and to not like it. In the closest approximation to this situation that is available in the literature, Goodstadt (1971) reports an experiment in which he found that when subjects were told that they liked a person, they helped that person less, and when they were told that they disliked the person, they helped that person more. These results are reminiscent of Haley's paradoxical injunction model and suggest that if the instructional approach, at least in this crude form, is to be used, it may be more effective when the prosocial behavior is derogated or forbidden in some way than when it is praised and advocated.

Modeling

Modeling is a popular approach to increasing prosocial behavior. The positive effects of modeling have been well demonstrated (Latané & Darley, 1970; Macaulay & Berkowitz, 1970). It is possible, however, for modeling to create reactance. Willis and Goethals (1973) report an experiment in which modeling of helping behavior led to reactance arousal and thus a reduction in helping behavior. They suggest that this occurred because following the model may have threatened other behavioral freedoms by implication. Fraser and Fuijitomi (1972) report a clever field study in which perceived prior compliance by others led to increased donations of money to a charitable cause when low reactance conditions (weak social influence and appropriate social characteristics) were in effect, whereas perceived prior compliance reduced giving when high reactance conditions (strong social influence and inappropriate social characteristics) were in effect.[1]

While there is no doubt that the use of modeling is an effective technique for increasing prosocial behavior, these studies suggest that reactance effects can accompany such modeling. The best ideas available on how to decrease these effects come from the experimental variables that have been used. Modeling should take place under low reactance conditions: the behavior to be modeled should be isolated from other behaviors, so that implications for future freedoms are reduced, and social influence factors (the prestige of the model, the attractiveness of the model, etc.) should be kept at a level low enough to avoid reactance arousal. In many instances, exact specification of such parameters prior to the modeling is probably impossible. Instead, the therapist should be guided by general principles such as those discussed above, his intuition about the appropriate operationalizing of these variables, and the knowledge that it may take a few trials and some errors before the best modeling presentation for a specific client is discovered.

Reinforcement

In view of the popularity among some therapists of using reinforcement techniques to promote just about any kind of behavior, this author feels somewhat timid about suggesting that reinforcement can create reactance and be detrimental to the production of behavior change. This timidity is perhaps better

---

[1] It's not clear to the present author why Fraser and Fuijitomi believed appropriate versus inappropriate social characteristics would affect reactance. Perhaps the implication principle was involved, e.g., "If I give to *that* person, who won't I give to?"

justified by the fact that a variety of theories (e.g., Lawrence & Festinger's effort justification paradigm, 1962; Amsel's theory of frustration, 1971; the traditional Skinnerian understanding; and J. W. Brehm's reactance theory) are currently in a state of flux as they contend for acceptance as ways to understand traditional learning effects such as the increased resistance to extinction that follows cessation of intermittent reinforcement as compared to continuous reinforcement.

Involvement in theoretical issues such as these is beyond the scope of this book. What should be considered is the simple point that reactance theory predicts that reinforcement (rewarding a behavior) may create reactance when such rewards threaten the person's freedom to engage in the alternative behavior that is not being rewarded and/or the freedom to not engage in the behavior being rewarded. The arousal of reactance will lead to efforts to restore the threatened freedoms, and direct restoration will be manifested in reduced engagement in the rewarded behavior. Bowers (1971) has provided some evidence of this effect.

If this point is granted, one would expect such reactance effects to vary according to already indicated variables relevant to the theory. That is, reactance as a response to reward should be more likely to occur if the importance of the freedom to not engage in the rewarded behavior and/or the importance to engage in an alternative nonrewarded behavior is high, if the agent delivering the reward is seen as intending to change the person's behavior, if implications for future freedoms are high, and so forth. Thus to avoid arousing reactance when rewards are being administered, the agent delivering the reward should not present himself as intending to change the person's behavior, implications for future behavior should be kept low; and rewards should be applied, if possible, to behaviors where the freedoms not to engage in the rewarded behavior and/or to engage in nonrewarded behaviors are not very important. This latter suggestion is probably not highly relevant to clinical practice since most of the behaviors that a clinician would reward would be quite important and the behaviors not being rewarded, often the symptomatic behaviors, would also be important to the client. Probably the simplest way to avoid arousing reactance during an operant treatment program is to keep the level of the pressure to engage in one behavior rather than another relatively low, that is, to keep the number of rewards as low as possible. Additional support for this suggestion of keeping the number of rewards to a minimum will be found in the chapters on cognitive dissonance.

SUMMARY

This chapter has examined three aspects of clinical practice to which reactance theory can be applied. First, reactance theory was considered for its relevance to the therapeutic persuasion of the client. Characteristics of the persuasive communication, of the therapist, and of the client were discussed in terms of their impact on the persuasion process. Second, the effects that social dependency might have on the interaction between the therapist and the client were examined. These effects were considered from the standpoint of the therapist and of the client. A reexamination of the Brehm and Cole (1966) experiment was provided as an additional example of how reactance effects can influence the therapist as well as the client. Finally, reactance theory principles were applied to the various methods—instruction, modeling, and reinforcement—that have been used to promote prosocial behavior.

CHAPTER
FOUR

CLINICAL APPLICATIONS OF REACTANCE THEORY

II Paradoxical effects, inexplicable behaviors,
and the minimizing of reactance effects

This chapter extends the application of reactance theory to areas of clinical interest by exploring some unusual events in therapy. These events are considered unusual either because the therapist does not expect them and they appear paradoxical to him, or because they refer to behaviors of the client that take the therapist by surprise and, while not paradoxical in appearance, are difficult for him to explain. The concluding section offers a summary of the ways in which reactance effects can be minimized and some new approaches to the avoidance of reactance arousal.

PARADOXICAL EFFECTS

Therapeutic Influence in the Absence of the Therapist

J. W. Brehm and M. Mann (1975) recently completed a study that, although explicitly designed to examine group influence, obtained results that are highly relevant to the dyadic interaction between therapist and client. Two variables were manipulated: the importance of the freedom that was threatened by an influence attempt and the attractiveness of the source of this attempt.

Brehm and Mann found that high attraction to the group increased public and private compliance with an influence attempt when the importance of the freedom to hold one's own position was low. When, however, the importance of the freedom was high, high attraction led to less public and private conformity than low attraction. Moreover, in one of the most intriguing aspects of this study, when the pressure to comply was removed, those subjects who valued highly their freedom to hold their own position, who found the group highly attractive, and who had demonstrated reactance on previous measures of their attitudes changed toward the position that had been advocated by the group.

This study has several implications for therapists. First, there is the seemingly paradoxical effect of attraction. A therapist would probably not be surprised if influence attempts failed when he felt his clients did not like or value him. On the other hand, a therapist probably feels that his influence attempts are more likely to be successful when his clients are attracted to him. This reasoning has been explicated by Goldstein, Heller, and Sechrest (1966).

> Our general proposition is that by heightening the favorableness of patient attraction toward his therapist, to that degree does the patient become more receptive to therapist influence attempts. (p. 81)

The findings by Brehm and Mann suggest a hitch in this reasoning. While it may be true under some circumstances that the more attractive a therapist is to his client, the more effective the therapist's influence will be, this would be so because attraction to someone can act as a pressure to agree with that person. It can be distinctly aversive to disagree with someone you like. However, because attraction produces social pressure to conform, it can also make that social pressure too strong and, in conjunction with an important freedom that is being threatened, create reactance. Thus, ironically, the therapist who is liked and respected by his client and who issues a strong communication recommending that the client engage in some activity that is important to the client runs the risk of being less successful than a therapist who is disliked by his client and offers the client the same recommendation. Over and over again in the reactance literature, we come across the message that the very variables that are usually thought of as furthering successful influence are also the variables that under some conditions can create reactance and reduce influence.

The second implication of the Brehm and Mann study, the delayed social influence they obtained, is perhaps even more interesting than the first. This delayed influence, sometimes called a "sleeper effect," suggests a rationale for the beneficial changes that can occur when therapy is interrupted or terminated. There is ample clinical folklore about "vacation cures," many of which may be ephemeral but some of which no doubt are genuine. From the viewpoint of the Brehm and Mann study, such "vacation cures" are readily understandable. It is quite likely that during ongoing therapy the client feels himself under strong pressure to change. This pressure may be so strong, in spite of the therapist's best efforts to the contrary, that reactance and thus resistance to change are created. Under these circumstances, change may be minimal and change in the opposite direction (e.g., "getting worse," "regression") may even occur.

Then the therapist leaves for vacation or the therapy is terminated. At this point pressures are reduced and positive influence variables can begin to have their effect without being reduced or negated by reactance. Without reactance, the client is free to change in the direction advocated by the therapist and, presumably, desired by the client himself. If such "cures" or at least therapeutic advances disappear when therapy resumes, any therapist who had read this book would know where to look for the culprit. With the renewal of therapy, social pressures have increased again to the point where reactance is induced, and the therapist should make every effort to reduce these pressures back to their optimal level. It is, in fact, conceivable that, instead of the hour or two a week schedule being institutionalized for all clients, frequent breaks or vacations from therapy can be extremely helpful for certain individuals. With a little help from reactance theory, the therapist will be able to utilize even his absence to benefit his client.

The Threat of New Freedoms

By this point, it should be clear that reactance theory has nothing to say about freedom as a global concept, but addresses itself to specific behavioral or attitudinal freedoms and to threats that can be directed toward these freedoms. Perhaps nowhere is this distinction better illustrated than in a study by J. W. Brehm and E. Rosen (1971). Most people think of freedom in global terms. Based on this, most people, and probably most therapists, think of the relationship between satisfaction and freedom as being direct, the more freedom the more satisfaction (Fromm, 1941, ranks as a notable exception to this consensus). By addressing itself to specific freedoms rather than to this global notion, reactance theory has been able to formulate the possibility that the issue may be considerably more complex than is implied by the hypothesis the more freedom, the more satisfaction.

Brehm and Rosen suggested that when a person has a repertoire of "old," established freedoms, the introduction of new, attractive freedoms can arouse reactance. These new, attractive freedoms, because they are new and attractive, create pressures on the person to adopt them and to forsake the old, established ones. If this pressure is great enough, reactance can be aroused and, instead of diminishing in attractiveness, those old freedoms can increase in attractiveness. Brehm and Rosen's experiment confirmed this reasoning and indicated that the old freedom that is most affected by this process is the one that was most attractive before the new freedoms were introduced.

Every clinician should recognize the clinical paradigm to which this study relates. The Brehm and Rosen experiment suggests that resistance to change, which is surely the most common problem in all of psychotherapy, may exist not only because of habit or fear or fixations or behavioral impoverishment, but because of the threat to a person's established freedoms that is posed when the possibility of gaining new freedoms by engaging in new behaviors is envisioned by the client and/or described by the therapist. This suggests a rather unhappy state of affairs. Most therapists for most clients want to increase their freedoms, to enlarge their spheres of action, to maximize, as some would say, their self-actualization. But in even the most skillful urging, the message is clear—gaining a new freedom by engaging in a new behavior threatens the freedom to engage in old behaviors that were free behaviors for the client. What can be done to reduce reactance in this situation? How can we open up new freedoms to our clients without enhancing the attractiveness of their old behaviors?

Probably the most effective strategy is to make sure that the freedom to engage in the old behaviors is not threatened by consideration of and attempts at new behaviors. The therapist can point out to the client that engaging in the new behavior does not, for example, preclude engaging in the old behavior; the new behavior can be presented as an addition to the client's behavioral repertoire rather than as a substitute for already existing behaviors. In many cases, reactance will probably be avoided if the client feels free to engage in the old behavior. In some cases, however, it may be necessary to demonstrate the client's freedom to him by urging him to actually engage in the old behavior.

The latter approach may have its limits when the therapist is working with a client whose old behaviors are grossly maladaptive or even dangerous to himself or others. What must be realized, however, is that the client is likely to engage in those old behaviors anyway—for many reasons, reactance being one—and that, in general, it's better to bring such behaviors under at least partial control by the therapist and to utilize them in therapeutic ways rather than to let them occur as they will. Indeed, from a reactance point of view, engaging in the old behaviors at the behest of the therapist is likely to be a particularly effective approach to eventually diminishing this behavior. First, relatively few actual acts should be sufficient to establish the client's freedom to act. This should counter the tendency for the introduction of new behaviors to arouse reactance and make the old behaviors more attractive. Second, urging the client to engage in the old behaviors may operate as a paradoxical injunction and threaten the freedom to engage in the new behavior, thus making the new behavior more attractive and increasing the probability of its occurrence.

In instances where engaging in the old behavior poses an extreme risk for the client and therefore cannot be urged by the therapist, the client can be urged to engage in substitute old behaviors that carry less risk. Again, the aim is to give the client the feeling of maintaining his freedom vis-à-vis the old behaviors and thus to help him relinquish these old behaviors in favor of the new ones. Another approach in the face of high risk, old behaviors is to offer new behaviors that are as similar as possible to the old ones but that are more beneficial to the client. This strategy makes use of the unique instrumental value postulate of reactance theory and assumes that if the new behavior is similar to the old behavior, that is, satisfies many of the same needs, the introduction of the new behavior will be less likely to arouse reactance.

INEXPLICABLE BEHAVIORS

Indirect Sources of Reactance Arousal

It was noted in the theoretical presentation that the principle of implication vastly extended the possibilities for reactance arousal. This principle, in the form of implications of one act for future behavioral freedoms, has already been seen to be of considerable importance. Other sorts of implications will be discussed in this section and the section Restoration of Freedom.

There are occasions when a client begins to act in ways that suggest to the therapist that reactance has been aroused, but the therapist is unable to uncover any direct reactance-eliciting event that has occurred to the client. For example, a client begins proclaiming vigorously his freedom to engage in some undesirable behavior and perhaps engages in this behavior at an unexpectedly high frequency and with unexpectedly high intensity. The therapist, however, after careful exploration with the client is unable to discover any significant threat to the freedom to engage in this behavior that has been directly experienced by the client.

Studies by Andreoli, Worchel, and Folger (1974), and Worchel (1972) suggest that the source of this behavior may be in what the client has lately observed. Andreoli et al. found that reactance can be aroused in an individual when he observes another person's freedom being threatened, even when the observer does not anticipate interacting with either the person (or event) that made the threat or the person who received the threat. All that is necessary is that the freedom that is threatened be of importance to the observer. Moreover, Worchel (1972), found that observing a film depicting a certain type of behavior increased the importance of the freedom to engage in that behavior and thus led to increased reactance effects when that freedom was threatened.

Presumably, then, people can experience reactance arousal by merely observing others' freedoms being threatened, and can become increasingly vulnerable to reactance arousal from even relatively mild threats if the importance of the threatened freedom has been increased through observing a filmed depiction of the behavior. Perhaps, although there is no empirical evidence on this, people may even have their freedoms threatened through observing actors in films or on television experience such threats.

We have here a compelling example of the well-known fact that while the therapist may have finely tuned control over the therapeutic sessions, he has much less control over events that occur outside therapy. Perhaps more disturbing, though not surprising to most therapists, is the suggestion that even relatively casual events such as observing the interactions of strangers or watching a movie can affect the client's behavior. There is no conceivable way, of course, that therapists can prevent such occurrences—short of placing the client in a controlled environment for twenty-four hours a day (and one wonders if there truly are any such environments, not to mention the obvious negative aspects of being thus restricted).

When a therapist is confronted with a client who appears to be experiencing reactance arousal, the possible sources of this arousal should probably be explored. If the client has experienced a direct threat to his freedom, especially if this threat stemmed from someone with whom the person interacts frequently, such as a family member, close friend, or business associate, the therapist and the client need to recognize both the threat and its consequences. It may be especially helpful in such cases for the therapist to explain the principles of reactance to the client. If the source is a familiar one, the client may be unable to avoid interactions with this person, and the therapist may have little control over the source's behavior. The client, then, is likely to be subjected repeatedly to reactance-arousing behavior on the part of this familiar person, and the amount of reactance experienced by the client is likely to be unpleasantly large.

Teaching the client the principles of reactance may help him, as presumably it will help therapists, to be more objective about his own behavior and to exercise more control over it. After all, if Mr. X always does A because Mr. Y tells him to do B, Mr X may be doing A to reestablish his freedom, but, in fact, Mr. Y has near-perfect control over Mr. X's behavior. When the client learns this, he may be able to decide whether he wants to do A or B, regardless of what the other person is urging him to do.

If, however, a careful exploration of the circumstances surrounding the client's reactance-like behavior reveals no evidence of a direct threat to the client's freedom, the therapist may decide to stop working on finding the source of the client's behavior and start concentrating on the behavior itself. It is important to carry out therapeutic interventions, such as reassuring the client that he can engage in the threatened behavior, so as to reduce the pressure on the client to engage in this behavior. There is probably no way to prevent the indirect arousal of reactance, but there are ways to reduce reactance, so that the client's behavior is not adversely affected.

Unexpected Behavior Change

Sometimes a client has indicated a clear preference for one thing over another and then suddenly chooses the less preferred alternative. Other times a client seems to vacillate endlessly between choosing one course of behavior or another and never arrives at a decision. These changes may be unexpected (although after a while the latter behavior becomes discouragingly predictable), but they may not be accompanied by either the frequency or intensity that would lead a therapist to suspect an external threat to freedom.

A number of studies (Linder & Crane, 1970; Linder, Wortman, & Brehm, 1971; Brehm, Jones, & Smith, in Wicklund, 1974) suggest that these behavior reversals can be understood in terms of reactance theory. Picture to yourself the psychological state of a person as he approaches a decision. In most cases, the person sees one alternative as preferable to the other alternative(s). This very preference, however, threatens his freedom to select the other alternative(s) as well as his freedom to reject the preferred alternative. As the time for making the decision draws closer, these threats become more salient to the person and the freedoms that are being threatened become more important. Reactance increases steadily as the time for decision draws closer and may even result in behavior reversal, that is, choosing a less preferred alternative over the originally preferred one.

There are certain parametric considerations in this sequence. If the choice is between a highly attractive alternative and a completely undesirable one, reactance arousal is likely to be minimal. This is because the freedoms to select an undesirable alternative and to reject a highly attractive one are not very important. When, however, the alternatives approach equality in their desirability (or undesirability), the possibilities for reactance arousal and behavior reversal are increased.

What is the therapist to do about such a situation? An obvious course, in cases where the therapist has a firm opinion about which behavioral alternative would benefit the client, is for the therapist to increase the differential between the decision alternatives. He can (hopefully, in ways that do not arouse reactance) emphasize the positive aspects of one alternative and the negative aspects of the other(s). Another possibility, in cases where the selection of one alternative doesn't mean the total relinquishing of the other, is for the therapist to indicate to the client that he still has the freedom to engage in the rejected alternative. Finally, for the vacillating client, the therapist may want to structure events in such a way that the client has to make a decision (one way to do this is to indicate that no decision is in fact a decision and then to proceed as if a decision has been made). Reactance effects may ensue, but there is a good probability that as long as the client feels he had some responsibility for the choice and makes some behavioral commitment to it, dissonance reduction will set in and the client will come to terms with the choice. (See Chapters Five, Six, and Seven for further discussion of these postdecisional effects.)

MINIMIZING REACTANCE EFFECTS

Restoration of Freedom

Once reactance has been aroused, what can a therapist do to reduce it? As has been noted, the therapist can help the client feel free to engage in the threatened behavior; he can also participate in helping the client directly restore his freedom by having the client engage in the behavioral freedoms that have been threatened. There are also some less obvious ways to restore freedom.

Worchel and Brehm (1971) report a study in which observation of another person restoring his freedom led to a reduction in reactance in the observers. This very significant point parallels the implication principle (discussed above) that allows for observed activity to threaten freedom. An individual whose freedom has been threatened may have it restored by observing another person who has experienced a similar threat restore his (the other person's) freedom. Even though the observer has not been directly involved, the observed restoration may, by implication, reflect back on him.

Child clinicians have an opportunity to restore the freedom of their clients, based on this principle. Children typically take great delight when their therapists don't accept parental directives. This delight may be composed of many features (indirect aggression, no doubt, being one), but it may also indicate that when the therapist restores his freedom vis-à-vis the client's parents, the client's freedom may be indirectly restored. This process reduces the pressure on the child to behave in counterparental fashion, which is beneficial because such counterbehaviors often are not in the child's best interest and create increased conflict between parents and child.

The therapist who works with adults may indirectly restore a client's freedom when he interacts with any significant other in the client's life (spouse, employer, etc.). In addition, the therapist can have the client role-play restorative behaviors. This may serve two functions. First, the therapist can model appropriate restorative behaviors and have them practiced by the client, so that if the client engages in direct restoration activities, they are less likely to be inappropriate or harmful. Second, the role-playing may in and of itself reestablish the client's freedom, thus reducing pressure on the client to engage in restorative behaviors and facilitating a more objective consideration by the client of what he really wants to do.

A second type of restoration effect has been described by Worchel and Andreoli (1974). In their experiment, subjects reduced reactance by attributing another person's reactance-inducing behavior to situational rather than personal causes. (Attribution processes are discussed in detail in Chapters Eight, Nine, and Ten.)

The investigators reasoned that some behaviors that occur in a continuing interaction evoke a norm of reciprocity, that is, friendly behavior requires reciprocal friendly behavior, and hostile behavior engenders reciprocal hostility. When a person is confronted with such norm-evoking behavior, his freedoms to not engage in the reciprocal behavior and to engage in the nonreciprocal behavior are threatened, and reactance is produced. In the Worchel and Andreoli study, this reactance was reflected in the derogation of the person initiating the reciprocal behavior. If, however, the person's norm-evoking behavior can be attributed to situational constraints, rather than to that person's own needs, motives, traits, and so forth, the obligation to return the behavior should be less—no particular reciprocity being evoked if the situation dictated the person's behavior—and reactance should be reduced. Worchel and Andreoli found that such a reduction of reactance did occur as a function of the opportunity to attribute the cause of the person's behavior to environmental characteristics rather than to personal characteristics of the person. This reduction in reactance was manifested in increased positive evaluation of the person initiating the reciprocal behavior.

Therapists should keep in mind the Worchel and Andreoli results when they are working with a client who is engaged in interactions in which reciprocal behaviors are likely to be initiated. The client may, upon perceiving the other person initiate a norm-evoking behavior, feel obligated to respond. This may create reactance and lead to hostility toward the other person. In order to reduce this hostility, the therapist can point out the situational characteristics that led the other person to behave the way he did. In accordance with the Worchel and Andreoli findings, this should lead to decreased reactance and decreased hostility on the part of the client.

It is possible to extend Worchel and Andreoli's reasoning to behaviors other than feelings of hostility. Let us consider what should happen to the reciprocal behaviors. If a person acts friendly toward us and we value our freedom to not act friendly toward him (or at least our freedom to make our own decision about how to behave toward him), reactance should be created, hostility should occur, *and* the likelihood of our acting friendly should be reduced. Similarly, a hostile act threatens our freedom to *not* respond in a hostile fashion and may thus create hostile feelings but reduce the probability of hostile behavior. In order to restore the freedom to not be friendly, one acts hostilely, while in order to restore the freedom to not be hostile, one acts friendly.

The reasoning behind the hypothesis that friendly behavior may lead to less friendly behavior has been confirmed by Brehm and Cole (1966). There are, indeed, occasions when being friendly will elicit both nonfriendly behavior and hostile feelings. Worchel and Andreoli found that these feelings may be mitigated by attributing the other person's behavior to environmental causes, and it may be that more friendly behavior also would result from such attributions.

When we consider the relationship between reactance and hostile behavior, however, we find a more complicated situation. For one thing, it is questionable whether less hostile behavior but more hostile feelings would ever be desirable, so the suggestion that less hostile behavior can be created through arousing reactance may not be very meaningful. In addition, if hostile behavior on the part of one person did, in fact, lead to reactance arousal and less hostile behavior on the part of the recipient, this could only occur under very special circumstances, such as when the freedom to *not* counteraggress was very important. There is abundant empirical evidence to indicate that hostile behavior usually evokes hostile behavior (see Hokanson, 1961). Furthermore, Nezleck and Brehm (1975) have found that when a person receives an insult, the freedom to counteraggress is created (rather than the freedom to not counteragress being threatened) and that hostility is heightened unless an opportunity to counteraggress is provided.

Thus the relationship among reactance, hostility, and aggression remains difficult territory. We do know that reactance leads to, or occurs simultaneously with, aggression (Worchel, 1974) and that attributing reactance-inducing behavior to external rather than personal causes reduces hostile feelings (Worchel & Andreoli, 1974). However, many questions remain for future research. At present, therapists are probably well advised to stick to known premises and to wait for future research to clarify the more complex relationships.

Suppression of Reactance

The notion that certain behaviors on the part of the therapist can minimize the possibility of arousing reactance in the client has been present throughout the discussion of reactance. Overly strong social pressure can be avoided, perceivable intent to persuade can be minimized, opportunities for prior demonstrations of freedom can be provided, communications can be tailored to the characteristics of the client, the continuing existence of the freedom to engage in old behaviors or rejected alternatives can be emphasized, social dependency and implications for future behaviors can be avoided, and so on. This section discusses two methods of suppression of reactance that have been investigated explicitly as suppressive mechanisms.

Grabitz-Gniech (1971) suggested that when a person commits himself to a group decision, and presumably is a part of the group's decision-making process, reactance will be reduced. While her study is obviously relevant to group therapy, the application to the dyadic therapeutic situation should be similar. A therapist who wishes to reduce undesired reactance arousal can do so by avoiding commands to the client and emphasizing joint, consultative decision-making. This type of reactance suppression may be useful in marital therapy.

A goodly number of marital conflicts may have their source in reactance arousal by one partner or the other. One of the more valuable lessons that can be learned from marital therapy is the necessity for mutual, consultative decision-making within the marriage. The therapist working with a married couple can emphasize the importance of this process both by explaining how unilateral decisions and commands can create reactance and thus resistance to the decision, and by modeling how one goes about involving both interested parties in a decision.

Pallak and Heller (1971) demonstrated a second type of reactance suppression. They showed that reactance can be suppressed by the implication of future interaction. This finding may be surprising, in view of all the attention that has been given to the evidence suggesting that future implications for behavior can increase reactance. To resolve this apparent conflict, consider the various elements that are involved when two people are engaged in a long-term relationship. For example, if the importance of the issue upon which partner A is exerting influence is relatively low, the importance of continuing in the relationship may reduce reactance effects in partner B, as shown by Pallak and Heller. Partner B may be willing to give up his freedom to hold an opposing opinion or engage in an alternative action in order to maintain a positive relationship with partner A. On the other hand, if the importance of the issue is high, reactance effects would be expected to occur in response to a reactance-inducing communication; due to the implications for future behavior that exist in a long-term relationship, these effects may even be increased.

If the results of Pallak and Heller are applied to clinical activity, it would seem that therapy may in general be a situation that reduces reactance effects. Most clients anticipate interacting with their therapists over a course of time; according to Pallak and Heller, this anticipation of future interaction should reduce reactance effects.

The therapist should be aware, however, that this reduction may depend on the importance of the issue being discussed. When the therapist attempts to influence the client on an important issue, the effect of anticipated future interaction may be to increase reactance arousal. If this proves to be the case, the therapist has some options. He can attempt to reduce the importance of the issue, although this may be difficult. He can, as has frequently been recommended, attempt to isolate the specific persuasion attempt from any implications for future behavior. Or he can arrange to deliver the persuasion attempt just before either the termination of therapy or a break in therapy. In the last instance, implications for future behavior are reduced because immediate future interaction is not anticipated and the sleeper effect of delayed positive influence (see p. 53) may contribute to reducing reactance and increasing persuasion.

SUMMARY

This chapter has focused on some unusual events in therapy that can be better understood through a reactance theory analysis and on ways to minimize reactance effects when they are not desired. Two seemingly paradoxical occurrences were described: the case in which the client shows the influence of therapy in the absence of the therapist and the one in which the introduction of new behaviors to the client leads to his engaging more vigorously in old behaviors. The application of reactance theory to these occurrences helped to explain them and provided methods to utilize them for the client's benefit. Two events that were difficult to understand were examined. It was shown that reactance theory explains such therapeutic surprises as reactance arousal in the absence of a direct threat to freedom, and decision reversals. The final topic dealt with the numerous ways in which reactance can be reduced once it has been aroused or can be prevented from being aroused.

SUGGESTED SOURCES

Brehm, J. W. *A Theory of psychological reactance.* New York: Academic Press, 1966.

Brehm, J. W. *Responses to loss of freedom: A theory of psychological reactance.* Morristown, N.J.: General Learning Press, 1972.

Wicklund, R. A. *Freedom and reactance.* Hillsdale, N.J.: Lawrence Erlbaum Associates, 1974.

PART TWO

DISSONANCE THEORY

CHAPTER FIVE

A THEORY OF COGNITIVE DISSONANCE

Karl Menninger (1964) quoting Nils Haak (1957) on the analytical situation:

"The analysis must involve a sacrifice, otherwise it becomes a matter of indifference in the patient's life." (p. 35)

Jerome Frank (1973) on psychoanalysis:

Finally the magnitude of the sacrifices the trainee has made to master certain methods and doctrines, and his public adherence to them, create a strong incentive for belief. For if the analyst were to abandon his position, his sacrifices would have been in vain and he would be under the painful necessity of admitting that he had been wrong. In this connection, that the method may not work well and that the doctrine is open to question may paradoxically strengthen the analyst's dogmatic adherence to them as a way of stifling his misgivings. It probably also contributes to the perpetuation of analytic institutes, irrespective of the actual merits of what they teach. For one of the best ways to allay self-doubts is to try to convert others to one's point of view, thereby gaining confirmation of its correctness from them. Conceivably this may be one factor in the energy devoted to the propagation of analytic doctrines. (pp. 175–176)

Clifford Madsen and Charles Madsen (1972) on a behavior modification approach to child- rearing:

It is much easier to act your way into a new way of thinking than to think your way into a new way of acting. (p. 31)

In many ways, reactance theory was an ideal theory with which to begin the substantive chapters of this book. It deals with a dramatic, not uncommon behavior in the clinical setting (i.e., behavior reversals), it has a literature that is broad enough to be interesting but is not so large as to be unmanageable, and its theoretical premises have remained relatively stable since their first enunciation by J. W. Brehm (1966). These characteristics facilitated presentation of the theory and its related findings and, it is hoped, enabled the reader to feel rather expert about reactance theory by the end of the chapters.

In Chapters Five, Six, and Seven our theoretical focus possesses many more difficulties than the previous focus had. The behavior that is described by the theory of cognitive dissonance is not as dramatic, by and large, as that described by reactance theory. The literature of cognitive dissonance is immense and to cover it in anywhere near its entirety would require a separate volume. Furthermore, cognitive dissonance is, for social psychology, a relatively "old" theory. During the years since Festinger's original formulation in 1957, there have been numerous modifications of the theory.

These difficulties will be reflected in our examination of cognitive dissonance and its relevance to the clinical setting. Considering the above features in reverse order, the following approaches will characterize this presentation. In order to provide some sense of continuity for readers who may at one time or the other have studied dissonance theory as well as to indicate the method in which a theory in social psychology can be developed, the presentation of theory will follow a historical outline. Festinger's original theory will be discussed and then modifications that have been made will be explicated.

To cope with the problem of a huge literature, coverage of dissonance theory has been severely restricted here. Although some mention will be made of the variety of experimental investigations that have been carried out under the dissonance rubric, only those investigations that appear most relevant to the clinical setting will be cited in detail. As the reader will see, this highly selective process still leaves a lot of territory to cover.

Finally, the provision of some general perspective may be appropriate. Although the behavioral focus of dissonance theory may not be as dramatic as that of reactance theory, this will not detract from dissonance theory's usefulness to the clinician. The reader is forewarned that some of the theory discussion may seem dry and overly cognitive. The clinical application chapters, however, will show that dissonance theory has tremendous implications for clinical endeavors and may, in some ways, be the most powerful theory for engendering desirable change examined by this book.

THE THEORY

The Original Formulation

Leon Festinger's book *A Theory of Cognitive Dissonance* was published in 1957. While there had been earlier published studies of dissonance processes (e.g., J. W. Brehm, 1956), Festinger's book marked the first full presentation of the theory. Festinger proposed that cognitions (i.e., information or knowledge about the self or the world) are related to each other in one of two ways. Cognitions may have an irrelevant relationship to each other, one cognition not implying anything about the other(s), or they may be relevant to each other. When cognitions are in a relevant relationship to one another, such relationships are either consonant or dissonant. A consonant relationship occurs when relevant cognitions "fit" with each other. When X implies Y, and, in fact, X and Y exist, X and Y are said to be consonant with each other. When, however, relevant cognitions do not "fit," when "the obverse of one element would follow from the other" (Festinger, 1957, p. 13), a dissonant relationship is created. Dissonance would occur when X implies Y, and when X and not-Y actually exist.

The words "follow from" are critical in this definition of relevant relationships among cognitions. Festinger stated that dissonance may be produced by logical inconsistencies (e.g., a person who prays but doesn't believe in God commits a logical inconsistency), cultural mores (e.g., being a Methodist and drinking represents dissonance between a person's behavior and the norms of his religion), specific opinions included in a general opinion (e.g., favoring a specific Democratic candidate doesn't follow from believing oneself to be a Republican), and past experience (having always been successful and then failing is dissonant). This list is certainly not exhaustive, but it should be sufficient to indicate that Festinger conceived of "follow from" to mean any circumstances under which two cognitions do not fit and, indeed, contradict each other.

Festinger proposed that whenever cognitions are in a dissonant relationship, a state of dissonance is created. This state was viewed as being aversive and as having motivational properties. Given its aversive qualities, a person would be motivated to avoid an increase in the arousal of dissonance and to reduce that dissonance that has been aroused.

Festinger stated that the magnitude of dissonance arousal is a function of two factors. The first is the importance of the cognitive elements. The more important the cognitions, the more dissonance would be aroused. The second is the proportion of dissonant elements. This factor is more critical because it represents a unique aspect of dissonance theory in comparison to any other cognitive consistency theory (e.g., Heider, 1958; Osgood & Tannenbaum, 1955). Focusing on one cognition, we can enumerate the other cognitions that are relevant to it. Among these, some will be consonant and others will be dissonant with the cognition of interest. As the number of dissonant cognitions increases, in relation to consonant ones, the magnitude of dissonance will increase.

Dissonance reduction attempts will be a function of the magnitude of dissonance arousal. As the magnitude of dissonance increases, so will the strength of the pressures to reduce that dissonance. Dissonance can be reduced by adding new consonant elements to increase the number of consonant elements in relation to dissonant elements or by eliminating dissonant cognitions. Dissonance can also be reduced by changing dissonant cognitions into consonant ones. Whether or not a cognition will be changed and which cognition it will be depend on the cognitions' resistance to change. Maximum possible dissonance is determined by the total resistance to change of the least resistant cognition; at the point of maximum dissonance, that cognition least resistant to change will change. It would also be possible to reduce dissonance by reducing the importance of one or more of the dissonant cognitions. These ways of reducing dissonance are called "modes" of dissonance reduction.

Having stated the bare bones of the theory, let us flesh it out a bit by applying these principles to the three traditional areas of inquiry for dissonance theory. The first is selective exposure to information. Festinger stated that dissonance arousal should trigger certain desires with respect to obtaining information. When a person experiences dissonance between cognitions, he should be motivated to seek consonant information and to avoid dissonant information. The first behavior would increase the number of consonant elements and thus reduce the existing dissonance; the second would avoid increasing the level of the existing dissonance. At a point near maximum dissonance, however, a person might well seek out dissonant information. He would be very close to changing one of the cognitions, and by availing himself of information that increased, temporarily, his level of dissonance, change in the least resistant cognition could be brought about and dissonance would be substantially reduced.

> *Example*: Mary has just bought a new car. She knows, however, that one of the cars she rejected gets better gas mileage than the one she bought. This knowledge arouses dissonance. In order to reduce dissonance, she can seek out information, say, in magazines or on TV, that tells her about

positive aspects of the car she bought, for example, that her car does not pollute the environment. She can also avoid information that reminds her that the car she rejected obtains superior gas mileage. If, in spite of her efforts to reduce dissonance, her state of dissonance increases close to the point of maximum dissonance, she might begin to seek out information about the other car's gas mileage. This additional dissonant information should change her attitude about the car she currently owns and allow her to eliminate dissonance by selling it and buying the other one.

Second, Festinger pointed to decision processes, especially those processes that occur after a decision has been made. Once a person has chosen X alternative over Y, dissonance is created between his knowledge that he has chosen X and his knowledge of the desirable aspects of Y and the undesirable aspects of X. Festinger suggests four ways in which postdecision dissonance can be reduced. The first is to change the decision. This should be relatively rare since a new decision would also create dissonance. Second, cognitive overlap can be established between the decision alternatives. If we believe that the properties of Y are found in X to a sufficient degree, we will experience little dissonance from having chosen X. Third, the importance of the unchosen alternative or the decision itself can be reduced. Last, and most important because it is designated as the most typical occurrence, cognitions about the alternatives can be changed, eliminating dissonant elements or, more probably, adding consonant elements. This process is likely to be reflected by the person's increasing the desirability of the chosen alternative and/or decreasing the desirability of the unchosen alternative(s) after the decision.[1]

Example: Mary's original decision to purchase her car was dissonant with the desirable gas mileage of the rejected car. She can change her decision by selling her present car and purchasing the other car. While this decision reversal would eliminate the original dissonance, it might create new sources of dissonance arousal—such as that between buying the second car and knowing that the first car does a better job of not polluting the environment. A way of reducing dissonance that would not entail a decision reversal would be for Mary to establish cognitive overlap between the two cars. For example, both cars are very comfortable. By focusing on this similarity and thus viewing both cars as satisfying the same need for comfort, Mary can reduce the dissonance from having bought one and rejected the other. As another alternative, Mary can try to convince herself that her decision about the cars was unimportant, that it did not matter which one she chose, or she can convince herself that it is unimportant

[1] The reader will recognize this as the exact opposite of reactance effects. The distinction to be kept in mind is that reactance effects are found most clearly in the predecision phase, while both dissonance and reactance effects are exemplified in the postdecision phase.

that the rejected car gets good gas mileage. Finally, Mary can focus on all the positive aspects of her present car, such as its smooth handling, and on all the negative aspects of the rejected car, such as its need for frequent tuneups. Her attention to these cognitions, which are consonant with her initial purchase, should reduce dissonance and be reflected in her raised evaluation of the car she bought and lowered evaluation of the one she did not buy.

Festinger's third major empirical focus was the forced-compliance situation. When a person is induced to behave in a manner that is discrepant with his beliefs and opinions, he has engaged in forced compliance. By definition, according to Festinger, dissonance is an inevitable consequence of compliance. Let us examine the forced-compliance situation where a person is led to say something he believes is not true. The dissonant element is obvious: the person's behavior is the opposite of what would follow from his belief. What, however, might be the consonant elements? Festinger states that the incentives that make the person's behavior appear justified are consonant with the behavior. Incentives might include the desire to avoid physical punishment, financial inducement, or, in an experiment, scientific importance. To state the extreme case, very little dissonance would be aroused in a person who says something he doesn't believe as a result of having a gun held to his head. On the other hand, substantial dissonance should be created when the person cannot determine any immediate, sufficient justification to account for his behavior.

Festinger noted that dissonance aroused by forced compliance can be reduced in two ways. One is to change one's own private, initial belief to conform with one's behavior. The second is to magnify the importance of the incentive, thus justifying the behavior. Note that a third method of dissonance reduction in the forced-compliance situation is at least theoretically possible. The person could deny his behavior. This should be rare, since it involves a distortion of reality, but it might occur in clinical settings.

Example: Let us assume that when Mary first went shopping for a car, she wanted one that obtained good gas mileage. While looking at a variety of cars, she talked with the sales representative of a company that was offering a rebate on some of their models. Mary had never before considered buying this company's cars because she knew they obtained poor gas mileage. Because of the rebate, however, she began to look at these cars. She looked at some on which the rebate was $100, but she did not feel $100 was sufficient to interest her in a car that obtained poor gas mileage. Then the salesman showed her a model on which there was a $500 rebate. This amount of money induced her to seriously consider purchasing the car and, after thinking about it for a while, she did so. Mary can reduce the dissonance resulting from being induced to purchase a low gas mileage car in several ways. She can change her attitude on gas mileage and come to believe that she does not really want a car that obtains good mileage. Or she can focus on the $500 rebate and come to believe that this was an offer she couldn't refuse. Or, although it is unlikely, she could deny that she bought the car.

Modification by Brehm and Cohen

Festinger's 1957 formulation stimulated a great deal of research designed to investigate the aspects of dissonance theory that he had explicated. By the 1960s, dissonance theorists were beginning to modify some of Festinger's original notions. Probably the most influential of these modifications was set forth in J. W. Brehm and A. R. Cohen's *Explorations in Cognitive Dissonance* (1962).

Brehm and Cohen suggested that the element of commitment was critical to dissonance and its reduction. Although Festinger had mentioned instances of commitment (for example, to the chosen alternative, to the discrepant behavior), he had not made commitment a central focus of the theory. Brehm and Cohen argued for such a central focus, and they based their argument on the following grounds.

Commitment, in the sense of engaging in an activity or choosing one thing instead of another, acts to aid one in specifying the psychological characteristics and implications of dissonance. If in considering the myriad cognitions that people may have, one anchors one end of a relationship among cognitions in a commitment and then considers whether the other cognitions "follow from" that commitment, the possible dissonances and consonances may be more accurately delineated. If, for example, the behavioral commitment is actually eating spinach, it is *obvious* that the attitude of not liking spinach is dissonant with and would not follow from this commitment. Brehm and Cohen note that actual behavior is not necessary for the effect of commitment, but it is necessary that the person perceive himself to be committed to the behavior, knowing that it occurred in the past or will occur in the future.

A behavioral commitment can act to make previously unrelated cognitions relevant to one another. For example, it is not clear that wanting to conduct research and wanting to work with clients are in any sort of dissonant or consonant relationship; without a behavioral commitment, they are essentially irrelevant to each other. However, once the person who desires both of these things has committed himself to a clinical job that takes up all his time doing clinical work, then wanting to do research becomes dissonant with the behavioral commitment, while the liking for clinical practice that led to his taking the clinical job is consonant.

Another important aspect of behavioral commitment discussed by Brehm and Cohen involves the specification of the resistance to change of relevant cognitions. As noted in the description of the forced-compliance situation, it is difficult to reduce dissonance by denying the discrepant behavior, since this requires a significant distortion of reality. Similarly, it is difficult to reduce dissonance by changing any cognition reflecting a behavioral commitment. Once we have specified the cognition that reflects a behavioral commitment, we can come closer to indicating which mode of dissonance reduction will be used in a given set of circumstances. We cannot, without further control over the situation, specify exactly which mode a person will use, but we can specify which mode he is unlikely to use, that is, he is unlikely to change his behavioral commitment. Commitments are by definition resistant to change. When a commitment forms one element of a dissonant relationship, the pressure for change tends to be greatest on the noncommitment elements.

Brehm and Cohen's focus on commitment clarifies the functional aspects of dissonance. Many people go around with all sorts of inconsistent cognitions in their heads without much appreciable evidence that this inconsistency bothers them. In addition, it may not matter very much in terms of survival whether one's cognitions are consonant or dissonant per se. When, however, dissonance is tied to the idea of commitment, a different picture results. When some factor, such as a thought, feeling, belief, or previous behavior, would lead one to commit oneself to acting in a Y fashion, or choosing Y, and one acts in a not-Y fashion or chooses not-Y, the discrepancy is hard to ignore. Committed behaviors tend to be salient and, thus, so are those cognitions that do not "follow from" them. Furthermore, we can speculate that it is generally functional for the organism to order the cognitions that are relevant to behavioral commitments. Any behavioral commitment has implications for subsequent behavioral commitments. It will facilitate future behavior if previous commitments are stabilized by bringing relevant cognitions into accord with them.

In addition to their focus on commitment, Brehm and Cohen discuss the importance of volition in dissonance processes. A given behavioral commitment can be more or less volitional, that is, can be viewed by the person as resulting from more or less choice on his part. Brehm and Cohen state that as perceived (by the person) volition increases, the magnitude of dissonance will also increase. That is, if two people are committed to engaging in the same attitude-discrepant activity and one has chosen this activity while the other has been assigned to it by some powerful other, the first person will experience a greater magnitude of dissonance than the second.

Modification by Wicklund and Brehm

In the years since *Explorations in Cognitive Dissonance* (Brehm & Cohen, 1962) was published, an enormous amount of research has been done on dissonance theory. Conflicting accounts of necessary ingredients, other than commitment and choice, have been promulgated, and conflicting evidence has been obtained. In *Perspectives on Cognitive Dissonance* (in press), Wicklund and Brehm review and reexamine these controversies.

One of the most significant theoretical problems for dissonance theory since *Explorations* is the matter of the person's responsibility for his dissonance-producing actions. Generally, a person will perceive himself as responsible for his actions and the consequences of those actions if he has chosen to commit himself to them. There may be, however, circumstances under which the person's responsibility for the consequences of his actions is not so clear. A person may choose a behavioral alternative only to find out that it involves certain consequences of which he was unaware when he made the choice. The person is committed, has chosen, but is he responsible? Under these circumstances, would we expect dissonance arousal to occur?

Wicklund and Brehm suggest that for dissonance to occur both commitment and responsibility must be present. While commitment can vary in degree, it is usually sufficient for minimal commitment if a person engages or prepares to engage in one activity instead of another. For responsibility, however, there are different ways in which it can occur. If a person chooses an activity and foresees its consequences, dissonance will be created. It is important to note that the person does not have to intend these consequences as long as he foresaw them at the time he made his decision. Thus, ordinarily, dissonance will occur only if the person can foresee attitude-discrepant consequences of a chosen activity. It appears, however, that there are special circumstances under which a person will feel responsible even if he has not foreseen the consequences of his behavioral commitment. One such circumstance is when the consequences of one's actions are directly connected to one's abilities. If an unchosen activity or unforeseen consequence of a chosen activity is presented as something that stems from the person's abilities, the person will perceive himself as responsible and dissonance processes can ensue.

Summary

This book will follow the lead of recent modifications of dissonance theory and consider only the processes that fit relatively stringent criteria for the arousal of dissonance. In general, dissonance will be viewed as a motivational state that is aroused when the person commits himself to a behavior that is discrepant with his beliefs, attitudes, opinions, and so forth, and when he perceives himself to be responsible for his commitment and for its consequences. The magnitude of this motivational state will depend on the importance of the cognitions involved and on the proportion of dissonant cognitions to consonant cognitions. If a person has not been able to avoid the arousal of dissonance and thus experiences such arousal, he will be motivated to reduce dissonance. He may add consonant cognitions, eliminate dissonant ones, or change a cognition. The mode of dissonance reduction that he uses will depend on the relative resistance to change of the cognitions involved and on the relative availability of such modes. In general, behavioral commitments will be highly resistant to change.

This position on dissonance theory leads to a focus on free-choice and forced-compliance situations. It is somewhat more difficult to examine the selective exposure to information paradigm within this framework. More important, however, the literature investigating the selective exposure hypothesis is fraught with confusion. Festinger's original hypothesis that selective exposure occurs as a function of dissonance arousal has not been clearly confirmed, and the whole question of selective exposure is quite complex. Furthermore, for the present purposes, information-seeking may not be a highly significant activity. The determinants and consequences of dissonance that affect attitude and behavior change seem much more significant for clinical endeavors. The free-choice and forced-compliance situations are, thus, the most relevant areas of dissonance research for the clinician, and, as such, will be the focus of the ensuing discussions of dissonance.

RELATED THEORIES

With regard to related theories, dissonance theory presents a different situation from that of reactance theory. For reactance theory, there are several theories or strategies of psychotherapy that were clearly similar, at least in basic conception. For dissonance theory, there are no such readily identifiable theories of psychotherapy. There are, however, important relationships between dissonance theory and a number of theories of psychotherapy. This section will examine these relationships.

Traditional Attitude Change

Psychotherapy has been discussed by Frank (1961/1973) as an attitude change paradigm. Frank examined the factors conducive to attitude change that have been explicated by social psychological research. Since this research was not conducted under the dissonance theory rubric, the factors noted by Frank constitute a limited review of more traditional perspectives on attitude change. Frank singles out four factors that have been shown to promote attitude change: participation (more specifically, role-playing), mobilization of initiative, improvisation, and anticipation of a future audience. These factors fit easily into dissonance theory notions of attitude change, a significant advance, since one theory can account for a variety of heretofore apparently isolated factors.

Role-playing, mobilization of initiative, and improvisation can be seen as factors increasing a person's commitment to a given behavior. The more involved a person is in an activity, the more public the activity, the more effort a person puts into an activity—all increase that person's commitment to the activity. Furthermore, the aspect of increased effort has special relevance to dissonance theory.

One of the most powerful of all dissonance formulations is the effort justification hypothesis. This hypothesis states that the more effort a person puts into an activity, the more dissonance is aroused. The assumption is that people do not engage in an effortful activity without needing to justify why they put forth that amount of effort. If there are external pressures to engage in the effortful activity, these pressures act as justifications. If, however, external pressures are small, the person needs to find other justifications. One commonly used justification is to enhance the intrinsic attractiveness of the activity. This process has been found to exist for both humans and rats (Lawrence & Festinger, 1962). As Festinger (1961) has noted, "Rats and people come to love things for which they have suffered" (p. 11). Thus, in the absence of strong external pressure, the more effort a person puts forth, the more the person will come to like the activity. In the case of attitude change studies, the more effort the person puts into presenting a certain attitude or opinion, the more the person will come to adopt that attitude or opinion.

Frank's fourth factor, anticipating a future audience, relates in several ways to dissonance theory. First, anticipating a future audience may increase a person's commitment to a given behavior and it may increase the importance of the behavior. Certainly, it will increase the number of dissonant cognitions. When one performs a discrepant activity in private, dissonance can be aroused. But when that activity is foreseen as resulting in a public display, that display adds to the dissonance between a cognition that would lead one not to behave in this way and the knowledge that one has, indeed, so behaved.

It is important to note that Frank's discussion was not presented in the context of dissonance theory and thus did not discuss the elements of commitment or responsibility. We can assume that most of the subjects in the studies he reviewed had some choice about their behavioral commitment and felt some responsibility for it. Without specific control over these elements we cannot be totally sure that dissonance theory can account for these findings, but it should be noted that under conditions in which responsibility is ensured, dissonance theory would predict these exact findings.

Operant Conditioning

Both operant conditioning and cognitive dissonance address themselves to behavior. Aside from this important similarity, there are significant theoretical differences. In the case of operant conditioning, it is held that behavior is maintained, or extinguished, by its consequences. Thus, rewards and punishments are utilized to affect the particular behavior. Cognitive dissonance takes a radically different view. Whereas a behavioral commitment provides an anchor for its analysis and its effects, dissonance theory stipulates that through the behavior comes attitude change and that long-range maintenance of any behavior is dependent on a favorable attitude toward the behavior. It is assumed that this attitude, this internalized value, will lead to continued engagement in the behavior and that this engagement, since it is promoted by the person's own attitude, will be resilient to the vicissitudes of the environment. Thus, for dissonance theorists, rewards and punishments should be minimal, as should all other external justifications for the behavior, and perceived choice should be maximal.

It may be helpful for the clinician to put this distinct and important controversy between operant conditioning and dissonance theory into a practical context. As is so often the case, what is hotly contested theoretically turns out to be not as much of a problem practically. Dissonance theory provides no particular advice as to how to elicit a behavior. If the person is simply unable to engage in the behavior but wants to, dissonance theory is not relevant, but neither is operant conditioning. The unskilled client needs to be taught skills; he does not need to be motivated. Rewards may be useful to highlight certain aspects of the skills to be learned (i.e., to act as cues) or perhaps to organize the social environment in which the skills are taught so that priorities are clear to everyone, but as long as the client wants to engage in the behaviors, this is a relatively trivial application of operant conditioning.[2]

A much more critical application occurs when the person is capable of engaging in the behavior but does not do so. If the behavior does not occur at all, the therapist will have to use incentives in order to get it to occur. At this point there is no disagreement between operant conditioning and dissonance theory; as noted, dissonance theory has nothing to say about how to elicit a behavior. Dissonance theory, however, does have something to say about the amount of incentive that should be used to elicit behavior. Incentives should be minimal, just sufficient to elicit the behavior and no more.

Once the behavior is occurring with reasonable frequency, both dissonance theory and operant principles would suggest a reduction in incentive. Operant principles stress that a variable interval schedule is optimal for maintaining behavior. Dissonance theory states that minimal justification is optimal for the same goal. In practice, both would reduce incentives at a certain stage of a therapeutic program.

Finally, here is a word about the idea of "making it easy," an idea that is widely held by practitioners of behavior modification. Again, initially this is probably a good practice. The goal is to have the behavior occur; it may increase the likelihood that it will occur if the first step is easy. On the other hand, once behaviors begin occurring, dissonance theory would advise "making it tough." According to the effort justification principle, the more effort, the more intrinsic value the behavior will take on.

Psychoanalysis

The comparison between dissonance theory and psychoanalytic theory is not in any way as fundamental as the comparison of dissonance theory and operant conditioning. Both dissonance theory and psychoanalytic theory share a concern with internal processes, such as values and attitudes that can affect behavior. Both address processes of rationalization. Beyond these general similarities, the two are based on such different premises and formulated in such different terms that any detailed comparison would be extremely difficult and possibly meaningless.

[2] Rewards can be utilized to shape into existence a behavior the client does not possess in his repertoire. True shaping, going through successive approximations, is an extremely laborious task and, as noted by Bandura and Walters (1963), is probably not very feasible nor frequently occurring in the real world.

It is possible, however, to take specific tenets of psychoanalytic theory and examine them in terms of dissonance theory. The best-documented example of this process occurred in the early 1960s when Bramel examined defensive projection from a dissonance theory point of view. Bramel suggested two modifications of traditional psychoanalytic analyses of projection (Adorno, Frenkel-Brunswik, Levinson, & Sanford, 1950; Bettelheim & Janowitz, 1950): (1) that a conflict between moral standards (superego functions) and knowledge of a forbidden impulse (in this case, homosexual arousal) would result in projection *only* when the person's self-concept was positive, and (2) that projection was more likely to occur onto respected others than onto people whom the person regarded with disfavor. Psychoanalytic views of projection had not emphasized the person's self-concept as an important mediator of projection and had suggested that members of disliked outgroups would be the most likely targets of projection.

Bramel investigated projection in two experiments. In the first (1962), he convinced college males that that they were exhibiting homosexual impulses. Using experimentally manipulated positive versus negative feedback about subjects' personalities to create high versus low self-esteem, he found that high self-esteem subjects attributed more homosexuality to others that did low self-esteem subjects. These data confirmed Bramel's dissonance analysis that had hypothesized that dissonance is created only when the belief that one possesses "bad" traits occurs in the context of one's having positive self-regard. It is dissonant for a "good" person to have "bad" traits, but consonant for a "bad" person to have such traits. When dissonance is aroused, projection can serve to reduce it by adding the cognition that "everybody does it"; this cognition is consonant with and helps maintain high self-esteem, while minimizing the "badness" of the trait that originally aroused dissonance. A further study by Bramel (1963) showed that defensive projection occurred more onto similar and respectable others than onto dissimilar and nonrespectable others. If believing that "everybody does it" reduces dissonance, believing that "nice people do it" is even more effective. (See related discussions by Berkowitz, 1960, and Festinger & Bramel, 1962.)

The importance of Bramel's work in terms of psychoanalytic theory is that it provides an example of examining a phenomenon of interest to psychoanalytic theory under laboratory conditions within a dissonance framework. It is probably less important that Bramel predicts and obtains results that contradict the hypotheses of some writers within the psychoanalytic tradition than that he has taken a clinical behavior and increased our understanding of the conditions under which it is likely to occur and the forms it is likely to take.

Such investigations mark a clear advance over purely speculative and case-study material.

PREVIOUS APPLICATIONS

There have been several previous direct applications of dissonance theory to clinical work. As will be shown, these applications have covered only a small part of the potential relevance of dissonance theory for clinical settings. Before explicating a broader view, however, it is appropriate to examine these previous applications.

Bergin: Inducing Changes in Self-Reports

The earliest direct application of dissonance theory to therapy was made by Bergin (1962) in a study on the effect of dissonant communications on changes in self-reports of masculinity and femininity. Bergin reasoned that a highly credible communicator who advocated a position discrepant from that of the subject would create dissonance and that the more discrepant the communication, the more dissonance would be created. One obvious way to reduce this dissonance would be to change one's own opinion about one's own characteristics. On the other hand, a communicator without much credibility would create little or no dissonance when he advocated a discrepant position and would thus lead to little or no attitude change as a way of reducing dissonance.

Bergin's results supported this line of reasoning. With a highly credible communicator, the more discrepant was the persuasive communication from the subject's original belief about himself, the more attitude change was produced in the direction of the communication. With a communicator of low credibility, there was little attitude change produced regardless of the communication discrepancy. This study is fairly typical of early work on dissonance theory in that the factors of commitment and responsibility were not examined explicitly.

Bergin's results appear to have direct relevance to therapy, and, indeed, he noted that his findings relate to therapeutic interpretations. In essence, his study shows that when the therapist is credible, he can produce significant attitude change and he can increase this change by making his communications highly discrepant with the client's original beliefs, opinions, attitudes, and so forth. When a therapist is of low credibility, things look generally dismal, no matter what position his interpretations take.

There is, however, some difficulty in attributing these findings to dissonance processes. Commitment and responsibility were not varied. If, for example, subjects had been allowed to choose whether or not they would listen to the communication, the results might have been dramatically different. In this case, dissonance would be created by choosing to listen to a communication discrepant with one's own beliefs, and the anchor of the dissonance would be one's own commitment and responsibility. In Bergin's study without such a commitment (presumably subjects were exposed to the communications without asking them whether or not they wanted to hear them), there is no such anchor, and the focus of dissonance was presumably on the communicator and the position of his communications. Given the circumstances of Bergin's study, the reader can probably accept and apply his findings, but when commitment is introduced, the reader is advised that the findings and the application will be changed.

Levy: Interpretive Dissonance

Subsequent to Bergin's study, L. H. Levy (1963) also considered the dissonance produced by psychotherapeutic interpretations. Levy maintained that all interpretations produced dissonance. He suggested that if the dissonance existing prior to an interpretation were less than the dissonance existing after an interpretation, the interpretation would be rejected or distorted and/or the therapist would be derogated. If, on the other hand, the dissonance existing prior to an interpretation were more than the dissonance existing after an interpretation, the interpretation and the therapist would be accepted.

Levy further postulated that if interpretations made by the therapist increased dissonance for the patient, the therapist would take on the negative qualities of the dissonant state, whereas if the interpretations made by the therapist decreased dissonance, the therapist would take on the positive qualities of the consonant state. The context of psychotherapy was presumed to be similarly affected by the dissonance-producing or -reducing features of interpretations, as were the interpretations themselves and any self-interpretations made by the client. Levy advocated, then, the general principle that any factor present when dissonance increased would become aversive to the client and any factor present when dissonance decreased would become favored by the client.

Levy's book *Psychological Interpretation* (1963) is the most thorough application of dissonance theory to clinical work that has thus far been written. Unfortunately, it is also a highly idiosyncratic application. There is no evidence that all interpretations produce dissonance. It depends on the content of the interpretation, its communicator, and its receiver. One can easily imagine a highly consonant interpretation that simply repeats what the client himself believes. Moreover, the whole business of preinterpretation dissonance and postinterpretation dissonance is exactly the kind of vague, general statement of psychological processes that dissonance theory enables one to avoid. For dissonance theory, the relevant cognitions must be pinpointed and the quality (i.e., dissonance or consonance) of their relationship specified. As for the hypothesis that anything in the presence of dissonance becomes aversive, the evidence for effort justification suggests that in the presence of at least some types of dissonance, factors in the environment will take on positive qualities. There is no evidence at all concerning the hypothesis that factors present when dissonance is reduced become attractive.

Thus, as an interpretation of dissonance theory, Levy's book has serious drawbacks. The power of dissonance theory is not that it allows the broad statements endorsed by Levy, but that it facilitates the examination of specific relationships and the predictions of behavior in light of these specifics. Dissonance theory is more complex and its application more limited than Levy's version suggests.

Goldstein, Heller, and Sechrest:
Dissonance and Attraction

Goldstein, Heller, and Sechrest (1966) also have considered the application of dissonance theory to clinical practice. In view of the criticisms of their application that will be offered, it should be noted that their coverage of dissonance theory is only a small part of their quite extensive examination of the relevance of psychological findings to behavior change in psychotherapy. The interested reader is encouraged to consult their book directly for the substantial part of their discussion that will not be examined here.

Goldstein, Heller, and Sechrest state three hypotheses that pertain to dissonance theory. Each of these hypotheses will be considered in turn.

> Patient attraction to the therapist may be increased by cognitive dissonance induced by patient participation in overt behaviors discrepant with resistive behavior. (p. 97)

In support of this proposition, Goldstein, Heller, and Sechrest discuss the broad range of dissonance literature suggesting that given commitment and choice, counterattitudinal behavior that is minimally justified can lead to attitude change in support of the behavior. It is assumed that this attitude change will promote continued behavior similar to that first engaged in under forced-compliance conditions. Much of the literature covered by Goldstein, Heller, and

Sechrest will be examined in subsequent chapters, and their discussion of dissonance theory is similar to that presented in this chapter. However, the specific focus of this Goldstein, Heller, and Sechrest hypothesis is a bit peculiar, and needs to be examined more closely.

The hypothesis concerning forced-compliance behavior by a client is found in a chapter exploring ways in which the client's attraction to the therapist can be increased. Goldstein, Heller, and Sechrest believe that attraction to the therapist and to the therapeutic situation is a cardinal prerequisite for successful therapy. This general context leads them to consider the forced-compliance hypothesis in terms of attraction to the therapist.

Goldstein, Heller, and Sechrest seem to advocate the client's engaging in minimally justified protherapy or protherapist behavior. By definition, this would be dissonant with the client's beliefs, because Goldstein, Heller, and Sechrest are focusing on "resistant" clients who manifest "resistant" behavior in therapy (i.e., presumably, are not doing what the therapist thinks they should do). Thus, one would envision using Goldstein, Heller, and Sechrest's paradigm in the following fashion. The client who dislikes the therapist/therapy would be induced to role-play how much he likes the therapist/therapy or to write an essay on how much he likes the therapist/therapy. All of this would be in order to increase the client's liking for the therapist/therapy, in order for the therapist to be able to change *other* behaviors.

This approach seems a bit inefficient, to put it mildly. A much more efficient method, utilizing the same principles, would be to focus immediately on those *other* behaviors and have the client engage in role-playing or essay-writing directly related to the attitudes and behaviors of interest. There is no need to work on increasing the client's attraction to the therapist prior to working on the focal behaviors. The client's feelings about the therapist are just one ingredient that needs to be considered when the therapist devises his attitude or behavior change strategy. Indeed, in later chapters we will consider evidence indicating that a client's lack of attraction toward the therapist is not necessarily a handicap and can be used to facilitate change.

> Patient attraction to the therapist may be increased by cognitive dissonance induced by overcompensation provided the patient for therapeutic participation. (p. 123)

This hypothesis is also found in the chapter on increasing client attraction to the therapist, and thus the content peculiarity noted above is continued. The reader is again advised that attraction to the therapist is only one of the behaviors that can be worked on and that there is no a priori reason to assume that attraction to the therapist is the first priority.

However, with or without a focus on attraction to the therapist, this hypothesis presents a problem. Goldstein, Heller, and Sechrest present evidence obtained by Adams (1963) in support of this hypothesis. Adams is a proponent of equity theory—people behave such that their inputs equal their outcomes—and as an application of equity theory, this hypothesis has merit. Unfortunately, as an application of dissonance theory, this hypothesis is directly opposite to what dissonance theory would predict. Dissonance theory would state that since the client is well justified, indeed, "overcompensated," for whatever attitude-discrepant behavior he performs in the therapeutic situation, he will experience no dissonance and no attitude change would be expected. In addition, if attraction is one's goal, the effort justification hypothesis states explicitly that

> higher organisms . . . will develop a special preference for certain features of the surrounding environment to the extent that effort is expended near these features that is not sufficiently justified by the provision of established rewards or reinforcements. (Jones & Gerard, 1967, p. 89)

Thus, according to dissonance theory, the more effort and the fewer the rewards, the more attraction to the therapist and therapy should occur.

It is beyond the scope of this book to conduct a detailed examination of the differences between equity theory and dissonance theory. The interested reader is referred to Adams (1965) and G. S. Leventhal (in press). In my opinion, Adams's equation would work best in situations where the concern is the relationship of work to wages, being most appropriate for industrial situations. For those situations in which some attitude, belief, or opinion is discrepant with a behavior and the goal is to change the attitude, belief, or opinion so as to facilitate recurrence of the behavior, there is considerable evidence that dissonance theory principles constitute the most appropriate and effective approach.

> The degree of effort required of the patient-candidate to gain therapy group membership will positively influence the subsequent initial attractiveness of membership status to him if he persists in completing the required premembership tasks. At the upper limit of this relationship, a curvilinear or asymptotic pattern will emerge. (Goldstein, Heller, & Sechrest, 1966, p. 345)

Again, the focus is on attraction, this time to a group rather than to a therapist. The reader has been adequately cautioned that this is not a necessary focus. Furthermore, this hypothesis is stated in terms of group therapy. The present book will not cover the group therapy situation and thus will disregard this other content aspect. The formal aspects of the hypothesis, however, are clearly relevant to individual as well as group therapy.

Recognize that in this hypothesis, Goldstein, Heller, and Sechrest leave the overcompensation principle of their preceding hypothesis and adopt the effort justification hypothesis. They focus on "premembership tasks," but this focus is not a necessary one. The general principle of the more effort the more attraction (or the more attitude change) is applicable at any time during the therapeutic process. The evidence for the specific effects of premembership tasks (Aronson & Mills, 1959; Gerard & Matthewson, 1966) cited by Goldstein, Heller, and Sechrest will be reviewed later.

There is a final point to be made about this particular hypothesis. Goldstein, Heller, and Sechrest state that "at the upper end of this relationship, a curvilinear or asymptotic pattern will emerge." They cite no evidence for this assumption and, indeed, the assumption is somewhat difficult to understand. The empirical evidence suggests that with increased effort, attraction will continue to increase, *up to the point where the effort is of such magnitude that the behavior is not performed.* The effect of effort on attraction is not curvilinear or asymptotic, as Goldstein, Heller, and Sechrest state, but performance does indeed limit the relationship. The behavior must be performed (the client must persist "in completing the required premembership tasks") for the relationship between effort and attraction to hold; if the behavior is not performed, obviously the relationship will not hold.

This concludes the present review of the Goldstein, Heller, and Sechrest application of dissonance theory. Their application is based on a good review of the then available empirical and theoretical literature, and they appear to understand the principles of dissonance theory rather well. Unfortunately, their application leaves much to be desired. They focus unnecessarily on attraction to the therapist or group; they are unclear, or ambivalent, about whether they advocate the use of dissonance or equity theory in individual therapy; and they make at least one unsupported assumption. The Goldstein, Heller, and Sechrest application fails to adhere consistently to the general principles of dissonance theory and does not indicate sufficiently that such principles are applicable to a variety of circumstances and goals.[3]

[3] The Goldstein, Heller, and Sechrest approach to dissonance theory has been continued in a later paper by Goldstein and Simonson (1971). Many of the earlier themes are repeated, including a focus on attraction to the therapist or therapy, and the simultaneous advocacy

Hattem: The Voluntary Client's State of Consonance

A final example of the application of dissonance theory to clinical practice is found in a paper by J. Hattem (1973). Hattem suggests that a client who comes into psychotherapy voluntarily is a person who, by definition, is worried, concerned, or anxious about some behavior. Given this definition, Hattem states that for the client it is consonant to believe that: (1) he has a maladaptive behavior, (2) he is worried, concerned, or anxious about it, and (3) he cannot change this behavior. It is suggested that in order to create change in this constellation of consonant beliefs, the therapist should tell the client that the maladaptive behavior is chosen, that it is not necessarily all that maladaptive since it reflects free choice on the part of the patient, and that there is no need to be worried over such freely chosen behavior. This should, according to Hattem, create dissonance that the client can reduce by changing the maladaptive behavior, reducing his concern about the behavior, or leaving therapy. Hattem says that a skillful therapist can reduce the likelihood of the last event and that either of the two former events constitutes beneficial change.

Hattem's paper is interesting and provocative. He shows sophistication about dissonance theory in his discussion about the need for the therapist to be undemanding in his communications so as to provide minimal justification for behavior change. There is, however, a significant problem with this paper. Hattem's presentation does not sufficiently anchor the creation of dissonance onto a behavioral commitment. Hattem's strategy is really for the therapist to simply say things with which the client disagrees. While this may approximate Festinger's original notions about dissonance, the present theoretical understanding is that it is not clear that such disagreements actually do create dissonance, and, in any event, behavioral commitment allows for greater precision of both the prediction and

---

of overcompensation as well as effort justification. One addition made by this more recent presentation involves an attempt to investigate empirically whether effort does, in fact, lead to increased client attraction to the therapist. The data discussed by Goldstein and Simonson are quite ambiguous, and no clear effect for effort is demonstrated. Unfortunately, however, their studies cannot be considered an adequate test of the effort justification process since they did not explicitly give the client choice about engaging in effortful tasks associated with therapy. If the client does not perceive himself to have chosen the effortful tasks, one would not expect dissonance to be aroused, and dissonance reduction through coming to like the tasks and their setting would not be predicted to occur. If, on the other hand, the client were given choice and he decided, in the absence of strong inducements, to engage in effortful, therapeutic tasks, one would expect dissonance arousal and its reduction through increased positive evaluation of therapy. The latter, very important experiment has yet to be conducted.

control of dissonance arousal and reduction. Hattem's paper would have been more compelling if he had specified some behavioral commitment that the client could have been induced into performing and that, therefore, would affect the client's belief that he has a maladaptive behavior, that he should worry over such behavior, or that he cannot change the behavior.

These comments about Hattem's use of dissonance theory are independent of Hattem's definition of who comes into therapy and of his notion that a decrement in concern over a "maladaptive" behavior represents improvement. These and other content aspects of his paper are for the individual therapist to read and form his own opinion about. What is important about Hattem's paper for this discussion is his formal utilization of dissonance theory. His paper cannot be considered a powerful application of dissonance theory because it lacks precision, specifically the precision of a behavioral commitment. In the beginning of his paper, Hattem makes reference to Albert Ellis's rational-emotive technique of therapy; unfortunately for our purposes, most of Hattem's suggestions turn out to be rational-emotive techniques in a dissonance disguise rather than dissonance techniques adequately utilized within a rational-emotive framework.

SUMMARY

This chapter has presented a survey of the development and modification of dissonance theory. The theory was traced from its origination by Festinger in 1957 to more recent modifications. A summary of the theory was provided, noting that the present discussion of dissonance theory will emphasize behavioral commitment and responsibility for that commitment and its consequences. Dissonance theory was compared to a number of other theories concerned with therapeutic change. Comparisons with traditional attitude change paradigms, operant conditioning, and psychoanalysis were examined. Finally, several previous applications of dissonance theory to psychotherapeutic behavior were discussed.

CHAPTER SIX

CLINICAL APPLICATIONS OF DISSONANCE THEORY

I Dissonance processes

In Chapters Six and Seven selected empirical studies will be presented in light of their relevance to clinical practice. It has already been indicated that this survey will not attempt an exhaustive presentation of the dissonance literature. For more extensive reviews of the literature, the reader is referred to the books listed at the end of Chapter Seven.

The studies described in this chapter are concerned with illustrating and clarifying fundamental principles of dissonance theory. They address themselves to relatively general dissonance processes and the conditions under which such processes are likely to occur. By examining this research, the complexity and precision of dissonance theory should be amply demonstrated and the application of dissonance principles to clinical endeavors can be faciliated.

"COUNTERATTITUDINAL" BEHAVIOR: FOREWORD

In the following sections, the notion of having a client engage in "counterattitudinal" (or "attitude-discrepant") behavior will be discussed frequently. Some readers may have initial difficulty translating this term, taken from the experimental literature, into terms relevant to the clinical situation. The translation envisioned by the author does rest on certain assumptions and these assumptions need to be explicated.

It has been noted that the major difficulty in therapy is that of getting clients to engage in behavior that they are capable of, but that they are not performing. Presumably, then, the reason they do not perform these desirable behaviors is that they have opinions, attitudes, beliefs, feelings, and so forth, that lead them to *not* so behave. It would be expected that when the client does perform the desirable behaviors, his performance will be dissonant with those cognitions that prevented him from performing the behaviors in the absence of therapeutic assistance. In this sense, novel, therapeutic behaviors are "counterattitudinal."

It is assumed that the dissonance arising from such counterattitudinal behaviors can be therapeutically beneficial. In subsequent sections, the major focus will be on how this dissonance arousal can evoke dissonance reduction in the form of changing the original attitude into one favoring the new behavior. Once such a favorable attitude is established, the client should engage in the therapeutically desirable behavior more frequently and without reliance on environmental influences. The client will have, to paraphrase Madsen and Madsen (1972), acted his way into a new way of thinking that will, in turn, promote additional similar actions.

COMMITTING THE CLIENT: HOW AND WHY

At this point, a certain mild duplicity on the part of the author must be acknowledged. In the presentation of the theory, the variable of commitment was treated as though the meaning of "commitment" were clear. It was defined simply as "engaging in an activity or choosing one thing instead of another." In truth, such an easy definition is not completely satisfying. Although this definition appeared sufficient to allow for a presentation of the general outline of the theory, it is now appropriate to consider the notion of commitment in more detail.

Different people have meant different things by the term commitment. Kiesler (1971) reviews these definitions and, indeed, uses several of them in his experimental investigations of commitment effects. Among the commonly used definitions are: choice ("I committed myself to the action"), public behavior ("By doing that in public, he was really committed to that"), and repeated behavior ("He was really committed to that because he'd done it so often"). Given this conceptual and operational complexity, some distinctions that will hold for the ensuing discussion will be helpful.

Commitment will be defined as the psychological state that exists when a person knows that he has engaged in a behavior, is presently engaging in the behavior, or strongly intends to engage in the behavior in the future. The behavior of interest will usually be overt and public, since this type of behavior most readily ensures that the person knows that he has engaged, will engage, or is engaged in the behavior. Overt and public behavior has the additional advantage that other people can know about the person's engaging in the activity.This public knowledge may make the commitment more salient to the person, and it will allow the interested observer (for present purposes, the therapist) to be sure that the person is, in fact, committed. It should be noted, however, that commitment can occur in the absence of overt and public behavior. The client who has, for example, engaged in a desensitization therapy that requires imaging can be considered committed to that imaging as long as the therapist is reasonably certain that the person has imaged, intends to image, or is presently imaging.

This definition of commitment does not solve all problems. The alert reader will have noticed the use of terms such as "know" and "intend." These terms, obviously, can introduce significant error into any application. The client may not "know," although the therapist thinks he does. The client may not "intend," although the therapist thinks he should. The best practical solution to these difficulties appears to be for the therapist, when he is engaged in making sure the client is committed, to strive for some overt, public, and highly salient behavior as the expression of commitment. One may obtain dissonance effects under other circumstances, but the therapist is interested in maximizing the likelihood that his predictions about the arousal and reduction of dissonance will be confirmed. This interest in confirmation is not an esoteric concern, but the heart of applying any theoretical scheme to the clinical enterprise. The therapist needs to be as certain as possible that he knows that will happen when any given therapeutic strategy is introduced.

MAXIMIZING THE CLIENT'S RESPONSIBILITY

There is evidence that the role of commitment in producing dissonance is quite powerful. Studies have been reported in which dissonance effects have been achieved solely by having subjects be committed to their behavior (e.g., J. W. Brehm, 1960; J. W. Brehm & G. S. Leventhal, in J. W. Brehm & Cohen, 1962). Developments in the refinement of dissonance theory, however, have suggested that while commitment is necessary for the occurrence of dissonance, it may not be sufficient. Increasingly in recent years, the role of the person's responsibility for his commitment has been emphasized. Anyone applying the principles of dissonance theory is, therefore, well advised to ensure that both commitment and perceived responsibility take place. The present discussion will examine the variety of ways in which a person can come to feel responsible for his commitment.

Choice

The easiest method to create felt responsibility is to give the person free choice, and, according to the above formulation, the more responsibility, the more likely it is that dissonance will be aroused. There is good empirical support for the direct effect of volition on dissonance arousal. In a number of studies, dissonance has been shown to increase as the person's volition increased (e.g., Brock, 1968; Cohen & Brehm, and Cohen & Latané, both in Brehm & Cohen, 1962; Cohen, Terry, & Jones, 1959).

Keep in mind that these relationships are stated in functional terms: the *more* volition, the more responsibility, the *more* dissonance. When one is attempting to induce a person to behave in a way in which he would not ordinarily behave, one may not be able to give completely free choice without running a substantial risk of the person choosing not to perform the behavior. Thus, in a therapy situation, it is not always feasible to provide absolutely free choice. The client comes to therapy for change, and for the therapist to simply observe the client continuing to make the same old choices and to engage in the same old behavior probably would not be very satisfying for either client or therapist. So, to induce new choices, the therapist may have to provide inducements. As has been noted before and will be discussed in detail below, dissonance theory suggests that these inducements should be kept to a minimum, that is, no more than what is necessary to induce the behavior.

In addition to keeping the actual level of inducements low, the therapist can support the client's perception of his own volition in the face of whatever inducements are being presented. An excellent way of doing this is for the therapist to make such statements to the client as "Of course, it's entirely up to you," "Are you sure you want to do this?" and "It's your decision." These verbal statements can foster the client's volition even while tremendous pressures ("Be a good client," "You're here for help and have to do what the doctor tells you," "Doctor knows best") act to induce the client to comply.

Justification

Whenever we give someone good reasons for his behavior (e.g., "This will help you," "This will help your family," "This will make me like you"), these verbal communications can act as justifications for attitude-discrepant behavior. Justification acts to reduce perceived responsibility for a counterattitudinal behavior, and many studies have shown that the more minimal the justification, the more attitude change results after attitude-discrepant behavior (e.g., Brock & Blackwood, 1962; Cohen, J. W. Brehm, & Fleming, 1958; Rabbie, J. W. Brehm, & Cohen, 1959).

We can be more specific about the operation of minimal justification. Freedman (1963) found that the low justification given before the person committed himself to an attitude-discrepant behavior produced more attitude change than high justification. When the justification was delivered after commitment to the task, high justification produced more attitude change than low justification. These results are what one would expect from a rigorous interpretation of dissonance theory. Justifications can only affect the dissonance aroused by a commitment if they are known at the time of the commitment. When they are known at this time, low justification creates a feeling of responsibility in the person for his commitment and is dissonant with performing the counterattitudinal behavior. Thus, low justifications received prior to the commitment contribute both to attitude change and to one's sense of personal responsibility for one's behavior that may be desirable on more general therapeutic grounds.

Justifications received after the commitment do not affect responsibility or the magnitude of dissonance. They may, however, affect attitude change. Once the person has committed himself to a counterattitudinal behavior, justifications supporting that commitment may facilitate his changing his attitude toward the position implied by the behavior. Thus, the therapist who uses high justifications in order to increase behavior-consistent attitudes should be careful to do so only after the commitment to the counterattitudinal behavior has taken place.

Justification was examined further in a study by Pallak, Sogin, and Van Zante (1974). Varying justification, choice, and the time when the justification was delivered, they found that when the justification was received before the commitment to the attitude-discrepant behavior, low justification produced more attitude change under conditions of high choice than under low choice. High justification produced more attitude change under conditions of low choice. Thus, high justification received prior to the commitment can produce desired attitude change, but the person's sense of volition must be eliminated or severely restricted. The chapters on psychological reactance strongly suggested that there may be other, deleterious effects of reducing a person's feeling of choice. Using dissonance theory, however, one can maximize choice, provide low justification, and produce attitude change as well as a sense of reponsibility.

Thus far we have considered what might be called positive justifications. There are also negative justifications. A threat is a negative justification. If we engage in certain behaviors or avoid certain behaviors because we have been threatened with dire consequences, our behavior or our avoidance is justified and should not arouse much dissonance. Aronson and Carlsmith (1963) examined this process with children. They found that when children refrained from playing with a forbidden toy under a mild threat, the children derogated this toy much more than children who refrained under the more adequate justification of a severe threat. Voluntarily refraining from playing with a desirable toy is dissonant; reducing the desirability of the toy serves to reduce the dissonance. This study has been amply replicated (Pepitone, McCauley, & Hammond, 1967; Turner & Wright, 1965; Zanna, Lepper, & Abelson, 1973), and it has been shown to be a strong effect, lasting an average of thirty days (Freedman, 1965).

Recently, there have been indications that the socioeconomic level of the children may affect these results (Dembroski & Pennebaker, 1975; Ostfeld & Katz, 1969) such that mild verbal threats will more predictably produce dissonance and derogation for middle-class children than for those from lower-class backgrounds. As yet, the reasons for this class difference are not clear, though one can surmise that at a general level they relate to children's previous experiences with verbal justification. What is clear is that, with the possible exception of lower-class individuals, the effect of a strong threat is to reduce dissonance arousal. Therapists probably don't need much empirical justification for refraining from threatening their clients; if they should need it, these studies certainly suffice.

Incentives. Financial incentives can be utilized to elicit desired behaviors from people and can act as a justification for such behaviors. While the use of such rewards is, presumably, not relevant to traditional dyadic psychotherapy, the employment of financial incentives is not an uncommon aspect of some types of behavior modification programs, such as token economies. The early dissonance studies on financial incentives found evidence that the smaller the financial incentive obtained for attitude-discrepant behavior, the greater the attitude change toward support of the behavior (Cohen, in Brehm & Cohen, 1962; Festinger & Carlsmith, 1959).

Later, when the variable of choice was appreciated as a crucial element in the arousal of dissonance, several studies showed that this inverse relationship between incentive and attitude change held when the person chose to engage in the attitude-discrepant behavior (J. Harvey & Mills, 1971; Holmes & Strickland, 1970; Linder, Cooper, & Jones, 1967; Sherman, 1970b). When the person did not choose, but was forced to engage in the attitude-discrepant behavior (i.e., assigned to the behavior by the experimenter), a direct relationship between incentive and attitude change (i.e., the more incentive, the more attitude change) was frequently obtained. This finding indicates that there is a way to produce attitude change with large incentives, but as with high justification prior to the commitment, this method requires the reduction of the person's sense of volition.

In one of the few direct studies of dissonance theory principles in a clinical setting, Bogart, Loeb, and Rutman (1969) examined the effects of varying magnitudes of incentives on a clinical population. In this study, postpsychiatric patients were given either large (worth up to $8.00) or small (worth up to $3.00) rewards for attending a rehabilitation program. When given large rewards, attendance increased from 90 percent to 95 percent. When the rewards were withdrawn, however, attendance dropped to 75 percent. When given small rewards, attendance increased from 82 percent to 88 percent and did not decrease when rewards were withdrawn. Bogart et al. (1969) cross-validated this finding with a different but similar population and used a within-subjects design. All patients in this second study went through all the conditions of interest: baseline, small rewards, withdrawal of small rewards, second baseline, large rewards, withdrawal of large rewards. It was found that the small rewards had beneficial effects during both maintenance and withdrawal, while the large rewards decreased attendance both when these rewards were offered and when they were withdrawn.

The Bogart et al. studies are certainly not without methodological problems. In the first study, the two different groups had different starting points of attendance prior to the introduction of rewards. In the second study, there is a question about order effects: Would the results have differed if large rewards had come first in the sequence? In spite of these problems, however, this study suggests that behavior change was promoted more with small rewards than with large rewards. This finding is highly consistent with the dissonance formulation.

In addition, the finding of decreased attendance in the second study suggests that the large rewards not only did not promote long-lasting behavior change, but that they may have threatened the person's freedom to *not* attend the rehabilitation program and may thus have created reactance. Whether one wishes to interpret these results in terms of dissonance or reactance theory, the import is the same: smaller incentives work better than larger incentives in creating lasting behavior change.

Communicator credibility. It was suggested in the chapters on reactance theory that much of the therapist's therapeutic action may consist of using verbal communications to persuade the client. Given this assumption, the findings on how dissonance theory relates to communicator credibility are clearly relevant to clinicians.

Some studies on communicator credibility (Aronson, Turner, & Carlsmith, 1963; Bochner & Insko, 1966) found what might be called the common-sense prediction (à la Bergin). Their results indicated that with a highly credible communicator, the greater the discrepancy between the communicator's position and the position of the subject, the more the attitude change in the direction of the communication. For a communicator with low credibility, Aronson et al. found that increasing discrepancy led to decreased attitude change in the direction of the communication, while Bochner and Insko found a curvilinear relationship between attitude change and discrepancy. These studies indicate that high discrepancy is dissonant only with high credibility and that increasing conformity to the highly credible communicator can reduce this dissonance.

On the other hand, Smith (1961) and Zimbardo, Weisenberg, Firestone, and Levy (1965) found that dissonance arousal was increased by a negative communicator. In these studies subjects were requested to eat an undesirable food (grasshoppers!). For subjects who agreed to eat the grasshoppers, more liking of the grasshoppers was displayed by those who heard an unpleasant person make the request than by those who heard a pleasant person.

The critical difference between the Aronson et al. and Bochner and Insko studies and the Smith and Zimbardo et al. studies is in the provision by the latter two of a behavioral commitment. It is dissonant to commit oneself to eating grasshoppers after hearing an unpleasant person request that one do this. The unpleasantness of the communicator is essentially a low justification for one's behavior; in the absence of sufficient justification, one attributes responsibility for one's behaviors to oneself and dissonance arousal can occur. For subjects who heard a pleasant communicator, it was less dissonant for them to agree to eat grasshoppers; the attractiveness of the communicator acted as a high justification. These subjects could always say (and believe), "I did it for him, nice guy that he is."

A study by R. A. Jones and J. W. Brehm (1967) further illustrates the importance of having the person be responsible for his own behavior. In this study, it was found that subjects who chose to listen to a counterattitudinal communication displayed more attitude change in the direction of the communication when the communicator was unpleasant. For subjects who did not choose, but were assigned to listen to the counterattitudinal communication, more attitude change occurred with the pleasant communicator. These results parallel previously reported findings on verbal and financial justifications.

This discussion of communicator credibility may then suggest some non-common-sense and perhaps not altogether welcomed information about the role of communicator credibility in attitude change. When a therapist wishes his client to feel responsible for his own behavior and when a behavioral commitment is involved, the therapist does not want to be too attractive to his client. Attraction may be necessary to elicit initial performance, but if kept high it may reduce the strength and stability of the desired behavior. Attraction to the therapist can act as a justification and, as such, can reduce attitude change and, presumably, the likelihood of continued engagement in the behavior in the absence of the therapist. Thus, rather than assuming, as did Goldstein, Heller, and Sechrest, that attraction to the therapist is always desirable and helpful in therapy, therapists will have to examine their attractiveness just as they would any other element in the therapeutic situation. At times, they may decide that they wish to keep this attractiveness high; at other times, in order to achieve specific therapeutic goals, they may decide that it is necessary that they be relatively unattractive to the client.

It should be pointed out that the above studies provide examples of an important difficulty in putting dissonance theory into practice. In none of these studies was it theoretically obvious which cognition was the most resistant to change and thus most likely to change as a function of dissonance reduction. In the early set of studies (Aronson et al., 1963; Bochner & Insko, 1966), the dissonance could have been reduced by reducing the credibility of the communicator. In the grasshopper (Smith, 1961; Zimbardo et al., 1965) and R. A. Jones and J. W. Brehm (1967) studies, dissonance could have been reduced by perceiving the supposedly unpleasant communicator as pleasant. In order to obtain the results that they predict, results that depend on the utilization of one mode of dissonance reduction instead of another, dissonance experimenters have learned to "block off" alternative modes of dissonance reduction.

The therapist who uses dissonance in the therapeutic situation will also need to learn to "block off" undesirable modes of dissonance reduction. If the desired effect is attitude change, it is important to make other cognitions (particularly, justifications) highly resistant to change. A therapist can do this by making these other cognitions highly salient and obvious. Unpleasant communicators can be highly unpleasant; high credibility communicators can be highly credible. This procedure does not absolutely ensure that these obvious cognitions will not be changed to reduce dissonance, but it makes it less likely.

In addition, a therapist, knowing his client well, should be able to create situations in which the target attitude is the cognition least resistant to change. This may mean beginning some distance from the ultimate attitudinal goal and working initially on less resistant attitudes. Through successive dissonance reductions, it may be possible to isolate the attitudinal goal from its former supporting attitudes and thus decrease its resistance to change.

THE CONSEQUENCES OF A BEHAVIORAL COMMITMENT

After a person has made a behavioral commitment, he is confronted with the consequences of this commitment. These consequences may occur immediately after the commitment or some time later, they may or may not be foreseen at the time of the commitment decision, and they may be positive or negative in character. A great deal of research has been directed at understanding more precisely the conditions under which the consequences of a behavioral commitment can influence the magnitude of dissonance.

J. W. Brehm (1959) reported a study in which subjects received information during their engagement in the behavior about unforeseen negative consequences of their behavioral commitment. Dissonance reduction was increased. Other investigators have focused on various types of negative consequences of attitude-discrepant behaviors. Helmreich and Collins (1968) and Carlsmith, Collins, and Helmreich (1966) found that the more public was the counterattitudinal behavior, the more attitude change in the direction of the counterattitudinal position was produced. Several investigators examined the effect of audience reactions to counterattitudinal behaviors delivered in public. Chase (1970), Cooper and Worchel (1970), Cialdini (1971), and Hoyt, Henley, and Collins (1972) found that when the person believed he was successful in convincing an audience, counterattitudinal behavior produced more dissonance and subsequent attitude change. In a related study, Nel, Helmreich, and Aronson (1969) found that attitude change tended to be greater when subjects addressed their counterattitudinal argument to an undecided and thus persuadable audience than when they addressed a less persuadable audience.

The meaning of these studies is somewhat unclear due to the variety of ways in which they were conducted. Some studies explicitly varied choice (e.g., Hoyt, Henley, & Collins); others did not (e.g., Carlsmith, Collins, & Helmreich). Some gave the information about the consequences of the behavioral commitment prior to the commitment (e.g., Nel, Helmreich, & Aronson); others gave the information about the consequences of the behavioral commitment after the commitment was made (e.g., Brehm). These methodological differences make it difficult to form a coherent assessment. Fortunately, in recent years, a number of studies have been performed that have clarified the role of consequences in the arousal of dissonance.

Responsibility

The hypothesis that people experience dissonance from negative consequences of their behavior only when they feel responsible for these consequences is supported by a study by Collins and Hoyt (1972). These investigators found that when subjects wrote a counterattitudinal essay under low incentive and high (negative) consequence conditions, positive attitude change (i.e., in the direction of the position of the essay) was found only when the subjects were told they were responsible for the consequences. When subjects were told they were not responsible for the consequences, attitude change did not occur.

Choice. Negative consequences of an unchosen behavior are not expected to create dissonance; not having chosen, the person does not feel responsible for either the behavior or its consequences. Calder, Ross, and Insko (1973) and Sherman (1970a) report studies indicating that negative consequences of a behavior increase dissonance only when that behavior is chosen.

Foreseeability. An important aspect of a person's responsibility for the consequences of a commitment is whether he foresaw the consequences at the time of the commitment. Watts (1966) and Cooper (1971) have found that only when a negative consequence of a behavioral commitment was expected did dissonance occur; when the negative consequence was unexpected, dissonance was not produced. A study by Goethals and Cooper (1972) indicated that while foreseeability of the occurrence of a negative consequence is necessary, intending the negative consequence is not necessary. Furthermore, Cooper and Goethals (1974) found that if the *non*occurrence of a negative event is *un*foreseen, dissonance is aroused.

Thus, it is not the type of negative consequence that is important. What is critical is that the negative consequence be foreseen, or at least, that the *non*occurrence of the negative consequence *not* be foreseen. Kruglanski, Alon, and Lewis (1972) have provided an interesting twist to this general principle. They found that when they told subjects that they had been forewarned, when in fact they had not been, the arousal of dissonance was increased by a negative consequence of a behavioral commitment. Thus, what is important is not the actual foreseeability, but the person's belief that he foresaw or should have foreseen the consequences of his commitment.

A study by J. W. Brehm and R. A. Jones (1970) indicated that the principle of foreseeability is not limited to negative consequences. Brehm and Jones found that additional, positive aspects of a chosen alternative decreased the usual postdecision dissonance effects (see p. 71) when the positive consequence actually occurred, but only when subjects had been forewarned of these possible positive consequences. In their examination of the Aronson and Carlsmith study (1963) of children's responses to threat, Lepper, Zanna, and Abelson (1970) found that a positive consequence was effective in decreasing dissonance only when the positive consequence was known prior to the behavioral commitment. Thus, to affect dissonance, positive or negative consequences must occur and must be foreseen as a possibility at the time of the commitment. When a person foresees consequences of his commitment, he will feel responsible for these consequences, and only when he assumes this responsibility, do these consequences affect the magnitude of dissonance.

There are, however, some circumstances under which a person can commit himself to an attitude-discrepant behavior that has clearly foreseeable negative consequences, but not experience dissonance. Davis and Jones (1960) conducted a study that indicated that a person will not experience dissonance when he is aware that he will be able to negate the negative consequences of his behavior. In this study, subjects chose or were assigned to deliver an insult to a stranger. When subjects chose to do this and knew that they would have no opportunity to speak with the target of the insult after the insult, dissonance was created and was reduced by derogating the person, insulting a negatively evaluated person being less dissonant. When, however, subjects chose to deliver an insult and knew they would have an opportunity to speak with the target person after the insult, no dissonance and no derogation resulted. Needless to say, no derogation was produced by an assignment condition, regardless of whether assigned subjects believed they would have an opportunity to speak with the target person. Thus, while subjects who chose and expected to speak with the person they insulted may have held themselves responsible for the insult, they knew that their behavior was relatively meaningless since they could negate it in the later conversation with the person. People must believe that their attitude-discrepant acts are "for real" in order for dissonance to be aroused.

While the general principle of foreseeability (in the absence of an opportunity to negate the consequences) is well supported, a few studies have obtained *fait accompli* effects (i.e., increasing dissonance with an unforeseen negative consequence or decreasing dissonance with an unforeseen positive consequence). For two of these studies, J. W. Brehm (1959) and S. J. Sherman (1970a), it is at present not well understood why they obtained results at odds with the currently held theoretical formulation. Two other studies that obtained *fait accompli* effects, however, can be interpreted in terms of there being a specific tendency for people to feel responsible for behaviors directly connected to their abilities, even when the consequences of these behaviors were unforeseen at the time of the behavior.

Pallak, Sogin, and Van Zante (1974) obtained a *fait accompli* effect, and their elicitation of this effect may have rested on impugnment of these subjects' abilities in the condition in which they obtained the *fait accompli*. Specifically examining the notion that people feel responsible for ability-connected behaviors, Worchel and Brand (1972) found that when subjects believed that their own abilities were involved in a behavioral commitment, an unexpected negative consequence produced dissonance. When their own abilities were not involved, an unexpected negative consequence did not produce dissonance.

It is likely that the studies of Brehm (1959) and Sherman (1970a) represent another, not yet understood, specific tendency for people to feel responsible for unforeseen consequences of certain types of behaviors. Regardless of this, however, and regardless of the ability finding, clinicians will do well to follow the general notion that foreseeability increases felt responsibility and thus affects the magnitude of dissonance.

Clinical Summary

Positive consequences. Most of the studies examining the effects of consequences of commitment on dissonance have used negative consequences. The use of such negative consequences, as compared to positive ones, would indeed seem more appropriate for clinical endeavors, and some discussion of positive consequences should demonstrate this. Positive consequences of a behavioral commitment act to decrease the magnitude of dissonance that is aroused. Let us consider some circumstances under which clinicians might wish to decrease the magnitude of dissonance that their clients will experience.

For example, a client is about to engage in a therapeutically undesirable behavior that is discrepant with his existing beliefs. The therapist may reason that if the client chooses to engage in this behavior, dissonance will be aroused. In order to reduce this dissonance, the client may come to change his existing belief and regard his behavior more favorably. This would be a highly undesirable outcome because this favorable attitude would promote further engagement in the behavior.

Theoretically, one could decrease the likelihood of the client coming to regard his undesirable behavior more favorably by decreasing dissonance arousal stemming from engaging in the behavior. From the preceding discussion of the literature, there are two ways for the therapist to do this. First, the therapist could "take control" of the undesirable behavior and forcefully urge the client to engage in it. This is a reactance strategy and is discussed in detail in the chapters on reactance theory. As noted there, one difficulty with such a strategy is that it puts the therapist in the position of advocating undesirable behavior. A beneficial aspect to this approach is that it reduces the client's volition in the matter and decreases the likelihood of dissonance arousal. Therapists who want to consider such a strategy should consult the reactance chapters for further examination of its effects.

If the therapist decides not to urge the client to engage in the undesirable behavior, he still has a way to decrease dissonance arousal. He can point out to the client, before the client commits himself to the behavior, positive consequences of the behavior that the client may not have considered. If in fact these consequences do occur (and, as part of the strategy, the therapist should point out only those that he thinks are likely to occur), dissonance arousal should be decreased, the need for dissonance reduction should be decreased, and the client should not change his belief in favor of his behavior in order to reduce dissonance.

Unfortunately, this approach of emphasizing positive consequences of the undesirable behavior has several troublesome aspects. First, the client who is tending to do something against his beliefs is in a high state of conflict. The therapist would prefer that the client decide not to engage in the behavior and, indeed, the client may, on his own, so decide. If, however, the therapist emphasizes positive consequences of the behavior, this may act as the just sufficient inducement to tilt the balance in favor of the client's engaging in the behavior.

Second, for dissonance to be decreased by positive forewarning, the positive consequences have to occur. When positive consequences to a behavior do occur, they reinforce the behavior at hand. Now, if in spite of the therapist's wishes, these positive consequences would have occurred anyway, it is probably better that the client be forewarned about them so that they at least diminish dissonance while they reinforce the behavior. On the other hand, if the therapist uses forewarning as a planned strategy, he would want to ensure that the positive consequences occur. In this case, he would be attempting to decrease dissonance, and presumably would do so, but he would increase reinforcement. In the case of undesirable behaviors, it is probably not wise to pit one theoretical formulation against another and take a chance on which process will be stronger.

This discussion should thus be sufficient to indicate that there are considerable difficulties in using forewarning of positive consequences as a way to decrease the arousal of undesirable dissonance. Undesirable behaviors are probably best approached in other ways, and many such ways are described in this book (see especially the discussion of destabilizing harmful decisions, pp. 110–111).

Negative consequences. Negative consequences present a more productive area of consideration for the clinician. In order to explore this area, it will be helpful to review some of the theoretical principles indicated in the discussion of the literature that preceded this clinical summary. The fundamental principle is that the person must feel responsible for the negative consequences of his behavior.[1] Felt responsibility for behavioral consequences depends on the person's choosing to engage in the commitment and on the person's foreseeing the behavior's consequences at the time of the choice. Negative consequences thus foreseen will increase dissonance when they actually occur and cannot be negated later.

Negative consequences can play a part in any strategy where dissonance arousal would be therapeutically beneficial. When the therapist is inducing the client, under conditions of low justification, to choose to engage in a *desirable* counterattitudinal behavior, he can maximize the dissonance that will be aroused by forewarning the client of possible negative consequences of this behavior. This forewarning has, of course, to be tailored carefully to the client; too much emphasis on negative consequences may prevent the client from committing himself to the behavior.

If, however, the therapist can tailor his communications such that he can forewarn the client without preventing the behavior, heightened dissonance should ensue, *provided* that the negative consequences do actually occur. The therapist should heed this proviso by only forewarning the client about negative consequences that he (the therapist) judges to be likely to occur or by arranging for the negative consequences to occur. In fact, however, the latter procedure is seldom necessary. Most new behaviors do have, at least

---

[1] These theoretical principles also apply to positive consequences, but need not be stressed in that regard, given the above discussion of the difficulties in using forewarning of positive consequences as a therapeutic strategy.

at first, some negative aspects. Dissonance theory suggests that rather than viewing these negative aspects as a problem in obtaining and maintaining the desired behavior, they can, if utilized properly, operate in the service of the client's therapeutic goals.

EFFORT AND DISSONANCE

In Chapter Five it was noted that the effort justification hypothesis has proven to be one of the most powerful aspects of dissonance theory. This hypothesis represents a special aspect of the person's search for justifications for dissonant behavior, such that the more effort expended, the more the person will need to justify his behavior. In the absence of external justifications, the person will attribute responsibility and volition to himself, dissonance will be aroused, and dissonance reduction can occur by coming to like the behavior.

The most detailed discussion of the effort justification paradigm is found in Lawrence and Festinger (1962). Since their work dealt primarily with rats rather than humans, it will not be covered in detail here; the interested reader is referred to the original publication. It should be noted, however, that Lawrence and Festinger found that resistance to extinction (i.e., how long the rat will perform the behavior without being rewarded) was a function of the *absolute* number of rewards during training: the fewer the rewards, the greater the resistance. When rewards were infrequent, the rats had to work harder for those that were made available. Lawrence and Festinger proposed that this increased effort led to the rat's increased attraction to the activity itself, thus promoting the activity's resistance to extinction. This finding is discrepant with the classic Skinnerian position that it is the *proportion* of rewarded to unrewarded trials that determines resistance to extinction. The import of this finding for clinicians is that it underlines the need to provide as few rewards as possible for a new, therapeutic behavior so that the behavior will endure. This basic principle applies to behaviors that are consistent with or counter to existing attitudes.

There are a number of studies that explore the effort justification paradigm specifically in terms of counterattitudinal behaviors. Cohen (1959), Zimbardo (1965), Zimbardo and Ebbesen (1970), and Linder and Worchel (1970) have all found that expending increased effort while taking a counterattitudinal position increased attitude change in the direction of the advocated position. Other studies have indicated that this effect is most pronounced when the person chooses to engage in the effort (Wicklund, Cooper, & Linder, 1967) and when the amount of effort the counterattitudinal task would take was known prior to the commitment (Linder, Cooper, & Wicklund, 1968). These are, of course, the typical circumstances under which we would expect dissonance arousal to be strongest.

These studies of the effects of effort on attitudes are quite relevant to the practicing clinician. Role-playing is an important therapeutic technique for many clinicians. We may, for example, need to role-play assertive behaviors with a client before he can be expected to assert himself in the real world. The literature cited above suggests that when role-playing is used to induce a new behavior, it would be helpful to make the role-playing an effortful endeavor. One might have the client role-play for a long time, role-play a particularly difficult anticipated interaction, or even take a page from Zimbardo's experiments and have the client role-play while receiving delayed auditory feedback. However the effort is induced, we can expect that the more effort expended, the more the client will believe in what he is doing and like doing it. It is, of course, important that the client choose to engage in the role-playing and that the external justifications for this choice be low.

The effort justification paradigm thus gives the therapist a powerful strategy for behavior change. Initially, it may be necessary to role-play the new behavior in the therapeutic setting. This role-playing can be made effortful. Then the client can attempt to engage in the behavior in the real world. This real behavior can be made effortful. The principles are clear and should create a strong behavior, resistant to extinction. The therapist, however, will have to be skillful in using these principles. There are no guidelines for what strength of effort for an individual client will be low enough to obtain the behavior and high enough to create dissonance. As has been emphasized repeatedly, the therapist must tailor these general principles to the particular client.

There are two other interesting dissonance studies involving effort. Yaryan and Festinger (1961) report a study in which high effort in preparing for an event that might not occur led subjects to convince themselves that the event would occur. This research may be relevant to the occasions in clinical practice when it is important that the client come to believe that something may indeed happen. On some occasions, this possible outcome may be positive; we may need to convince some clients that they really may obtain the job, the spouse, or the skill at a task they desire. On other occasions, we may want the client to more realistically assess the possibility of some negative outcome occurring, for example, losing that job, that spouse, or that skill.

Whatever the particular circumstances, the Yaryan and Festinger study suggests a possible therapeutic approach. The therapist can begin by having the client contemplate that the outcome may or may not occur. In terms of its possible occurrence, the therapist can suggest that the client work on preparing himself for it, but also stipulate clearly that they both know that it might not, in fact, occur. According to Yaryan and Festinger, if the client does begin to prepare for the event, voluntarily and with low external justification, this will be dissonant with his knowledge that it might not occur. The dissonance that is aroused should be reduced by the client's coming to believe more strongly that the event may occur.

A study by Weik (1964) indicates that effort can be a consequence of dissonance arousal as well as an instigator. Weik found that under conditions of high choice, low justification, and the expectation of an unpleasant task, subjects worked more effortfully on the unpleasant task. Working harder in this case may reflect the person's reduction of dissonance by coming to believe that he both likes and is interested in the task. Thus, in preparing our clients for an experience in which they will benefit from working hard, it will be especially important that they engage in the behavior voluntarily, with low external justifications, and they know ahead of time about the unpleasant aspects of the experience. These prior conditions should increase the effort they expend.

THE DECISION PROCESS

Thus far our consideration of dissonance theory and its application to the clinical setting has focused primarily on the forced-compliance situation. Indeed, the forced-compliance paradigm with its focus on eliciting behaviors and changing attitudes is probably the aspect of dissonance theory that is most clearly relevant to clinical work. Before going on to more specific clinical applications of the forced-compliance model, however, some consideration will be given to the theory and literature on the decision process. Throughout therapy, our clients make decisions, some very easy and some very difficult ones; it is therefore important to understand the psychological processes involved in decision-making.

Free Choice

As has been noted, dissonance theory hypothesizes that after a decision is made, the attractive aspects of the rejected alternative and the unattractive aspects of the chosen alternative are dissonant with the decision. Probably the most typical way to reduce this dissonance is to enhance the value of the chosen alternative and/or diminish the value of the unchosen alternative, that is to increase the difference between the alternatives such that postdecision evaluation of the alternatives is consonant with the decision that was made. Beyond this basic model, one can be more specific about related factors. The closer in attractiveness are the decision alternatives at the time of choice, the more dissonance is aroused and the larger is the postdecision spread between alternatives (J. W. Brehm, 1956). The more volition the person experiences in making the choice, the greater is the dissonance and the larger is the postdecision spread (G. S. Leventhal & J. W. Brehm, in J. W. Brehm & Cohen, 1962). The more alternatives one chooses from, the greater is the dissonance and the larger the postdecision spread (J. W. Brehm & Cohen, 1959b). The more dissimilar in actual characteristics (but similar in attractiveness) the choice alternatives, the greater is the dissonance and the larger is the postdecision spread (Brehm & Cohen, 1959b). Each of these postulates rests on the principle that dissonance increases as the number of dissonant elements relative to consonant elements increases. Attractive aspects of the rejected alternative, responsibility for the decision, many alternatives with attractive aspects, and unique attractive features of rejected alternatives are all cognitions that are dissonant with having chosen one alternative and rejected the others.

Occurrence of Dissonance

It has been found that dissonance arousal does not occur when people make a decision unless this decision is irrevocable. Jecker (in Festinger, 1964) and Allen (in Festinger, 1964) report studies indicating that unless the person has clearly given up on obtaining the rejected alternative, dissonance is not aroused. With the slightest chance of obtaining the rejected alternative (1 out of 20 in Jecker's experiment), there will be no increased postdecision spreading of evaluations.

There is another factor that has been shown to affect the magnitude of postdecision spreading of evaluations of decision alternatives. Davidson and Kiesler (in Festinger, 1964) and Davidson (in Festinger, 1964) have shown that the more deliberation time spent prior to the decision, the greater the postdecision reevaluation of decision alternatives. It is not clear why this effect occurs, but we can speculate that the more time spent in evaluating decision alternatives prior to a decision, the more salient will be the dissonant elements of the decision. It has been well estalished that the more salient are the dissonant elements when one makes a behavioral commitment or a decision, the greater is the dissonance aroused and, thus, subsequently reduced (J. W. Brehm & Wicklund, 1970; Brock, 1962; Zanna, Lepper, & Abelson, 1973). In addition, Gerard (1967) has found that during the predecision phase, more attention is paid to the alternatives eventually not chosen than to those eventually chosen. Thus, we can infer that given more time in the predecision phase, there would be more attending to the alternatives eventually rejected, more salience of the positive aspects of these alternatives at the time of the decision, more dissonance aroused by the decision and, thus, more postdecision dissonance reduction by reevaluating the alternatives in line with the decision.

Regret

"Regret," in dissonance theory terms, is that situation where the attractive aspects of the rejected alternative are, at least momentarily, more potent than the attractive aspects of the chosen alternative. Festinger and Walster (in Festinger, 1964) found that an implicit decision led to a high frequency of actual reversals of choice on the "real" decision. Walster (in Festinger, 1964) found that 4 minutes after a decision, there was a tendency to evaluate the unchosen alternative more positively than before the decision and to evaluate the chosen alternative less positively.

Given the well-documented reactance effect that can occur in the predecision phase (see p. 57), it is probably theoretically more sound to regard all predecision effects (such as the implicit decision paradigm of Festinger and Walster) as reactance rather than dissonance effects. For postdecision effects, however, there is no such clear road to theoretical coherence. Reactance theory would predict a regret-like phenomenon, the decision having eliminated the freedoms to have the rejected alternative and to not have the chosen alternative. The notion of postdecision regret is, however, also quite consistent with dissonance theory. At the moment there is simply no empirical evidence that strongly indicates one theoretical explanation instead of another and, indeed, postdecision regret could be a joint function of both reactance and dissonance processes.

Timing

There have been several attempts to work out the timing of the occurrence of dissonance reduction. Thus far the results have been rather confusing. Walster (Festinger, 1964) found a slight amount of dissonance reduction immediately after a decision, a large amount 15 minutes after the decision, and very little 90 minutes after. Gailon and Watts (1967) found dissonance reduction immediately after the behavioral commitment for foreseen consequences and no dissonance reduction for a *fait accompli;* 20 minutes after the commitment, however, there was dissonance reduction for the subjects who were given a *fait accompli*.[2] Crano and Messé (1970) found dissonance reduction upon immediate measurement, but no dissonance reduction 15 to 20 minutes later. As has been noted, Freedman (1965) found dissonance reduction effects lasting a mean of a month (the actual range of measurement was 23 to 64 days).

At present, then, there are no general theoretical principles as to when dissonance reduction will occur after a decision or behavioral commitment, nor as to how long dissonance reduction processes would last. Clearly, it can be a very stable process with long-lasting effects (Freedman, 1965) or a very ephemeral occurrence (Crano & Messé, 1970). One suspects that the experiences of a person after initial dissonance reduction would have an impact on the durability of the outcome of dissonance reduction. If the new attitude, created through dissonance reduction, is worked into the person's ongoing life, dissonance reduction efforts can endure. If, however, the new attitude is itself dissonant with other long-standing behaviors or attitudes, the effect is likely to be short-lived.

Clinical Summary

In order to apply the findings on the decision process to the clinical setting, it is necessary to consider two possible therapeutic goals. Let us consider first the occasions on which a therapist wishes to solidify and promote the impending choice of an alternative that would be beneficial to the client. First, the therapist should ensure that the client spends a good deal of time thinking about the decision because this should promote postdecision reevaluation. Second, the therapist should try to promote the client's perceiving the choice alternatives as having certain characteristics. They should be fairly attractive and relatively close to each other in attractiveness, and they should be dissimilar in terms of their actual physical or psychological characteristics, that is, in terms of the needs they satisfy. In addition, it would help to maximize dissonance if the client had to choose only one of a fairly large array of alternatives. Third, at the time of the decision the client should perceive himself as having free choice (high volition) and should perceive the decision as irrevocable (the rejected alternatives cannot be obtained). Furthermore, the dissonant elements in the choice should be made highly salient.

---

[2] This finding contradicts the present understanding of dissonance theorists that dissonance is not aroused by a *fait accompli*. The suggestion is that the time of measurement may be critical and that if measures were taken some time after the commitment, it might be found that a *fait accompli* would arouse dissonance. Until this suggestion is better documented, however, we will retain our present position (see p. 101) that a *fait accompli* will not arouse dissonance.

Finally, there are some considerations about the postdecision phase. The therapist should attempt to minimize the possibility of a decision reversal (regret) and maximize the durability of the increased evaluative spread betweeen the chosen and rejected alternatives. Probably the most effective way to do this would be to tie the decision into other, ongoing behaviors. A decision that is seen as consonant with other major behaviors (e.g., one's work, one's romantic activities, one's living situation) is unlikely to be revoked.

Note that some of the above suggestions are not without risk. If, for example, decision alternatives are too close in attractiveness, it may be difficult for the therapist to be confident that one rather than the other will be chosen. Again, the therapist must tailor the parameters of these variables to the particular client and his decision.

Now, let us examine the occasions on which a therapist might wish a client not to make a firm, enduring decision. If a client appears to be on the verge of choosing a decision alternative that may be harmful to him, the therapist may first try to ensure that the harmful decision alternative is not chosen. Various approaches to this include reactance manipulations threatening the client's freedom *not* to make the bad decision (i.e., the therapist tells him he must choose the harmful alternative) and a dissonance approach trying to get the client to engage in a behavioral commitment that would lead to attitude formation dissonant with the impending "bad" decision alternative.

If, however, the therapist believes that the harmful alternative will be chosen in spite of any strategies he uses to prevent it, he can still work to make this decision unstable and unenduring. First, he can attempt to shorten the time the client spends contemplating the decision. Second, he can promote the client's perception that the decision alternatives are similar in terms of their actual physical or psychological characteristics and that there is a fairly small array from which to choose. Third, at the time of the decision he can enhance the client's perception of himself as having low volition and his (the client's) feeling that the decision is potentially changeable at a later date. Furthermore, the dissonant elements in the choice should not be made salient. Fourth, the therapist can attempt to affect the postdecision phase. The decision should be isolated from ongoing behavior so that it will not create much dissonance to revoke it.

No doubt the reader recognizes these suggestions as the exact opposite of the ones given for stabilizing choice. Only one is missing. It was not suggested that decision alternatives be greatly different from each other in attractiveness. While dissonance is enhanced by attraction similarity of alternatives and attraction dissimilarity will decrease the arousal of dissonance, it is presumed that the problem at hand concerns a therapeutically undesirable choice alternative that is very attractive to the client on other grounds. If it were not so attractive, the therapist would have been able to dissuade the client from his anticipated choice. Thus, attraction dissimilarity would translate into pointing up unattractive alternatives. This, of course, would simply increase the client's tendency to choose that therapeutically undesirable but attractive alternative. In trying to reduce the stability of an anticipated harmful choice, the therapist should emphasize other, *attractive,* therapeutically desirable alternatives that are available to the client and that can substitute for the initially preferred alternative.

It is not being suggested that every desired or undesired decision should be exposed to this variety of therapeutic strategies. The therapist needs to be aware of the range of strategies that he has at his disposal and then choose the ones that he judges will be most effective with each client. What should be clear from this presentation is that dissonance theory offers therapists a variety of options when they wish to support a beneficial decision or to weaken a harmful one.

OTHER DISSONANCE PROCESSES

Before examining specific dissonace situations, some remaining theoretical points about processes of dissonance need to be specified.

Modes of Dissonance Reduction

In planning dissonance strategies, therapists will be most concerned about the mode of dissonance reduction that the client utilizes. For, in fact, it is not the intervening variable of dissonance and its arousal that the therapist is aiming for; rather, it is the outcome of dissonance arousal, that is, the specific behavioral or attitudinal changes that take place as the person works to reduce dissonance. Thus, it is critical in the therapeutic strategy to control for which mode of dissonance reduction is used.

Steiner and Rogers (1963) conducted a study examining different modes of dissonance reduction. They found these modes to be negatively correlated; when one mode is utilized, it becomes less probable that other modes will be brought into action. Furthermore, Götz-Marchand, Götz, and Irle (1974) report that if subjects are unaware of multiple modes of dissonance reduction, they will tend to use the first mode presented to them. If, however, they are aware of other modes, they will use the mode that is the least resistant to change and that involves the least reorganization of other cognitive elements.

These findings are quite important for clinicians. Usually a therapist will be working with his client on cognitions that are resistant to change and that are part of a network of other cognitions. Given complete freedom and complete awareness of alternative modes, the client might prefer to reduce dissonance in ways other than the way that constitutes the therapeutic goal. The therapist will have to ensure that these other avenues of dissonance reduction are adequately blocked. General suggestions for blocking alternative modes of dissonance reduction have been offered earlier (see p. 97). At this point, it seems appropriate to add to these suggestions by noting that the therapist, by focusing the attention of the client on the desired mode of dissonance reduction, may be able to keep the client somewhat unaware of alternative. modes. The results of the study by Steiner and Rogers suggest that once the client has begun to utilize this desirable mode of dissonance reduction, the therapist does not have to concern himself unduly about alternative modes.

Recall of Dissonant Elements

Most of our consideration of dissonance processes has focused on relatively immediate responses to dissonant cognitions. The question has been raised as to what happens to these cognitions over time. A study by J. W. Brehm (in Brehm & Cohen, 1962) indicates that over time people tend to forget dissonant elements more quickly than consonant ones. Similarly, Walster and Festinger's subjects (in Festinger, 1964) tended to forget about a dissonance-provoking, unavailable ideal decision alternative. These two studies strongly suggest that a therapist needs to reinstate dissonant elements frequently, at least through the period when dissonance reduction is taking place. It will generally be ineffective if a therapist creates dissonance in the client in one session and then expects dissonance reduction to occur a week later in the next session. For one thing, the client will be exposed to other modes of dissonance reduction outside of therapy; for another the client may forget about the dissonant elements (another undesirable mode of dissonance reduction). The therapist would be well advised to constantly reinstate the dissonant elements by bringing them to the attention of the client, or, better yet, to work toward eliciting dissonance arousal and reduction within the same session. The latter procedure will give the therapist maximum control over the mode of dissonance reduction utilized by the client.

Avoidance of Dissonance

The typical paradigm in examining dissonance is for dissonance arousal to be created and then for dissonance reduction to be employed. There is, however, an alternative paradigm: namely, for dissonance-arousing situations to be avoided. Braden and Walster (in Festinger, 1964) report a study on this issue in which they found that subjects who anticipated a dissonance-arousing decision preferred to be randomly assigned a decision alternative rather than to choose. Subjects who did not anticipate a dissonance-arousing decision preferred to choose.

This study is important for clinicians in at least two ways. First, clinicians should not be surprised if during the course of a therapy oriented toward maximizing choice and responsibility, clients begin to indicate that they would prefer to avoid choice and responsibility. This can happen for any number of reasons (fear, dependency, etc.), but will most certainly happen if the therapy is intentionally or unintentionally creating dissonance-arousing decisions for the client. Second, the client may begin to avoid not only choice and responsibility within the therapy, but the actual therapy setting as well.

Although there are multiple ways to deal with such problems, a method that should be considered is the use of dissonance strategies to reduce any such avoidance behaviors. One strategy would be to commit the client to being a decision-maker. For example, once a client makes some easy decisions in therapy, it should be dissonant for him to avoid choice and responsibility for other, tougher decisions. The therapist should, therefore, provide the client with enough easy decision-making experiences in therapy so that the client remains committed to decision-making per se. This will not necessarily eliminate the client's tendencies to avoid making tough decisions, but if prior decision-making is kept salient by the therapist, these avoidance tendencies should be reduced to manageable proportions (i.e., to proportions that increase the dissonance aroused by a difficult decision without preventing it from being made).

Furthermore, the therapist should keep the client committed to coming to therapy. One way to do this is to make each session or at least every few sessions into a "go or no-go" decision for the client. The client should be asked frequently to reassess whether he wishes to keep coming to therapy. If this is done enough in the early stages of therapy, when it is easier for the client to decide to keep coming, then when dissonant decisions begin to be prominent in the therapy, the client should have become strongly committed to therapy and should be unlikely to drop out precipitously. Every time the client makes the decision to continue therapy, dissonance should be created and should be reduced by the formation of an increasingly favorable attitude toward therapy. This attitude may be extremely important during the more uncomfortable stages in therapy where the client is confronted with changing long-standing attitudes or behaviors. Beware the unexamined habit of coming to therapy; the mere habit may not be sufficient to keep the client in therapy at exactly those times when it is most important for him to be there.

SUMMARY

This chapter has focused on general dissonance processes and the conditions under which these processes occur. In regard to counter-attitudinal behavior, commitment to and responsibility for such behavior were defined as the necessary conditions for dissonance to be aroused. Choice and external justification were examined as the major factors on which the person's perception of responsibility depend. Once a person has made a behavioral commitment, he is confronted with its consequences. In order for these consequences to affect the magnitude of dissonance, the person must feel responsible for them. It was pointed out that people typically feel responsible only for those behavioral consequences that they believe they could foresee at the time they chose to make the behavioral commitment.

Several other dissonance processes were reviewed. The effort justification paradigm was described, indicating that dissonance is created by effort that is chosen and not externally justified. Reduction of this dissonance results in liking the effortful behavior. The decision process was discussed, and suggestions were made about how to stabilize beneficial decisions and how to mitigate against harmful ones. Finally, other dissonance processes were examined, including modes of dissonance reduction, recall of dissonant material, and avoidance of dissonance arousal.

CHAPTER
SEVEN

CLINICAL APPLICATIONS OF DISSONANCE THEORY

II Specific topics

Chapter Six provided many general notions about how dissonance theory can be used by clinicians. In this chapter, a variety of specific topics relevant to clinical practice will be discussed. Little new theoretical material will be presented, but it is hoped that by focusing on more specific content areas, understanding of the application of dissonance theory to clinical endeavors will be promoted.

RANGE AND POWER OF THE THEORY

Range

Although there have been only a few empirical tests of its clinical utility, dissonance theory qualifies for consideration by clinicians on many grounds. Not the least of these grounds is the extensive empirical literature generated by the theory. The range of topics to which dissonance theory has been applied is truly amazing. Dissonance theory has been used to understand young men's attitudes toward the draft when they were not drafted (Notz, Staw, & Cook, 1971), to examine the moral attitudes of students who were induced

115

to cheat versus those of students who did not cheat (Mills, 1958), to increase subjects' disbelief in ESP (Raven & Fishbein, 1961), to investigate the psychological behavior of members of doomsday sects (Festinger, Riecken, & Schachter, 1956; Hardyck & Braden, 1962), and to explore people's reactions to the Supreme Court's decision banning prayer in the public schools (Muir, 1967). Even in the absence of direct empirical evidence for the therapeutic efficacy of dissonance theory, the clinician should be encouraged to try out dissonance theory strategies in therapy. Dissonance has been found to be applicable to so many human behaviors that it would be strange indeed if it did not apply to those very human behaviors of importance in therapy.

Power of the Theory

The range of dissonance theory is impressive; so too is its power. In order for a theory to be useful in a therapeutic setting, it must be capable of producing powerful effects. Therapy typically does not deal with trivial, inconsequential behaviors and feelings. Psychopathological behaviors and feelings are strong and of great significance to the person; psychotherapeutic techniques need to be quite powerful if they are to be effective in promoting change in these behaviors and feelings. Given this necessity, it is important to assess the power of dissonance theory as it can be judged from the present literature. This section will provide a brief review of this issue.[1]

How might one define the power of the theory? For our purposes, this section will focus on the ability of dissonance manipulations to affect such apparently stable processes as physiological responses, primary drives, and classical conditioning. A relatively weak manipulation of the environment might affect such behaviors as paper-and-pencil ratings, but only a powerful manipulation can alter bodily states and processes related to them.

In examining the effect of cognitive dissonance on physiological responses, two studies are of greatest interest. M. L. Brehm, K. W. Back, and M. D. Bogdonoff (1964) have found that subjects who were hungry in the beginning of an experiment and who chose to continue deprivation under conditions of low justification, showed a smaller increase of free fatty acids in the blood than subjects who were initially hungry and who continued deprivation with high justifications being provided. Free fatty acid increase is an accepted physiological sign of hunger. It appears that choosing deprivation

---

[1] For the reader interested in the power of dissonance theory, an excellent review of some of the most powerful dissonance effects that have been obtained is provided by Zimbardo (1969). Descriptions of all of the studies that will be examined in this section can be found in Zimbardo's book.

that is only minimally justified is dissonant with being hungry, that this dissonance is reduced by convincing oneself that one is not hungry, and that this cognitive activity is accompanied by the appropriate physiological state. Examining a different physiological response, Zimbardo, Cohen, Weisenberg, Dworkin, and Firestone (in Zimbardo, 1969) found that subjects who chose to undergo painful electric shock for low justification showed a lower GSR response than subjects who were assigned to this painful experience or who chose it in the presence of high justification. Again, the physiological state appears to have reflected the cognitive process of dissonance reduction, of coming to believe that the experience one has freely chosen is not that unpleasant.

There is considerable evidence that cognitive dissonance processes can affect primary drive states. J. W. Brehm (1962) found that male subjects who agreed to go without liquids for low pay and for whom the issue of thirst was made salient (a pitcher of water in sight during the experiment) showed a greater decrease in self-ratings of thirst and tended to drink less than those who were paid a substantial amount and for whom thirst was salient. In addition, Mansson (1965) found that subjects who agreed, under conditions of low justification, to deprive themselves of liquids rated themselves less thirsty, drank less water, perceived and preferred fewer thirst words, and learned thirst words less rapidly than subjects who had agreed to thirst deprivation in the presence of high justification. Finally, Brehm and Crocker (in Brehm, 1962) found that subjects who agreed to minimally justified hunger deprivation decreased their ratings of food, while subjects who agreed for highly justified reasons increased their ratings. The low justification subjects also ordered less food to eat after their fast. These three studies together provide strong support for the effect of cognitive dissonance on primary drives. Within physiological limits, people who choose to undergo deprivation of desired substances that is not justified by external rewards will decrease their desire for these substances, and when given the opportunity, they will consume less of these substances than they would if they had undergone the deprivation involuntarily.

Investigating the effect of dissonance on classical conditioning, Grinker (1967) noted that subjects who expect an intensification of the unconditioned stimulus in eyelid conditioning will usually show an increase in their rate of eyelid conditioning. This effect was indeed found for subjects who did not choose, but were assigned, to continue the experiment under these new conditions or who chose to continue for highly justified reasons. For subjects who chose to continue under low justification conditions, however, Grinker found that their eyelid conditioning was decreased. Again, it is dissonant to freely choose to undergo an unpleasant experience, and one can reduce dissonance by minimizing the unpleasantness. Physiological states can reflect this minimization, primary drive behavior can be modified, and, as indicated by Grinker, classical conditioning can be affected.

Several inferences for clinical practice can be made from these studies. First, at a general level, they indicate the immense power of cognitive dissonance manipulations. More specifically, they indicate that the clinician may be able to use dissonance theory to modify clinical behaviors that involve strong affect and important physiological components. For example, voluntarily behaving in a fashion that is discrepant with being afraid should reduce fear. Further, these studies highlight the powerful effects that can be achieved when people are motivated to justify their voluntary participation in an unpleasant experience. The following section explores the specific results this motivation can have when employed in therapeutic activities.

THERAPEUTIC IMPROVEMENT AS A FUNCTION OF DISSONANCE AROUSAL

In two recent studies,[2] Cooper examined the relationship between commitment to participate in a supposedly therapeutic experience and subsequent behavior. The subjects in the first study were people who reported themselves to be afraid of snakes and who met an experimental criterion of snake-avoidance behavior during a pre-experimental approach test. The selected subjects then participated in one of four experimental treatments. Half of the subjects were forewarned that the coming procedures might be anxiety-producing and effortful, and were then asked if they wanted to continue. The other half were asked if they wanted to continue and only after they committed themselves were told about the possible unpleasant aspects of the coming procedure. The supposed therapeutic procedures cross-cut these conditions. All subjects were told that they would participate in a therapy focused on reducing their fear of snakes. For half of them, this therapy consisted of a brief version of implosive therapy. For the other half, a bogus therapy was administered. Subjects were given a convincing rationale explaining that physiological arousal would reduce ability to exhibit fear of snakes; these subjects then participated in simple physical exercises, supposedly to increase their physiological arousal.

[2] Cooper, J. Personal communication, May 1975.

After the "therapy" sessions, all subjects engaged in a second approach test. It was found that subjects who had been forewarned about the upcoming arduous experience exhibited more approach to the snake than those who had made the decision to continue in the absence of forewarning. Type of treatment made no difference in approach behavior.

These results show that the forewarned subjects experienced dissonance arousal when they agreed to continue in the experiment in spite of knowing it might be unpleasant. One way to reduce this dissonance is to come to believe that the therapy experience was, in fact, "good," that it "worked," that it reduced their fear of snakes. No matter what the supposed "therapy" actually consisted of, these new attitudes would promote increased approach behavior to snakes. For those subjects who agreed to continue without warning prior to the commitment, any dissonance aroused would be quite low, they would have little need to believe in the therapy, and they would show few effects of therapy on their approach behavior.

Cooper's second study dealt with a different type of problem behavior but utilized a quite similar methodology. Subjects who reported themselves to be very unassertive were selected. Half of them were forewarned of a possibly unpleasant experience and were asked if they wished to continue. The other half of the subjects were not given any decision freedom in regard to continuing and were not told anything about the characteristics of the upcoming therapy. Subjects then participated in either a role-play therapy focused on sit- utations in which the subjects desired to be more assertive or a series of physical exercises that again were presented as therapeutically beneficial. After the "therapies," the subject encountered what appeared to be a real-life incident, unrelated to the experimental procedure, in which he was treated somewhat badly by another person. The dependent measure was the amount of assertiveness subjects showed in coping with this apparently real situation.

It was found that subjects who had received choice concerning their participation in therapy showed more assertiveness than subjects who had not received choice. Once again there was no effect from the particular therapy the subjects had received. These results are, of course, the ones that would be predicted by dissonance theory and are highly consistent with the results from Cooper's first study. In this case, however, receiving choice and forewarning was compared to receiving neither, while in the first experiment receiving choice with forewarning was compared to receiving choice without forewarning.

The results of the studies by Cooper are of major importance to therapists. They indicate that the manner in which clients make their commitment to therapy may be more critical to their improvement than the type of therapy that they receive. Clients who make a commitment to therapy under dissonance-enhancing conditions (high choice and forewarned about the effort that will be involved and the unpleasant aspects that may occur) should come to reduce their dissonance by believing in the therapy and should show the effect of this belief in an improvement in the behavior that is the focus of therapy. On the other hand, clients who make a commitment to therapy under conditions that do not enhance dissonance (low choice and not forewarned) will not be motivated to believe in therapy and therefore may not improve.

This method of creating beneficial dissonance in therapy should be quite acceptable to most therapists. It is highly preferable from an ethical standpoint for clients to choose to participate in therapy and to know that it will take effort (as it does) and that it may be unpleasant at times (which it may). This discussion should also, however, alert the therapist to expect slow progress, if any, from clients whose participation in therapy is not voluntary. For these clients, therapists should work on creating as much perceived freedom of choice as possible in order to facilitate therapeutic change.

CONFORMITY

A study by Gerard (1965) examines the issue of conformity from the perspective of the person who feels that he is or is not conforming to the positions advocated by others. Gerard gave subjects feedback indicating that they were high or low in ability on the experimental task. Subjects then participated in a series of judgments during which they heard the supposed responses of other subjects (actually these responses were controlled by the experimenter). While listening to these responses, the subject was hooked up to an apparatus that supposedly measured (again, actually was controlled by the experimenter) the subject's first tendency to conform or not conform to the judgments made by the other subjects. The dependent measure in Gerard's study was the liking of the other subjects by the real subject.

Before we examine the results of this study, it should be noted that Gerard's experiment was not designed to test dissonance theory. Thus, commitment and responsibility were not explicitly varied. However, it seems that these two variables were at least minimally present. Subjects probably did feel an implicit commitment to their responses; they were led to believe that they did have the tendencies indicated by the machine. Furthermore, the subjects are likely to have felt responsible for their tendencies, since they probably viewed them as heretofore unknown personality traits in themselves. Thus, even though subjects did not choose to make their responses, the conditions of commitment and responsibility appear to have met the minimal requirements of a dissonance-evoking situation.[3]

For people with high abilities who deviated and for those with low abilities who conformed, not much dissonance should have been produced. The high ability deviators should have thought the other subjects were rather inept, while the low ability conformers should have thought the others superior in performance and should have felt badly about their own comparative abilities. In Gerard's study, both of these groups of subjects evidenced relatively low levels of liking for the other subjects.

Dissonance should be created for high ability subjects whose first impulse is to *conform*; such people should feel that they should make their judgments "objectively" and not be influenced by others. One way to reduce this dissonance is to increase one's liking of the others; conforming to well-liked others should be seen as consonant. On the other hand, it should be dissonant for low ability subjects to *deviate*. In order to reduce this dissonance, the subject could reduce the importance or acceptance of the ability information, deny his deviation, or minimize the behavioral implications of his deviance by increasing his liking of the other subjects. Perhaps because it was the most readily available mode of dissonance reduction or because the other modes were difficult to use in light of the distortion of reality that would have been required, Gerard's data indicated that the low ability deviants also reduced dissonance by increasing their liking of the other subjects.

These results can be applied clinically in several ways. First, for a client who feels he conforms to others, the therapist can increase or decrease the probability of his liking the others to whom he conforms. If liking would be beneficial, the therapist can emphasize the client's high abilities; if not liking or liking to a lesser degree would further therapeutic goals, the therapist can emphasize the client's lack of ability on those issues on which he conforms. For a client who feels he deviates from others, the reverse would be the case. The probability of liking would be increased by emphasizing the client's lack of abilities and decreased by emphasizing the client's possession of high ability. Furthermore, for a client who interacts with others around some task or issue and who doesn't particularly feel that he conforms or not, the therapist can increase liking by

---

[3] Wicklund and Brehm (in press) have also interpreted the results of this experiment in terms of dissonance theory.

emphasizing conformity impulses in conjunction with high ability or deviancy impulses in conjunction with low ability. Conversely, the probability of this sort of client's liking the others can be decreased by emphasizing conforming impulses in conjunction with low abilities or deviancy impulses in conjunction with high abilities.

FAILURE

Most therapists at some point in their practice work with clients who feel themselves to be failures and who may, in fact, fail in a great many of their life enterprises. Cohen and Zimbardo (in Brehm & Cohen, 1962) report a study that suggests one way in which these feelings and acts of failure may maintain themselves. Cohen and Zimbardo found that when people committed themselves to a failure experience with little external pressure to do so, they tended not to take advantage of a later opportunity to improve their situation, thus continuing to fail. It was suggested that committing oneself to failure leads to dissonance between that commitment and the person's need for achievement; one way to reduce this dissonance is to reduce one's need for achievement. With a lowered need for achievement, one would be less likely to respond to opportunities to improve one's performance. Schlachet (1965) also found that under high dissonance conditions (greater likelihood of failure on the task; minimal justification for participating in the task) subjects showed less negative affect associated with failure and reduced need to succeed.

It is not suggested that all feelings and acts of failure arise from a similar process, but it is possible that dissonance reduction through lowering one's need to achieve may account for some of these behaviors and feelings. If this is so, the therapist can attempt to modify the client's unhappy state. First, engagement in failure activities should be attributed to external pressure ("They made you do it") so as to reduce the client's sense of commitment to and responsibility for these acts. Second, success experiences should be provided for the client, and the client's volitional engagement in these activities should be stressed. Committing oneself to a successful experience is dissonant with a low need for achievement and should elicit some raising of one's need to achieve.

DEPRIVATION

Most clinicians have had experience with clients who feel deprived. There are several studies on deprivation in the dissonance literature that suggest that the effects of such feelings vary greatly depending on the type of deprivation involved and on the circumstances of the involvement.

First, deprivation can act as a condition of low justification. Brehm and Cohen (1959a) found that subjects who chose to participate in an experimental procedure in which they were deprived of incentives that others received expressed more satisfaction with the experimental procedure. Cooper and Brehm (1971) report a similar study in which they found that this increase in dissonance, and therefore in task satisfaction as a reducer of dissonance, occurs only when people know about the deprivation before the commitment. Relative deprivation, not getting what others obtain, is an aversive condition for most people. To justify choosing such a circumstance, a person can come to believe that he must really like doing the task on which he is deprived. This amounts to a sort of deprivation justification hypothesis—we come to love that on which we are deprived.

Therapists can apply relative deprivation similarly to any low justification procedure: the more relative deprivation known at the time of the commitment, the more dissonance and the more liking for the behavior. Note, however, that this should work only for people who dislike feeling relatively deprived. For anyone who enjoys or at least fully accepts relative deprivation as his lot in life, relative deprivation will not act as a low justification; indeed, if the person liked it, it would act as a high justification and reduce the possibilities for dissonance.

There is another sort of deprivation: social deprivation, being alone. Studies by Cohen, Greenbaum, and Mansson (1963) and Epstein (1968) have explored the relationship between this type of deprivation and dissonance processes. The results showed that if people choose to deprive themselves of contact with others, social approval loses strength as a reinforcer, while if people do not choose social deprivation but are assigned to it in the experiment, social approval gains power as a reinforcer.

Again, a sort of deprivation justification principle appears operative. If one chooses to be socially deprived, one can justify this choice by coming to like the chosen activity, that is, liking being alone. If one likes being alone, social approval will decrease in effectiveness in promoting behavior. If, on the other hand, one is forced to be alone, this state of deprivation acts in a way similar to that of deprivation of primary reinforcers and increases the reinforcement power of social approval. These processes are not necessarily dependent on social deprivation being aversive to the person. In general, one comes to like more that which one chooses, while being forced to do something may well result in liking it less.

This finding, as most dissonance findings, can be utilized differently depending on the therapist's specific goals. If the therapist wishes to rely on social reinforcement, he can increase the power of this reinforcement by minimizing the person's voluntary social deprivation—either by providing external justifications for self-induced social deprivation or by enforcing social deprivation without the client's consent (the latter technique resembles the "time-out" procedure employed by behavior therapists). On the other hand, the therapist who finds that his social approval is too great—interfering with his abilities to utilize dissonance strategies and/or creating reactance effects—should be able to reduce the power of such social approval by getting the client to commit himself, under conditions of high volition and low justification, to social deprivation. One readily available form of this approach is for the therapist to get the client to voluntarily suspend therapy for a while. There is, of course, the risk that the client will not return, but this risk is probably slight if the original problem is that the therapist's social approval is too powerful. Assuming the client does return, the power of the therapist's social approval should be reduced following this voluntary therapeutic deprivation.

MARITAL CHOICE

Cohen (in Brehm & Cohen, 1962) examined how dissonance might affect the process of marital choice. In one of the relatively rare correlational studies of dissonance, he had male students fill out questionnaires before and after they became engaged. His results indicated that the more negatively the future fiancées were perceived prior to the engagement, the more positive was the change in the subjects' feelings about the fiancées after the engagement.

Theoretically, this study reflects the effect of knowing about negative consequences prior to making a decision. Practically, they again, but this time in a more "real world" manner, point out the paradoxical fact that negative consequences of a chosen alternative can lead to increased favorability toward that alternative. The therapist should be able to use this principle in effecting strong, stable decisions, whether they involve choosing a marital partner or any other choice alternative significant in therapy.

PRETHERAPY BEHAVIOR

As has been noted, one of the few Goldstein, Heller, and Sechrest suggestions (1966) for the use of dissonance theory in therapy with which the present author can agree is found in their discussion of premembership tasks for group therapy members. The suggestion is simply that the more effortful the premembership tasks, the more attraction to the group will occur. This notion was based on studies by Aronson and Mills (1959) and Gerard and Matthewson (1966). These investigators found that subjects who went through an unpleasant initiation task in order to join a group found the group more attractive than subjects who did not go through such a task. Thus, a strict interpretation of the results indicates that the more unpleasant the initiation task, the more attraction to the group will result. However, Goldstein, Heller, and Sechrest are probably correct in extending the notion of "unpleasant" to the more general concept of effort. Unpleasant activities require more effort to get through, and the effort justification principle has been found to have wide utility.

It has been pointed out that such premembership tasks can apply to dyadic as well as group therapy. If the therapist desires to have a client enter therapy with high attraction to the therapist and the therapeutic situation, one way to generate this high attraction is to put the client through some effortful pretherapy behavior. It should be stressed that this positive effect of effort on attraction will only occur when the client voluntarily commits himself to the effortful task in the absence of powerful external justification. Thus, the therapist should not indicate that the effortful pretherapy task is necessary for therapy or will help the client "get better"; both of these rationales would justify the effort and reduce dissonance arousal. Instead, the therapist has the more difficult role of inducing the client to perform the effortful pretherapy tasks with minimal external justification for his performance.

HYPNOSIS

This section will not attempt to explain hypnosis in terms of dissonance theory or, indeed, any other theory. It will, however, examine a study in which hypnosis was utilized to create dissonance. Thus, whatever the hypnotic process is, and this is a highly controversial and unresolved issue, it seems that it can, under some circumstances, affect the arousal of dissonance.

Brock and Grant (1963) performed a study in which they had subjects eat hot sauce or some mild food. After this, they hypnotized the subjects. Some of the subjects were told that their stomachs were full and bloated, while others were told that their stomachs were not full. All subjects were then instructed not to recall the hypnotic instructions. After they had been awakened, subjects were allowed to drink as much water as they wanted.

Brock and Grant reasoned that dissonance would be created for the subjects who ate hot sauce and were thus thirsty, and who were told their stomachs were full. It was predicted that subjects would reduce this dissonance by coming to believe they were not thirsty and thus not drinking much water. The results confirmed this prediction. High dissonance subjects drank less water than subjects who had not eaten hot sauce, whereas low dissonance subjects (i.e., those who ate hot food but were told their stomachs were empty) drank more.

These results are quite intriguing. The behavioral commitment in this experiment was eating hot sauce. Since subjects did not choose to do this but were told to do so, their commitment should not have been very strong. Subjects were then told something about the condition of their stomachs, and listening to this was certainly not a volitional experience; they were hypnotized for the message! It is intriguing that the mode of dissonance reduction, that is, reducing thirst, indicated that the hypnotic communication was the element most resistant to change. Subjects did not distort this message by coming to believe their stomachs were not full; they distorted the logical and physiological outcome of eating hot sauce, that is, being thirsty. The Brock and Grant study suggests that hypnotic communications can act to anchor dissonance reduction in a fashion similar to that of a chosen behavioral commitment. The therapist who cannot obtain his client's participation, under low justification conditions, in a behavioral commitment might try a hypnotic suggestion that he has engaged in the behavior. The finding that hypnotic suggestions can lead to actual behavioral change in a strong drive state indicates that such suggestions may be quite powerful dissonance inducers.

PERSONAL INVOLVEMENT
IN THE COMMITMENT

In Festinger's original formulation of dissonance theory, he stated that the more important the cognitions in a dissonant relationship, the greater would be the magnitude of dissonance aroused. Several studies have shown that one way to increase the importance of these cognitions is to tell people that their behavioral commitments and decisions reflect on important aspects of themselves, such as their personality and values. Zimbardo (1960) found that the greater the self-involvement of a subject on an opinion issue and the greater the discrepancy between the subject's opinion and that advocated in a communication from a positive source, the greater was the opinion change toward the source's position. It should be noted that this experiment did not explicitly vary choice and is thus a less than fully adequate examination of dissonance. However, it may be that high personal involvement led to greater dissonance not only because the importance of the dissonant cognitions (i.e., own belief and opinion of positive source) was increased, but also because the highly involved subjects felt more responsible for their opinions, these opinions being represented as reflecting their personality, social values, and outlook on life.

In a study of decision processes, Deutsch, Krauss, and Rosenau (1962) found that the more self-involvement, the greater was the postdecision reevaluation of choice alternatives. Since this study focused on free decisions, it involves dissonance more clearly than the Zimbardo study. The results of the two studies are, however, perfectly consistent: the more self-involvement, the more dissonance and the greater the dissonance reduction.

These studies indicate that the therapeutic situation is at least potentially one of high dissonance. Most clients already believe that their behavior and attitudes during therapy reflect their "personalities," and are highly self-involved. It may be, then, that not only can therapists utilize dissonance strategies effectively and easily, but also that therapy may create unintended dissonance and undesired dissonace reduction. There are, of course, many ways to decrease the arousal of dissonance. The therapist familiar with dissonance theory and its effects should recognize unintended dissonance and its reduction when they occur and, through knowledge of the theory, be able to guard against the recurrence of any such undesired effects. Nicely enough, then, knowledge of the theory should make possible both intentional utilization as well as intentional avoidance of dissonance arousal.

INCREASING EXTREMITY
OF INITIAL BELIEF

Thus far the chapters on dissonance theory have assumed that therapists will desire to use dissonance strategies to bring about attitudinal and behavioral change. The notion has been that clients have certain beliefs and opinions that may create difficulties for them; that by having the client engage in a counterattitudinal behavior under conditions of high commitment and high responsibility, the client's opinions and beliefs will change; and that this change will promote the stable occurrence of what was originally counterattitudinal behavior and other similar behaviors. What, however, about those instances when a therapist wishes to strengthen existing beliefs? Will dissonance theory aid the therapist in this aim?

The literature on this issue is somewhat problematic. Cohen (1962) reported a study in which subjects tried to convince other people of their (the subjects') beliefs. The less successful they were at this, the more extreme subjects became in their own belief, especially if the other person was originally well liked. An additional finding was that the subjects showed less interest in their unconvinced partner. Cohen reasoned that to try to convince another person of one's own beliefs and to fail creates dissonance. How, then, can dissonance be reduced? One way is to devalue the other person, and it seems that some dissonance reduction did occur this way, as expressed in losing interest in the partner. Another way seems to be to become *less* extreme in one's own beliefs, bringing them more into line with the partner's reaction. This did not happen. Instead, subjects became *more* extreme in their initial beliefs. In order to view this as dissonance reduction, one must accept that the failure to convince others acted as a negative outcome reducing the justification for the behavior and increasing the perceived effort of the behavior. The person would then be confronted with dissonance between his engaging in the behavior and his achievement of a negative outcome. In order to justify engaging in the behavior, he would come to believe more strongly in his original position.

It is hard to judge whether it is reasonable to expect that dissonance would operate in this fashion. Cohen did not explicitly vary choice, although subjects should have felt responsible for their behavior since they were arguing their own beliefs. In addition, although the outcome was not explicitly foreseen, subjects probably felt they should have foreseen the possibility of failure; in any advocacy behavior, failure is always possible. Thus, the minimal requirements for dissonance arousal were probably met. The critical issue is whether the focus of the dissonance would be on justifying the behavior or on coping with the conflict of opinions. The finding of decreased interest in the unconvinced partner suggests that the focus was on both, but that only changing one's opinion toward the other person was untenable, because it left unresolved the problem of justifying the behavior.

If one accepts this line of reasoning, Cohen's study makes two very important points for clinicians. First, a method of increasing the strength of a client's initial belief is revealed. The method is for the therapist simply to listen to the client's opinion and tell him that his arguments are unconvincing. Second, and perhaps more important, therapists often view this procedure of listening and then telling the client that his arguments are unconvincing as a way to "reality-test" for the client and as a method of changing his initial beliefs. Unfortunately, Cohen's study suggests that this may result in just the opposite outcome. The client may justify his unproductive and unpleasant behavior by becoming more extreme in his original belief, and by devaluing or at least losing interest in the therapist.

Dissonance theory suggests that a more effective strategy for the therapist who wishes to change the belief of a client is to use the forced-compliance paradigm. If the client voluntarily engages in counterattitudinal behavior, change in the direction of this behavior is likely to take place. As long as there is high commitment and responsibility on the part of the client for counterattitudinal behavior, there is very little likelihood of strengthening the undesired, original belief.

Jellison and Mills (1969) suggest a less problematic way of strengthening initial beliefs. They found that when subjects made tape-recorded speeches consonant with their own opinions, initial beliefs became stronger. In the terms of the previous discussion, the belief-consonant behavior produced negative outcomes—in this case, embarrassment and discomfort—and subjects justified their behavior by becoming more extreme in their original opinions. Again, and this time without competing modes of dissonance reduction, the point is made that belief-consonant behavior can strengthen original beliefs and thus should be encouraged only when this is the goal.

FEEDBACK ON THE CLIENT'S BEHAVIOR

The notion of feedback as a therapeutic variable is becoming increasingly interesting to clinicians (e.g., Kanfer, 1966; Leitenberg, Agras, Thompson, & Wright, 1968; Rutner, 1973). The dissonance theory literature contains several studies examining the effects of feedback on dissonance and attitude change. Greenbaum, Cohn, and Krauss (1965) conducted a study in which it was found that for subjects who chose to engage in an experimental task, negative feedback on their performance led to greater liking for the task than positive feedback. For those who were assigned to the task, feedback made no difference in their evaluation of the task. Choosing what turns out to be an unpleasant behavior (assuming that the subject foresaw at least the possibility of this unpleasantness) arouses dissonance and is justified by liking the behavior.

Examining feedback received about counterattitudinal behavior, Heslin and Amo (1972) found that praise for such behavior increased dissonance and led to more attitude change than did criticism. A successful, convincing counterattitudinal behavior acts as a negative outcome and increases attitude change in the direction of the behavior. Thus, for belief-consonant behavior (Cohen, 1962) and for neutral tasks (Greenbaum, Cohn, & Krauss, 1965), *negative* feedback is a negative outcome and increases dissonance. For counterattitudinal behavior (Heslin & Amo, 1972), however, *positive* feedback is a negative outcome and increases dissonance.

Belief-consonant behavior that produces a negative outcome is justified by believing more strongly in the original belief. Counter-attitudinal behavior that produces a negative outcome is justified by reducing the strength of one's original belief and moving in the direction of the belief implied by the behavior.

These findings indicate that simple notions of giving positive feedback to the behavior one wishes to encourage and negative feedback to the behavior one wishes to discourage may at times be ill founded. A critical variable is the relationship between the original belief and the belief implied by the behavior. For consonant or neutral behavior that is voluntarily engaged in, negative feedback may strengthen a positive attitude toward these behaviors. For behavior that is discrepant with one's initial belief, positive feedback will create a positive attitude toward these behaviors. Feedback, thus, can be an important therapeutic variable, but it must be understood and utilized in the context of the complexities of human behavior.

AGGRESSION

Aggressive responses are, in general, considered by dissonance theory to be counterattitudinal activities in opposition to a person's belief about himself (i.e., that he doesn't hurt other people). While there have been several dissonance studies on aggression (e.g., Brock & Buss, 1964; Buss & Brock, 1963), this section will examine only the two studies that appear most unambiguous from a theoretical standpoint and most interesting from a practical one.

Brock and Buss (1962) found that subjects who chose to deliver painful electric shocks to another person minimized the shock more than subjects who did not choose but were assigned to deliver the shock and more than subjects who chose to deliver less painful shocks. Interestingly, this result was found only when the victim was male. When the victim was female, high dissonance subjects did not minimize the pain of the shock, but instead perceived that they had been under great external constraints and had had to deliver the shock. Thus, for the person who ordinarily doesn't think of himself as some-one who hurts others, it is dissonant to choose to hurt someone else, especially someone who has not provoked the aggression. One way to reduce this dissonance is to minimize the pain that the aggression causes the other person. Under some circumstances, however, it is difficult to do this. Presumably the reality of delivering electric shocks to a female is so strong that one cannot persuade oneself that the shock did not hurt. What one can do to reduce dissonance is claim that one is not responsible, by saying that "someone made me do it."

Firestone (1966) conducted an interesting study on aggression and dissonance. He found that if subjects chose to enter an interaction with a hostile person (knowing about the hostility at the time of choice) and then that person acted in a provocative manner, there was less likelihood of the subject's retaliating against the hostile other than if the subject had not chosen to enter the interaction. Firestone's reasoning was that it is dissonant to voluntarily enter an interaction with a person known to be hostile; provocation by the person simply increases that dissonance. To retaliate would presumably increase the dissonance even more by making salient what a bad decision the person had made. If, however, the person can minimize the other person's negative characteristics to himself, he can make his decision appear less bad and he will be less likely to respond to provocation. This is what appears to have happened in Firestone's study. We do not usually think of provocation as *decreasing* the chances of a person retaliating against another, but under certain circumstances this is what can occur.

Therapists usually have two major concerns about aggression.[4] The first is with clients who are not assertive enough, who allow themselves to be trampled on unnecessarily. Such a client may indeed make the kind of bad decisions illustrated by Firestone's study and voluntarily interact with hostile people and then reduce dissonance by not retaliating. In addition, if the person does behave assertively, he may act similarly to the subjects in the study by Brock and Buss and reduce dissonance by minimizing the aggressiveness of his response or by decreasing his responsibility for the behavior. What is clear from these studies is that it may be difficult to increase a person's assertive responses. In working with nonassertive clients, the therapist may have to start out with having them engage in assertive behaviors of very low magnitude. In some ways, this is a strategic disadvantage: not as much dissonance will be aroused by low-level assertion as would be by higher levels. But in another way this is an advantage. Since dissonance arousal will not be as great, the pressures to reduce dissonance will not be as powerful and the therapist can more likely succeed in blocking off undesirable modes of dissonance reduction. In carrying out this procedure, the client's choice to engage in the behavior should be made highly salient, and the exact effect of the assertive response should be designated in

---

[4] For the purposes of this section, aggressive and assertive responses will be considered as similar in quality and different in degree, with assertive responses a mild form of aggression. This does not deny the importance of teaching clients how to assert themselves without provoking aggression from others. What this approach does imply is that for many clients both assertion and aggression are seen as moves "against other people" and that this notion is not necessarily in error.

advance so that it will be difficult to distort this effect. By gradually increasing the strength of the assertive response, the therapist should be able to gradually effect some changes in the person's attitude. The person should come to believe that he is an assertive person, quite capable of standing up for his rights and thus quite likely to do so.

As for the bad decisions nonassertive people may make, a two-pronged approach may be necessary. First, the client should be instructed to examine the environmental pressures that cause him to agree to interact with an unpleasant person. If the client feels little volition in these interactions, provocations will not act to increase dissonance and decrease retaliation. In addition, if through the dissonance procedures described above, clients begin to actually be more assertive, they will be more able to refuse to interact with hostile others. To avoid such interactions may be the best possible choice.

Therapists' second concern is with clients who are overly aggressive. The dissonance strategy that would be useful with this type of client is essentially the opposite of the above techniques. Dissonance should be utilized by getting the client to voluntarily engage in nonaggressive behaviors. These nonaggressive behaviors may at first need to be only slightly nonaggressive, with a gradual approach to the desired level of behavior. Moreover, if the client typically aggresses against particular people whom he, and the therapist, consider hostile and provocative, the therapist can emphasize the fact that the client knows these people are hostile and yet he voluntarily interacts with them. By thus highlighting the client's volition in these bad decisions, the therapist should obtain one of two results. The client should experience dissonance and retaliate less. Or, better still if such people are indeed provocative and hostile, the client will use his newly recognized freedom of choice to avoid such people.

INCREASING PROSOCIAL BEHAVIOR

In suggesting ways to affect assertion and aggression, it was noted that the therapist may need to start the client out on approximations to the ultimately desired behavior. We might term such a procedure "dissonance shaping," since it resembles the successive approximation procedure used within a reinforcement paradigm. Freedman and Fraser (1966) conducted an experiment that suggests that such dissonance-shaping techniques may be especially helpful in eliciting desirable prosocial behavior. Freedman and Fraser term their approach the "foot-in-the-door" technique. Their study found that when people complied first with a small request for volunteering assistance, they were later more likely to comply with a large request than those people who had not been exposed to the small request. It seems that complying with a request for help creates dissonance between, on the one hand, the chosen behavioral commitment and, on the other, the effort required to engage in the behavior, preferences to do other things, and, perhaps, concerns that more helping behaviors will be required. To justify their compliance, people can come to like the helping behavior. Liking this sort of behavior, they are more likely to comply with a subsequent request for help that requires a greater expenditure of time and effort.

It would seem, then, that dissonance-shaping procedures have merit, certainly for prosocial, helping behaviors and probably for other behaviors as well. The therapist can program out the new behaviors he wants to elicit from the client—new behaviors that are valuable in and of themselves or are important because of the attitudes they imply—and he can start at a low level of behavioral engagement. Freedman and Fraser's study suggests that these low-level, easy behaviors will make it easier to elicit more difficult behaviors. Theoretically, this principle should be capable of virtually infinite segmentation, with therapists free to build in as many steps as they feel are needed in order to maximize chances of eliciting the desired behavior.

It should be pointed out that "dissonance shaping" differs on several dimensions from the kind of shaping based on principles of reinforcement. In dissonance shaping, it is important to minimally reward each behavioral step, whereas reinforcement principles call for rewarding behavior at an unspecified, but presumably rather high, level. Moreover, dissonance shaping should be accompanied by high voluntary commitment to each behavior and would be enhanced by having the behavior be as effortful as possible (i.e., great enough to arouse dissonance without preventing voluntary commitment). Reinforcement principles do not specify the volitional state of the person that is necessary, and they imply that the effort involved should be minimal.

These theoretical differences reflect the different types of behavior to which dissonance shaping and reinforcement shaping are applicable. Shaping by reinforcement is most appropriate when the goal is to train the client to perform a behavior that he *cannot* perform.[5] Dissonance shaping, on the other hand, is most appropriate when the goal is to induce the client to perform a behavior that he *will not* perform. In the former case, the client wants to perform the behavior, but lacks the skill. In the latter, the client will

---

[5] This application may be quite difficult in practice. See footnote, p. 79.

benefit from performing the behavior, but lacks the appropriate attitude that would lead to its occurrence.

Marlowe, Frager, and Nuttall (1965) conducted another study examining the relationship between dissonance arousal and prosocial behavior. Subjects were asked to fill out an attitude questionnaire dealing with a topical issue. When this questionnaire was completed, subjects were told they could not participate in a further part of the study because they had the "wrong" attitudes. Some subjects believed they lost $1.00 because of their beliefs, others believed they lost $20.00. After this, a seemingly independent interruption occurred and subjects were asked if they would volunteer for a task related to their original attitudes. It was found that volunteering was greater for subjects who had lost $20.00 than for those who had lost $1.00. In a control study, Marlowe et al. found that this effect did not occur when the volunteering task was unrelated to the original beliefs.

The Marlowe et al. study can be understood in terms of dissonance principles already discussed. Subjects who acted in accordance with their original beliefs—that is, filling out the questionnaire—suffered the negative outcome of losing money as a consequence. It has been noted that negative outcomes for belief-consonant behavior can create dissonance and that this dissonance can be reduced and the behavior justified, by coming to believe more strongly in one's original position. The Marlowe et al. study indicates that the more negative the consequence (losing $20.00 versus losing $1.00), the more dissonance is aroused and the more strongly one holds to one's original belief. The more strongly one holds to one's belief, the more likely one is to perform actions consistent with it.

The clinical application of this study is quite straightforward. The therapist can increase the strength of a client's initial prosocial belief and the likelihood that the client will act in accordance with this belief by having the client endure some unpleasantness as a consequence of his original belief. It should be noted that this strategy is only effective with clients who already have a prosocial belief, albeit a weak one; for clients without a prosocial belief, this procedure would be inappropriate and the dissonance-shaping technique described above more appropriate.

INDIVIDUAL DIFFERENCES

As one would expect for an older theory that has an extensive literature, there have been many more studies of the relationship between individual differences and cognitive dissonance theory than there have been examinations of individual differences and reactance theory. As will be seen, however, these studies have generally been disappointing: effects have been unclear, attempted replications have failed, critical variables have been misused and so on. Furthermore, at a more general level, all of the problems mentioned when discussing reactance theory and individual differences are present when examining the relationship between dissonance theory and individual difference variables: the effects obtained may be limited to extreme types, other variables correlated with the individual difference measure may be equally or even more important in leading to the results than the individual difference that is being studied, and many of the individual difference measures in these studies are not individual differences with which therapists are typically concerned.

The following summary is presented to give the reader an idea of what has been done. The literature discussed will probably not be very helpful as it stands. Clearly, new research is needed that isolates variables of interest to therapists and that is directly related to tenets of the theory. More important, perhaps, therapists should realize that individual differences do not provide the magic road to success in applications of social psychological theories. Even with some pointers gleaned from more sophisticated and relevant individual difference research, therapists will still need to rely on their own understanding of the specific characteristics of their clients in order to tailor their clinical strategies and maximize their success.

Self-Esteem

There have been a number of studies examining the relationship between cognitive dissonance and self-esteem. The basic notion behind all of these studies is that self-esteem reflects a group of cognitions and that these cognitions should affect dissonance arousal and reduction.

Focusing on the free-choice situation, Malewski (1967) conducted a study that employed two measures of self-esteem. For self-ratings of self-esteem, there was no effect on dissonance and its reduction. For sociometric ratings (i.e., popularity choices made by others), there was a clear effect: subjects with high "self-esteem" (i.e., chosen more by others) evidenced the typical postdecision spread of evaluation of the alternatives, while subjects with low "self-esteem" (i.e., chosen less frequently by others) showed no such spread. Thus, one can reason, as has Aronson (1968), that only people with high self-esteem will expect to make good (i.e., correct) choices, will experience dissonance from those elements inconsistent with the choice, and will then justify their choices by increasing their liking of the chosen alternative and decreasing their liking of the rejected alternative(s). People with low self-esteem, on the other hand, do not expect to make good choices, do not experience dissonance, and do not attempt to justify their choices. Malewski's study, while suggestive, does not provide very good support for this idea in that his measure of the subject's own cognitions about themselves had no effect whatsoever on dissonance reduction. It is not clear what psychological process in the person was measured by the sociometric measure nor how this unknown process may be related to dissonance.

Glass (1964) and Glass and Wood (in Zimbardo, 1969) examined the relationship among aggression, self-esteem, and dissonance. Glass found that aggression led to decreased liking of the person the subject aggressed against only for subjects with high self-esteem. Presumably, only subjects with high self-esteem would find it dissonant to do something against their principles, and, therefore, only they would be motivated to derogate the victim in order to justify their behavior. It should be noted that "self-esteem" in this case was a manipulated variable, some subjects receiving positive reports about themselves, others receiving negative ones. Glass and Wood replicated this effect under high choice; under low choice, self-esteem had no effect. Again, self-esteem was experimentally manipulated. In a second study, Glass and Wood utilized the subjects' own premeasured self-esteem, gave all subjects choice, and varied the attractiveness of the victim. This time no effects were found on liking of the victim. Combining high attractiveness of the victim and high self-esteem did lead to the greatest increase in the favorableness of using shock, this increase being considered an alternative way to reduce dissonance.

These two studies indicate yet another problem of individual difference variables. In some ways it is more elegant experimentally to manipulate individual difference variables; then, at least, one knows what the variable is. Unfortunately, the manipulated variable may have little or no relationship to the personality characteristic of interest. One can learn from studies with manipulated variables what will happen when people receive certain types of information about themselves and this can be useful. Therapists, for example, may find it helpful to give a client positive feedback about himself (the client) before the client makes a commitment to a counterattitudinal behavior. What one does not necessarily learn from studies of manipulated individual differences is anything about the effect of chronic personality variables on the psychological process of interest.

The total confusion about how self-esteem affects dissonance processes is exemplified by studies by Greenbaum (1966) and Cooper and Duncan (1971). Using a pre-measure of chronic self-esteem, Greenbaum found that dissonance occurred only for subjects with low self-esteem who made a counterattitudinal speech. This result is totally contradictory with Aronson's theoretical position that would expect dissonance to occur only for people with high self-esteem. Finally, Cooper and Duncan found that with manipulated self-esteem there was no effect on dissonance reduction. All subjects who made a counterattitudinal speech for low incentives showed the typical pattern of reducing dissonance by moving toward the attitude implied by the behavior.

Thus, one can have one's pick. Dissonance occurs for everyone regardless of level of self-esteem; dissonance occurs only for people high in self-esteem; dissonance occurs only for people low in self-esteem. Given the present state of knowledge, the therapist is well advised not to follow any of these principles in his therapeutic applications.

Other Types of Individual Differences

The existing literature on other individual difference measures is hardly more reassuring. There are studies that find individual difference effects on dissonance only for one sex (Rosen, 1961); that fail to connect the justification to the commitment (Bishop, 1967), thus failing to create a dissonance-provoking situation; that examine people's responses to other people's behavior (O. J. Harvey & Ware, 1967), thus calling "dissonance" something that has nothing to do with dissonance theory; that mix one difference with another (Wolitzky, 1967), making any conclusion about either one impossible. There are, however, a few studies that are somewhat more promising.

O. J. Harvey (1965) found that a measure of concrete versus abstract thinking differentiated among situations under which people would show more dissonance reduction. All subjects engaged in counterattitudinal behaviors. For concrete thinkers, more dissonance reduction was found when these behaviors were public; for abstract thinkers, more dissonance reduction was found when they performed their counterattitudinal behaviors privately.

Glass, Canavan, and Schiavo (1968) and Gordon and Glass (1970) examined repressors versus sensitizers. Initially, Glass and his colleagues predicted that sensitizers should show more dissonance arousal and reduction than repressors. They found in both studies that repressors showed more dissonance reduction than sensitizers. These results are interesting and now have been achieved in two studies with differing formats. Unfortunately, it is extremely difficult to understand the relationships producing these results. One can speculate that repressors are people who defend and that dissonance reduction is essentially a defensive process; without converging data, however, any interpretation remains highly speculative.

Bogart, Geis, Levy, and Zimbardo (in Zimbardo, 1969) report some evidence indicating that people high in Machiavellianism (Christie & Geis, 1970) may not behave in accordance with dissonance principles. Subjects low in Machiavellianism did behave in accordance with dissonance principles, indicating that the investigators were successful in arranging a dissonance-evoking experimental situation. High Machs, however, either behaved in a fashion opposite to that expected by dissonance theory or showed no change in their attitudes. Unfortunately, the problems of knowing exactly what "Machiavellianism" is and what aspect of it relates to dissonance processes remain.

Cooper and Scalise (1974) conducted a study examining the relationship between introversion versus extroversion and dissonance. They predicted that for introverts more dissonance should be created if they believed their first impulse in a group judgment task was to conform, while for extroverts more dissonance should be created when they believed their first impulse was to *not* conform (information about the subject's "impulses" was controlled by the experimenter). These results were confirmed and showed that those subjects who had been predicted to experience the most dissonance showed the greatest opinion change in the direction of their first impulse.

The study by Cooper and Scalise (1974) can be taken as support for the comments made in the beginning of this section. What is interesting about their study is not what it says about introversion and extroversion per se, but the general point that it makes—namely that for some people, some types of events are dissonant, while for others, other types are dissonant. No dissonance theorist would quarrel with this and, indeed, the original theory's being formulated in terms of cognitions held by the person allowed considerable room for such individual variation. The most powerful strategy, however, is not to tailor applications according to personality type as indicated by a personality test, but to tailor them according to individual cognitions. Therapists can find out if their clients expect to make bad decisions, think of themselves as people who do not hurt others, feel more uncomfortable about counterattitudinal behavior in public or in private situations, and are bothered more by conforming or nonconforming impulses. They can, indeed, find out about any cognitions that they believe may affect some planned therapeutic strategy employing dissonance arousal. Once the individual cognitions are assessed, the strategy can be made to fit the particular individual rather than a type.

EXPECTANCY VIOLATIONS: DISSONANCE OR NOT?

There are any number of studies indicating that people will behave in accordance with their expectations (e.g., Aronson & Mettee, 1968; Carlsmith & Aronson, 1963; Marecek & Mettee, 1972). The most well known study of expectations was conducted by Aronson and Carlsmith (1962). They found that people who did poorly in the initial phases of an experimental task would, when confronted with a change to a good performance, redo their performance to make it conform to their expectancies, that is, to make it bad instead of good. People with an expectation of doing well redid a bad performance to make it a good one. Thus, instead of behaving in accordance with a self-enhancement motive to always do as well as possible, subjects in the Aronson and Carlsmith study acted in accordance with a consistency motive, behaving in such a fashion as to make any particular performance conform to their expectations. The Aronson and Carlsmith study has been examined by many other investigators (Beijk, 1966; Brock, Edelman, Edwards, & Schuck, 1965; Cottrell, 1965; Lowin & Epstein, 1965; Moses & Marcia, 1969; Silverman & Marcantonio, 1965; Ward & Sandvold, 1963; Waterman & Ford, 1965). The sum of these studies suggests that both self-enhancement and consistency motives exist and that situational particulars will determine which motive has primacy.

The purpose of this section is not, however, to explore in detail the literature on expectancy effects. It is, instead, to attempt to put these effects within the perspective of dissonance theory. For while expectancy violations clearly create inconsistency, it is debatable whether such violations should be considered dissonance-arousing. At one level, expectancy violation and dissonance appear highly similar. Cognitions are dissonant when the "obverse of one follows from the other," in other words, when one cognition is not expected, given the other cognition. People who believe in X do not expect to engage in behaviors implying not-X.

On the other hand, expectancy violations appear to have nothing to do with the free-choice paradigm. People expect to choose Y and they do, but under certain circumstances they still experience dissonance. One could argue that the positive aspects of the unchosen alternative make it unexpected to choose the chosen alternative, but this would seem to be stretching the expectancy notion further than parsimony and logic would warrant.

Perhaps more important than the difficulty that the hypothesis of expectancy violation has in accounting for the dissonance effects in the decision process is the problem of fitting important aspects of dissonance theory such as commitment, choice, low justification, high responsibility, and effort into an expectancy violation framework. No doubt this could be done, but again it would require an awkward stretching of a basically simple notion.

Thus, there seems to be little to be gained from viewing dissonance theory as being subsumed by expectancy violation, and a good deal to be lost in theoretical precision. It also does not seem to be profitable to view all expectancy violations as creating dissonance. No doubt there is some general motive toward consistency and toward keeping one's behavior in line with one's expectations. Therapists may wish to use this principle in their therapeutic strategies, for example, preventing some undesirable behavior by emphasizing how inconsistent it is with the person's beliefs or previous behaviors. This principle is probably most effective, however, when it is kept separate from dissonance theory. Dissonance theory is rich, complex, and precise; use of the theory should follow the existing theoretical understanding instead of trying to make it follow a related but theoretically independent principle such as the need to avoid the violation of expectancies.

DISSONANCE AND REACTANCE

In concluding this discussion of dissonance theory and its clinical application, a brief comparison between reactance theory and dissonance theory will be helpful. In many ways, the two theories are similar and lead to similar applications. Both are motivational theories that posit the creation of an unpleasant state that the person then seeks to reduce. Both theories underline the importance of having the client perceive himself as acting freely, without being subject to external pressures. Perception of personal volition will prevent reactance arousal and facilitate dissonance arousal.

There are, however, a few conflicts between the theories. One is the already noted jurisdictional dispute about which theory best accounts for postdecision regret. This conflict is probably of minimal importance in terms of application. Another conflict between the theories, concerning decision-making, is of more practical significance. In Chapter Four, it was recommended that for the client who will not make a decision, the therapist might help him by emphasizing the positive aspects of the beneficial alternative and the negative aspects of the undesirable alternative. This procedure was recommended to reduce predecision reactance. The reader will recognize, however, that this procedure would decrease dissonance arousal from the decision, decrease its postdecision reduction, and possibly lead to some instability in the decision.

In order to resolve this conflict, the clinician will have to scrutinize the circumstances of the particular client. For the client who has great difficulty making any decision at all or for whom delaying a particular decision would cause significant difficulties, it would probably be best to lean toward the reactance-reducing side of the fence and and work to get the decision made, even though the resultant dissonace reduction and stability may be less than desirable. Once the decision has been made, it can be anchored in other important life events in order to make it more resistant to reversal. On the other hand, for the client who can make decisions or for whom delaying a particular decision causes no particular damage, the clinician may want to lean toward the dissonance side of the fence. This may mean it will take longer for the client to make the decision, but once made, the decision should be quite stable.

A final conflict between dissonance theory and reactance theory involves the notion of getting the client to do something "for the therapist." This was discussed in considerable detail in the reactance chapters, which described how clients might be induced to perform behaviors "for the therapist." One might ask, however: Wouldn't having the client do a "favor" for the therapist justify the behavior and reduce the magnitude of dissonance arousal and reduction? Again, this apparent conflict can be resolved by a parametric examination of specific therapeutic situations. If, in order to induce the client to perform a desirable behavior, it is necessary to have the client do it "for the therapist," this is not discrepant from dissonance theory principles. A discrepancy arises only when the justification of doing it "for the therapist" becomes more than minimal. If a client could be induced to perform the behavior on other grounds, obviously the therapist would not add the "for me" to the existing justification. The guideline is simply to use whatever is necessary for performance, but not enough for satisfactory justification.

SUMMARY

This chapter has examined a variety of specific applications of dissonance theory to clinical practice. A selection of widely different content topics was offered as an example of the range of the theory, and a number of studies indicating dissonance effects on basic physiological and psychological processes were cited as examples of the power of the theory. Recent studies were presented indicating that voluntary commitment to therapy and being forewarned about possible unpleasant aspects of therapy can achieve therapeutic improvement no matter what type of "therapy" is employed. Following these sections, some specific content areas were examined including conformity, failure, deprivation, marital choice, pretherapy behavior, hypnosis, personal involvement in the commitment, increasing the extremity of initial belief, feedback on the client's behavior, aggression, and increasing prosocial behavior.

In the concluding sections, some theoretical and methodological issues were discussed. Studies relating individual differences to dissonance processes were reviewed, and the conceptual and methodological problems of these studies were indicated. Some consideration was given to distinguishing violations of expectancy from dissonance. Last, the relationship between the theories of psychological reactance and cognitive dissonance was discussed.

SUGGESTED SOURCES

Brehm, J. W., & Cohen, A. R. *Explorations in cognitive dissonance.* New York: Wiley, 1962.

Festinger, L. *A theory of cognitive dissonance.* Stanford, Calif.: Stanford University Press, 1957.

Festinger, L. *Conflict, decision and dissonance.* Stanford, Calif.: Stanford University Press, 1964.

Wicklund, R. A., & Brehm, J. W. *Perspectives on cognitive dissonance.* Hillsdale, N.J.: Lawrence Erlbaum Associates, in press.

Zimbardo, P. G. *The cognitive control of motivation.* Glenview, Ill.: Scott, Foresman, 1969.

PART THREE

THEORIES OF ATTRIBUTION

CHAPTER EIGHT

THEORIES OF ATTRIBUTION

George Kelly (1955) on "man-the-scientist":

Might not the individual man, each in his own personal way, assume more of the stature of a scientist, ever seeking to predict and control the course of events with which he is involved? Would he not have his theories, test his hypotheses, and weigh his experimental evidence? (p. 5)

Otto Fenichel (1945) on projection:

In general, the organism prefers to feel dangers as threats from without rather than from within because certain mechanisms of protection against overly intense stimuli can be set in motion against external stimuli only. Many projections give the impression that internal stimuli are misapprehended as external ones. (p. 147)

Donald Ford and Hugh Urban (1963) on the therapist's considerations in choosing a conceptual framework:

The therapist is faced with a number of choices. One of the things he might do is use the patient's way of analyzing and construing what is happening. The patient's analysis of events, his "view," becomes the set of concepts that the therapist employs. On the other hand, the therapist can adopt a set of concepts advocated by some theorists.... Finally, he can be "eclectic" and employ some of the concepts of the patient, some of his own, and those of a variety of systems.... He knows that he must exercise care, however, because the concepts he uses will determine what he listens to, what he considers to be important, and how he relates all the different kinds of events to one another. (pp. 34–35)

In turning our attention from dissonance and reactance theories to the theories of attribution, we enter a vastly different theoretical arena. Both dissonance and reactance theories are motivational; they posit the creation of a motivational state and thus the induction of behaviors designed to reduce or satisfy this motive. Attribution theory, on the other hand, is largely without motivational properties. General background motivational trends are sometimes noted, such as the need for a person to have knowledge about causal relationships so that he can affect these relationships or the need for a person to enhance his view of himself, but there is no single, specific motivational state with which the theories of attribution concern themselves. Theories of attribution are, in essence, theories of information processing; they seek to describe the ways in which people reach conclusions about causation. The effects of varying motivational states on such information processing remain largely unformulated.

The reader will have noticed that for the first time in this volume theories (of attribution) are designated. Dissonance and reactance were each designated as a theory. This distinction reflects an important theoretical difference. Attributional behavior, as currently presented in the literature, has been interpreted by a number of theories, each with some similarities to and some differences from the others. There exists today no single coherent attribution theory, but rather a number of individual attribution theories.

This lack of theoretical coherence makes the theoretical presentation section of this chapter a somewhat difficult undertaking. Ideally perhaps, an attempt at a theoretical reconciliation should be made, meshing all existing attribution theories. While the intellectual vigor required for such an undertaking would be admirable, the result might be less praiseworthy, for, in effect, such an approach would simply add one more attribution theory to the already existing array.

Thus, a more conservative approach seems appropriate. Out of the existing array, a number of theories have been chosen, and these will be explicated individually. This approach will not bring order into a somewhat chaotic area, but it has the merit of preserving the original formulations and presenting them for the reader's inspection. Each reader is then free to create his own integration.

In the face of theoretical confusion, one cannot expect empirical work to reflect coherence, and, indeed, the empirical work on attribution processes tends to be characterized by a similar lack of generally accepted premises. Researchers have tended to adopt one attribution theory instead of another and then conducted their empirical investigations accordingly. Thus there is very little of a common reference point for an increasingly burgeoning empirical literature.

Again, choices must be made. Rather than attempt to present all studies of attribution processes, only the studies judged by the author to be most relevant to clinical work will be presented. Fortunately, in the case of attribution theories, there are ample signposts to help make this selection. Of all the theories considered in this book, theories of attribution have been most directly and explicitly concerned with clinically relevant behavior. Thus if the reader can tolerate the somewhat fragmented theoretical presentation, he is promised the reward of applications that will speak quite directly to clinical interests and concerns.

THE THEORIES

Heider: An Analysis of Causation

Fritz Heider is the father of all attribution theories. In his work (1944, 1958) he laid the foundation for all later theories of attribution. These later theories often differ radically from Heider's in terms of content and methodological implications, but they owe the very notion of examining people's attributions of causality to Heider's pioneering ideas.

Heider (1958) presented what he termed a "naive analysis of action." He proposed that people tend in general to seek to understand the effects in the world about them in terms of underlying properties or "invariances." By understanding these invariances, the person gains a powerful prerequisite to effective action. Temporary, transitory events can be understood in terms of enduring properties, allowing for prediction and control of future events.

In taking the perspective of the naive observer, Heider suggested that the search for invariances leads to a division in the attributions associated with purposive action. Action can be seen to result from the two conditions of "can" and "trying." In the condition of can, action will be influenced by both the state of the environment and the power, or abilities, of the person. A facilitating environment, or at least a noninhibiting one, and personal ability are necessary for the person to be able to perform some action. In the condition of trying, two personal factors are involved: intention and exertion. Given that an action *can* be performed, it *will* be performed if the person intends it and exerts himself in its performance.

The result of an analysis of causation is the attribution of responsibility. Heider postulates that people will be held responsible for the acts that they intend and exert themselves to accomplish, but that they will be held less responsible for the events that primarily reflect abilities or the lack thereof. Furthermore, events determined largely by environmental factors are not considered to be the person's responsibility. As the role of environmental factors, such as task difficulty or luck, increases, the role of personal responsibility decreases.

Obviously, this review of Heider's attribution theory is exceedingly brief. It omits consideration of Heider's theory of balance relationships as well as discussion of the complexities he perceived in the attribution process. It should be sufficient, however, to indicate the factors and processes that he emphasized and to give the reader the general orientation of Heider's attribution theory.

Jones and Davis: Dispositional Attributions

As can be seen in the above review, Heider discussed both personal and impersonal attributions. Attributing the causes for a person's behaviors to environmental forces (i.e., forces external to the person, including other people) would be an impersonal attribution, whereas attributions of intention, exertion, and, to a lesser extent, abilities represent personal attributions. In "From Acts to Dispositions: The Attribution Process in Person Perception" (1965), Jones and Davis undertake a detailed examination of how people come to make personal attributions in accounting for another's behaviors.

Jones and Davis agree with Heider that people seek to understand the invariances in the world, and they note that a fundamental invariance in personal attribution is the attribution of a disposition. According to Jones and Davis, other variables such as the intention to commit a behavior and the ability to commit it do not offer the predictive power of dispositions. Thus, whereas Heider focused on the personal invariant of intention, Jones and Davis push the analysis back one step and focus on dispositional characteristics of the person that may underlie his intended acts.

The inferential calculus that Jones and Davis propose for observers is termed "correspondent inference." Correspondence is defined as "the extent that the act and the underlying characteristic or attribute are similarly described by the inference" (p. 223). If, for example, an honest act is inferred to have been caused by the honesty of the actor and the observer is very confident about attributing honesty to the actor, this would be a highly correspondent inference.

What are the characteristics of the acts that allow for correspondent inferences? Jones and Davis propose that the best type of action from which to infer a dispositional attribute is when the person makes a choice. Chosen acts serve two purposes. First, the observer can reliably infer that when an actor has free choice, his behavior is not accounted for in terms of environmental pressures; thus a personal attribution is deemed appropriate. Second, choices made by the actor allow the observer to take note of noncommon effects among choice alternatives. This latter characteristic of choice is a critical ingredient in the correspondent inference process.

If the actor is observed to choose between two alternatives that have highly similar consequences for him, the observer obtains very little information about specific outcomes considered desirable by the actor. If, on the other hand, the actor chooses between alternatives that are highly dissimilar, the observer has too much information about preferences from which to distill a dispositional attribution. But when two choice alternatives share many effects and differ on one or just a few, the observer obtains maximum information about the person's preferences. For example, the person who chooses a car that gets good gas mileage but is identical in every other respect to one getting poor gas mileage has conveyed to an observer his (the actor's) clear desire to obtain more miles to his gallons of gas.

Another important feature in the correspondent inference process is the assumed desirability of the chosen alternative. If, to use the same example, the observer is aware (or thinks, even mistakenly) that virtually everyone would choose the car with good gas mileage, the significance of the actor's choice is greatly diminished. The choice of alternatives that are assumed to be universally desirable tells the observer only that the actor is similar to other people; it tells very little about the actor's unique dispositional characteristics.

Thus, Jones and Davis maintain, the situation that will allow for highest correspondent inference can be specified. It entails the actor's making a free choice among alternatives containing a low number of noncommon effects and that the noncommon effects of the chosen alternative *not* be assumed to be universally desirable. Given these circumstances, the observer can infer that the actor intended his behavior and that this behavior can be described in terms of dispositional attributes of the actor.

To this point, the Jones and Davis formulation deals exclusively with objective observers, that is, observers who can view the actor's behavior dispassionately and who are not directly affected by the actor's choices. There are, however, circumstances under which the actor's behavior does have consequences for the observer. These circumstances are discussed by Jones and Davis in terms of actions with "hedonic relevance."

In examining the effects of hedonic relevance on correspondent inference, Jones and Davis propose that relevance acts to increase correspondence. They suggest that faced with an actor's behavior that has positive or negative consequences for himself, the observer will tend to "package" the effects of the actor's action such that noncommon effects are reduced; with reduced noncommon effects more correspondence should result. In other words, if from a dispassionate observer's viewpoint there are five noncommon effects between two choice alternatives and only one of these effects has hedonic relevance for the affected observer, the affected observer may tend to package or ignore the other four effects and be aware of only that noncommon effect that was relevant to him. This reduction process should in and of itself increase the affected observer's tendency to attribute dispositional properties to the actor.

In addition to this logical effect on correspondence, Jones and Davis propose a more complex, psychological effect. The meaning of the attributed disposition may be affected by the sign of the hedonic relevance. If a person does something on impulse that benefits us, we may perceive him as generous. If, on the other hand, the same impulsive action harms us, we may perceive him as thoughtless. In both cases, relevance has acted to increase our tendency to make dispositional statements, but the meaning of the disposition is altered in accordance with the nature of the act's hedonic relevance.

Jones and Davis take their analysis of the relationship between relevance and correspondence further when they state that given high relevance and high correspondence (derived from features of the actor's behavior other than relevance), extreme evaluations are most likely to occur. If, on other grounds, we feel confident about a dispositional attribution and then, in addition, the action has direct consequences for ourselves, we should be led to extreme dispositional attributions: for example, the actor is seen as *very* generous or *very* thoughtless.

Extremity of attribution also can be affected by the factor of personalism. Jones and Davis note that in principle, relevant actions can be viewed as intended or as not intended by the actor. A relevant action that would be viewed as intended and thus as "personal" in the Jones and Davis sense is one where the actor's choice is viewed as having been affected by the presence of the observer. An unintended act or one of "low personalism" would be one where even though the actor's choice affected the observer, it was not seen as having been influenced by the presence of the observer. Jones and Davis state that with high personalism and high relevance, extreme dispositional attributions to the actor will occur.

Kelley: The Principle of Covariance

The Jones and Davis formulation focused on dispositional attributions. The next theory examines attributions to environmental entities. Kelley (1967, 1971, 1972, 1973) has considered the problem of how one decides that the cause of an event most likely resides in the environmental object with which the actor interacts, be it car, food, another person, or whatever. Kelley's analysis is suitable both for attributions made by an observer to account for an observed other's behavior and for attributions made by actors themselves seeking to understand their own actions.

Kelley, like Heider and Jones and Davis, posits that the basis of attributional behavior is found in determining invariances. He elaborates this basis into his principle of covariance. In relating effects (sensations, perceptions, responses) to entities (cars, food, other people), variations in effects are examined in relation to variations in entities. The effect is then attributed to the state of affairs that is present when the effect is present and absent when the effect is absent.

More specifically, Kelley focuses on four factors where the principle of covariance can be applied. For the factor of distinctiveness, the effect is attributed to the entity if the effect uniquely occurs when the entity is present and does not occur when the entity is absent. The other three factors concern consistency: attributions will be made most confidently to entities when there is consistency over time (when the entity is present, the effect always occurs), over modality (the effect always occurs when the person interacts with the entity even though his way of interacting—e.g., seeing versus hearing—with the entity differs), and over other people (virtually everyone experiences the same effect when interacting with the same entity). Thus if the four criteria of distinctiveness, consistency over time, consistency over modality, and consensus are met, Kelley states that people will, with confidence, attribute causality for the event to the entity. The entity attribution can then be said to satisfy the search for invariance in that a durable, reliable causal relationship has been ascertained.

Kelley also addresses the problem of self-attributions of volition— the sense of free choice. He states that, in general, a sense of volition is created by those conditions that are opposite to those conditions that create entity attributions. According to Kelley, one's sense of free choice is enhanced by low consensus (doing something different from what others do), low consistency over time (doing something at the time that differs from what one did at other times), and low consistency over modality (doing something under one set of circumstances that differs from what one did under other circumstances). Kelley does not explicate what the status of the factor of distinctiveness should be in order to create a sense of volition. It is clear, however, that it cannot simply be the opposite of the high distinctiveness factor required for entity attributions. Low distinctiveness, responding in the same way to many objects, could as easily be attributed to habit as to free, considered choice.

Bem: Self-Perception Theory

Kelley's theory of attribution takes no uniform position on the issue of self-attributions versus attributions about others. As has been noted, both actors and observers can utilize the same principle of covariance in determining whether attributions of causality to entities are appropriate to account for the actor's behavior. On the other hand, Kelley's discussion of volition uniquely applies to self-attributions, since presumably only the person himself would have adequate information concerning such historical factors as consistency over time and modality.

The most explicit theory of self-attributions is offered by Bem (1965, 1967, 1972) in his self-perception theory. Interestingly enough, however, while the theory's stated purpose is to explore how people come to attribute attitudes to themselves, the theory rests on Bem's assumption that actors and observers may use the same inference process.

Bem bases his theory on Skinner's distinction (1957) between tacts and mands. Tacts are verbal responses under the discriminative control of some portion of the environment. Presumably, tacts have been taught by social training and are provided generalized social reinforcement. A person "tacts" his environment when he gives a verbal description of internal or external stimuli that impinge on him. Mands, on the other hand, are verbal or nonverbal responses under the control of specific reinforcement contingencies. Commands, demands, and request for specific reinforcers are classified as mands. Tacts, then, are descriptive and are maintained by generalized social reinforcement given for being descriptively accurate. Mands are behaviors maintained by a specific consequence for their performance.

Bem suggests that every person, be he actor or observer, discriminates, as well as possible in any given situation, tacting behavior from manding behavior. Tacting behavior would be seen as true, valid responses to existing stimuli. Manding behavior would be seen as taking place in an effort to obtain a reward (or, presumably, to avoid a punishment). Thus, for the observer, an endorsement of a product by someone who stands to gain from the product's sales would be seen as manding behavior, and consequently the communicator and his communication would be seen as less credible. The atttribution of causality would be to environmental factors (i.e., financial gain) and not to the person's own beliefs. A spontaneous endorsement of the same product, however, by someone who did not stand to gain in any way from its promotion would be seen as tacting behavior. Credibility would be enhanced and attribution to the person's own beliefs would be appropriate.

Now that we have considered the behavior of observers, how does this apply to actors? Bem notes that this discriminating and inference process applies to actors only "to the extent that internal stimuli are not controlling" (1967, p. 186). Thus, in the presence of strong internal stimuli, actors would necessarily see their behavior as tacting and as representing their true feelings. Presumably, in this case, actors might make different attributions than observers, who would not have direct access to the internal stimuli impinging on the actor.

Except for this instance, however, Bem states that actors and observers employ the same process of inference in attributing attitudes. Given no internal stimuli, the actor will observe his own behavior and discriminate its manding versus tacting nature. If the act is perceived as manding, that is, occurring in the presence of strong environmental forces, the actor would conclude that his behavior does not have significant relevance to his true attitudes. But if the act is perceived as tacting, that is, occurring in the absence of strong environmental rewards or punishments, the act is seen as conveying information about the actor's attitudes. To use Bem's example, the answer to the question "Do you like brown bread?" can be "I guess so, I'm always eating it."

Bem originally used his theory of self-perception to provide an alternative explanation to dissonance theory findings. After a long and, at times, quite tedious debate in the literature, it would seem that the issue of who is right, Bem or the dissonance theorists, is unresolvable in that neither side is particularly impressed by the other side's arguments. The interested reader is referred to the extensive literature on the subject—for example, Arrowood, Wood, and Ross (1970); Bem (1968); Bem and McConnell (1970); Green (1974); R. A. Jones, Linder, Kiesler, Zanna, and Brehm (1968); Ross and Shulman (1973); and Snyder and Ebbesen (1972). For purposes of our discussion, Bem's theory will be considered on its own merits, without regard to whether it also explains dissonance phenomena.

Jones and Nisbett: Actor-Observer Differences

While there exists a lack of coherence among the attribution theories, there does exist a certain symmetry. Now that we have considered a theoretical position that argues for the similarity of actor and observer attribution, we will discuss a theory that, fittingly enough, argues for the dissimilarity between the attributions made by actors and observers. E. E. Jones and R. E. Nisbett (1971) have stated a basic principle of actor-observer attributional difference. They propose that actors will tend to attribute their actions to situational influences, while observers will tend to attribute the actor's actions to personality dispositions of the actor.

According to Jones and Nisbett, there are two bases for this dissimilarity. First, there are cognitive differences. Actors have access to information not possessed by observers (e.g., historical information, internal stimuli). Also, even with the same information available, different parts of this information may be more salient for actors than for observers. The actor's attention, for example, will be focused on the environment so that he can respond to changes in it. Both the actor and the rest of the environment constitute the "environment" of the observer, and his attention to the actor's behavior is increased accordingly.

A second basis for actor-observer differences lies in motivational considerations. An actor may be reluctant to define himself in terms of personality traits. As Jones and Nisbett have suggested, such self-definitions may threaten his behavioral freedoms and induce psychological reactance (J. W. Brehm, 1966). For an observer, however, no such reluctance should exist, and trait attributions would be a convenient way of organizing an actor's behaviors. In addition, the actor and the observer may be motivated by the desire to maintain self-esteem, and this same motive may produce differential attributions. The actor who fails at a task may maintain self-esteem by attributing his failure to the difficulty of the task. The observer of this behavior has the opportunity (especially if he believes he can succeed at the task or knows he will not have to engage in it) to enhance his self-esteem by attributing the actor's failure to the actor's stupidity and viewing the actor as intellectually inferior to himself (the observer).

RELATED THEORIES

As will be discussed in the chapters on clinical applications, there have been explicit attempts to relate attribution processes to clinical situations. The purpose of this section is not to focus on such applications, but to explore the relationships between the theories of attribution and other theories of psychotherapy. This relationship turns out to be rather complex. There are no theories of psychotherapy that clearly focus on the exact same psychological issues as are addressed by theories of attribution. There are, however, several theories of psychotherapy that have generally similar orientations and concerns.

In order to explicate these similarities, it is necessary to pull out three major themes that seem to be shared, implicitly or explicitly, by all theories of attribution. These are emphases on cognitive processes, on the person's desire to control his environment, and on the person's need to understand cause and effect relationships in order to control this environment. If, with these three general themes in hand, we review theoretical work in psychotherapy, we can come up with three theories that seem to have somewhat similar orientations.

First, there is the personal construct theory of George Kelly (1955). Kelly's theory is highly cognitive, focusing on the way in which man "construes" his world (i.e., places an interpretation on objects and events). The theory of personal constructs also shares the emphasis of attribution theories on the person's desire for control and need for predictive understanding. As indicated in the quotation at the beginning of this chapter, Kelly views people as scientists who seek to predict and control whatever is relevant to their lives.

Apart from these significant similarities, however, the theory of personal constructs and attribution theories are quite different. Kelly's cognitive framework is exceedingly broad: "construing" appears to apply to interpreting everything; there is no particular emphasis on interpreting causation. Moreover, the theory of personal constructs, as exemplified by its leading to the creation of a personality test (The Repertory Test), is very concerned with individual differences. Attribution theories, like the other theories discussed in this book, have been interested primarily in formulating general principles that can be generally applied.

The second theory similar to attribution theory is that of Albert Ellis's rational-emotive therapy (1962). Again, the focus is on cognitive processes and control. Again, one does not find the attribution emphasis on determining causality; Ellis has some interest in atrributions of causality, but they are not of primary interest to him. A major difference between Ellis's theoretical orientation and that of attribution theorists is in their consideration of emotions. Both Ellis and attribution theorists believe that cognitions are critical in emotional experience. Ellis, however, has worked mainly on how people can exert direct, conscious, cognitive control over their emotions. Attribution theorists, as will be seen, have focused on how causal attributions can influence emotions without personal awareness of this influence.

Finally, a word should be said about Beck's theory of depression (1967). In suggesting that the causal sequence in depression can go from cognitions to emotional states, rather than the other way around, Beck has alerted clinicians to the importance of cognitive factors in emotional response. Attribution theories have not yet been examined in specific relation to depression, but, as noted, their relation to emotional events has been investigated, and the findings have pointed up the critical role of cognitions in emotional experience.

SUMMARY

This chapter has presented a variety of social psychological theories of attribution. The ideas of Heider—the father of all of these theories—concerning the analyses of causation and responsibility were discussed. Jones and Davis's theory of correspondent inference was examined in the context of its emphasis on making dispositional attributions. Kelley's notion of the principle of covariance was described as a method of determining entity attributions. Two theories concerning the relationship between the attributions of actors and those of observers were presented. Bem's theoretical perspective stresses the similarity of the attribution processes for actions and observers, while Jones and Nisbett stress the differences between these processes. Last, the clinically oriented theories of Kelly, Ellis, and Beck were discussed in terms of their similarities to the social psychological theories of attribution.

CHAPTER
NINE

CLINICAL APPLICATIONS OF ATTRIBUTION THEORIES

I Emotional states and self-observation

This chapter will focus on attributions concerning the person's emotional state and on the attributions that a person may make in light of his own behavior. Both of these types of attributional events occur primarily within an intrapsychic framework, and the contribution of interactions with other people is relatively minimal. The empirical findings and clinical applications that more strongly emphasize the social component in the attribution process will be found in Chapter Ten.

Before examining the specific findings dealing with attribution topics, a few general words about the place of attribution theories in the clinical setting may be helpful. In his book on attribution processes, Shaver (1975) has noted,

> After all, what is "insight" if not a correct attribution of the causes of behavior? (p. 130)

Shaver's remark is an appropriate one. Attribution is in many ways synonymous with insight. Now, different clinicians have different views about insight. Some love it and some loathe it. In addition, insight may be differentially helpful to different clients. It may greatly assist some, be irrelevant to others, promote damaging intellectualization or obsessiveness for still others. These chapters on clinical application will not attempt a global assessment of the helpfulness or harmfulness of attribution or insight. Instead, suggestions will be offered to assist with specific clinical problems. Attribution and insight are clinical tools like any others, to be used on some occasions and avoided on others.

If attribution is similar to insight on the client's side of the fence, it is equally similar to therapeutic understanding on the therapist's side. In the beginning of Chapter Eight, Ford and Urban (1963) were quoted on the importance of the therapist's choice of a conceptual framework. To paraphrase Shaver: After all, what is a conceptual framework if not systematic attribution of the causes of behavior? All of the social psychological theories examined in this book can be applied to the behavior of the therapist as well as to the behavior of the client. Attribution theories may, however, bear a special relevance to the behavior of the therapist. Therapists utilize some method, some system, in understanding the ongoing therapeutic process. They make multiple attributions of causation—about what brought the client to therapy, what led to his problems, and what affects his present behavior. These attributions are subject to attributional analysis and, although no special effort has been made to apply the subsequent findings to therapists' conceptual frameworks, it is hoped that the reader will bear such possible applications in mind while reading this chapter and the one that follows.

ATTRIBUTION AND EMOTIONAL STATES

In 1962 Schachter and Singer published what came to be a highly influential paper on the role of cognitive factors in the development of emotional states. Schachter and Singer proposed that emotional states are the product of an interaction between cognitive and physiological factors. Typically, one might expect that physiological arousal and an adequate cognitive explanation for that arousal would exist simultaneously. A more interesting, though perhaps less common, situation would be one in which physiological arousal existed without an explanation for it. In such cases, Schachter and Singer hypothesized that the person would search for an adequate explanation and that he would tend to use as an explanation whatever environmental factors were present at the time of arousal. Similar hypotheses have been suggested by earlier writers familiar with clinical practice.

We are not used to feeling strong affects without their having any ideational context, and therefore, if the content is missing, we seize as a substitute upon another content which is in some way or other suitable. (Freud, 1946, p. 314)

It was as if the subjects, experiencing an emotion without adequate stimulus, sought something in the external world to justify it. (Murray, 1933, p. 324)

In their now classic experiment, Schachter and Singer tested this proposition by injecting subjects with either epinephrine or a placebo. All subjects believed they were receiving an injection of a vitamin compound. Subjects in the epinephrine condition were then given one of three explanations of their bodily condition: epinephrine-informed subjects were told to expect side effects typical of physiological arousal ("Your hand will start to shake, your heart will start to pound, and your face may get warm and flushed"), epinephrine-ignorant subjects were told nothing about the injection other than that it was harmless and had no side effects, and epinephrine-misinformed subjects were told that they would have side effects that were in fact quite unlikely to occur from the epinephrine injection ("Your feet will feel numb, you will have an itching sensation over parts of your body, and you may get a slight headache"). At this point all subjects waited, supposedly for the vitamin injection to have an effect; in fact, the waiting period was necessary to provide an opportunity for subjects to be exposed to a confederate who by his behavior might supply an explanation for their physiological arousal. For one set of subjects (comprising all the epinephrine conditions described above, plus a placebo condition), the confederate acted in a euphoric manner; for another set of subjects (comprising epinephrine-informed, epinephrine-ignorant and placebo conditions), the confederate acted in an angry fashion. The results of the study indicated that subjects who were informed of the appropriate side effects of epinephrine showed the least emotion (i.e., self-reported the least anger or the least happiness). Subjects who received a placebo showed intermediate emotion. Subjects who were ignorant or misinformed about the appropriate epinephrine symptoms showed most emotion. This pattern of results was also confirmed by behavioral ratings made while the subjects were with the confederate.

This experiment provided compelling evidence that emotional response to an environmental event is least when one has another explanation of bodily arousal and is most when one has no satisfactory explanation of this bodily arousal. In addition, the nature of the emotion reflected the nature of the environmental event: an angry stimulus produced anger, and a euphoric stimulus produced happiness. Schachter and Singer argued strongly for the relative plasticity of emotions, in that the same physiological arousal could be channeled into different emotions as a function of one's cognitions about the environment.

Further evidence for this point of view was provided by a study by Schachter and Wheeler (1962). They found that a slapstick film was judged most amusing by subjects who had received the arousing drug epinephrine, moderately amusing by subjects who received a placebo, and least amusing by subjects who received an arousal-reducing drug, chlorpromazine. All subjects believed they were receiving a vitamin injection, and none were informed of any side effects to expect.

How do these studies relate to the attribution theories that have been presented? The papers by Schachter and his colleagues were done without explicit reference to any specific attribution theory. The relationship between these studies and attribution theories is, however, apparent. It is posited that people seek to understand the cause and effect relationships in their world, in this case, the cause for their bodily states. When a bodily state occurs without the person clearly understanding its origin, the person seeks a cause in the environment and attributes his arousal to some feature of the environment that might reasonably account for the arousal. In attributing his arousal to an environmental entity, the person forms what we call an emotion, that is, a specific statement about the nature of his arousal. This view of emotion has provided a stimulating research focus for attribution theorists.

Cognitive Desensitization

If physiological arousal plus a cognitive explanation for that arousal can induce an emotional experience, what might be the effect of simply telling a person that he is aroused and then providing a reasonable explanation for that event? This question has been addressed by Valins (1966). Valins exposed male subjects to false heart-rate feedback (i.e., audio recordings of increased or decreased heart-rate responses that they thought were actually their own responses but that were, in fact, prerecorded tapes controlled by the experimenter) while they observed slides of nude females. Subjects reported liking these slides more than slides where they heard no heart-rate change, and they chose pictures of these slides to take home with them.

Valins suggested that his results showed that when someone *thinks* he is aroused, he will seek an explanation of this arousal and attribute it to his response to environmental entities. Barefoot and Straub (1971) confirmed this reasoning. They found that the Valins effect was elicited only when subjects had time to visually scan the slides. Presumably, an active search for a reasonable attribution of arousal is taking place (something like, "Let's see, I must really like this slide, my heart- rate is going crazy, what is it about this girl, oh, I see, it's her legs, she has really great legs"), and if the subject is prevented from making this active search, attribution to the environmental feature does not occur.

These studies are quite provocative and are important in themselves for clinicians, who deal daily with their client's and their own emotional responses. The relevance of this work for clinical practice was, however, greatly enhanced by a study by Valins and Ray (1967) and the subsequent controversy it elicited. Essentially, Valins and Ray hypothesized that if telling someone he is aroused can affect his emotional response, then telling someone he is *not* aroused may also affect emotions.

In their experimental investigations of this hypothesis, Valins and Ray worked with phobic subjects. Subjects who believed themselves to be afraid of snakes and who reported this on a questionnaire were shown a series of slides. For the slides of snakes they heard what they believed to be their own heartbeats continue at an unchanged rate (these heart rates like all others were in fact prerecorded tapes). For other slides, which said "shock," they received a mild electric shock and heard their supposed heart rates increase. Afterward these subjects, in comparison with subjects who had the same experience but believed they were hearing only noise and not their own heartbeats, showed more approach behavior to a live snake.

Obviously this study has direct relevance to clinical settings. It suggests that by providing compelling evidence to a client that he is not afraid, he will alter his emotional response and then act not afraid. Unfortunately, the value of such a simple and potentially powerful therapeutic technique has been called into question by a series of follow-up studies to Valins and Ray (e.g., Borkovec & Glasgow, 1973; Gaupp, Stern, & Galbraith, 1972; Kent, Wilson, & Nelson, 1972; Rosen, Rosen, & Reid, 1972; Sushinsky & Bootzin, 1970). These studies have raised a number of issues: the role of a behavioral pretest (Valins and Ray did not use one), the relationship between self-ratings of fear and approach behavior (increased approach behavior not necessarily correlating with reduced fear ratings), and the possibility of accounting for the original results by an aversion relief model (the chance that since snake slides followed shock slides, these snake slides signaled that shock was over and thus took on reinforcing properties). Out of all this controversy, the most important finding was that the Valins and Ray results were repeatedly not replicated.

A recent study by J. C. Conger, A. J. Conger, and S. S. Brehm (in press) may have brought some clarity into this confusion. First, an explicit test of the aversion relief hypothesis was made within the exact framework of the original Valins and Ray paradigm and found not to account for the Valins and Ray results. Second, the Valins and Ray results of more approach behavior for false heart-rate feedback subjects than for noise subjects were replicated, but only for low fear subjects. High fear, false feedback subjects showed no such increased approach behavior. In addition, low fear subjects, as compared to high fear subjects, did report emotional feelings (lessened fear, increased pleasant feelings about snakes) consistent with their approach behavior. Thus the failure to replicate Valins and Ray in studies using a preexperimental behavioral approach test may have resulted from the fact that these studies selected a more fearful group than the one that participated in the Valins and Ray studies.

The Conger, Conger, and Brehm finding of the high versus low fear differential is, in fact, quite consistent with Schachter's original position and also with suggestions made by Bem. Schachter stated that the search for cognitions with which to label the arousal would be set in motion by having physiological arousal and no explanation for this arousal. Thus the entire Schachterian position depends on having an unclear or ambiguous psychological setting. The work by Valins also took place under psychologically ambiguous conditions. Subjects who didn't think they were aroused were told (by the heartbeats they heard) that they were aroused.

Thus, low fear subjects may be seen as being presented with a psychologically ambiguous event: they think they're "sort of" afraid of snakes, and then they find that their physiological response says they're not. In contrast to these ambiguous situations, the high fear subject is subject to no such ambiguity. He *knows* he is afraid of snakes. His physiological response in this one situation seems inconsistent with his fear, but placed against his strong conviction of being afraid, it's unlikely that one piece of inconsistent information would have much effect. In Bem's terms, the high fear subject is impinged upon by internal stimuli. Accordingly, he would not engage in searching his own behavior (in this case, his physiological response) to find out how he feels. He knows how he feels.

This finding and its theoretical underpinnings are quite discouraging in terms of the proposed clinical use of cognitive desensitization. Clients who seek therapeutic assistance because of excessive fear are unlikely to be in the low fear condition. As with high fear subjects, clients know they are afraid. A technique that is only effective with nonclinical levels of fear is unlikely to be of much use in clinical endeavors.

Additional findings in the Conger, Conger, and Brehm study suggest, however, that the reports of the death of cognitive desensitization may at least be premature, if not grossly exaggerated. In the low fear, false heart-rate feedback condition, there was a high correlation between behavioral approach and fear of shock. This finding may indicate that a contrast effect is at least partially responsible for the behavior of the low fear subjects. That is, the greater their fear of shock (preexisting and then confirmed by their supposed physiological response to shock), the less their fear of snakes seemed and the more approach behavior was possible. It may be, then, that if high fear (of snakes) subjects had been confronted with a stimulus that they feared greatly, clearly more than they feared snakes, increased approach behavior to snakes could have occurred.[1] This possibility, as noted by Conger, Conger, and Brehm, is similar to implosive therapy, where the subject imagines highly aversive situations as contrasted with the *relatively* mild aversive event that he originally reports fearing.

What can the clinician gain from this work on cognitive desensitization? Let us separate our consideration of this issue into two client populations. For clients who have relatively low level, but still bothersome, fears, a direct clinical application of the Valins and Ray procedure seems feasible. If the clinician does not wish to deceive the client by using bogus feedback, he can take a less dramatic approach and verbally emphasize to the client the aspects of his behavior (physiological or otherwise) that are inconsistent with his stated claims of being fearful. This approach may be most effective when used in situations of contrast—with demonstration of or reference to objects that elicit greater fear.

For high fear clients, cognitive desensitization techniques only merit consideration if the clinician can employ an effective contrast stimulus. It remains an unanswered and empirical question whether the Valins and Ray false-feedback technique, when used with contrast stimuli, would be more effective than implosive therapy imaging techniques.

As a therapeutic technique, however, cognitive desensitization must recognize its strongest competition. Systematic desensitization is a widely used and apparently effective (see Paul, 1966) technique for the reduction of excessive fears. Clinicians are obliged to employ the technique with the best-demonstrated effectiveness for coping with their clients' problems. At this time, in any choice between cognitive desensitization and systematic desensitization,[2] the conscientious clinician could only choose the latter.

---

[1] This possible effect was not testable within the Conger et al. study due to the ceiling effect for both fear of snakes and fear of shock that existed for high fear subjects.

[2] This discussion assumes that the clinician does not wish to or is unable to use *in vivo* desensitization techniques.

Cognitive desensitization techniques become a viable alternative only if there is some reason that systematic desensitization cannot be used. Such a circumstance could arise with children, where the controlled concentration on and attention to images required by systematic desensitization may be difficult to obtain. The Valins and Ray cognitive desensitization technique, on the other hand, provides an easier procedure for a child. All he has to do is look at slides and listen. He would have to be taught that increased heart rate usually means that he is afraid, but through demonstration this probably would not be difficult. Thus with children and perhaps under other specific instances where systematic desensitization is difficult to implement, it may be reasonable to consider using cognitive desensitization techniques.

The Therapeutic Use of Redirecting Attributions

The original Schachter and Singer study indicated that drug-induced physiological arousal is manipulatable in terms of the environmental factors available for labeling this arousal. In a variation on this theme, Nisbett and Schachter (1966) showed that naturally occurring physiological arousal, in this case, the fear of electric shock, is also manipulatable as a function of accompanying cognitions explaining this arousal. In the Nisbett and Schachter study, subjects were given a placebo before experiencing electric shock. One-half of the subjects were told that the pill would cause arousal symptoms ("You may have some tremor, that is, your hand will start to shake, you will have some palpitation, that is your heart will start to pound, and your rate of breathing may increase . . . you will probably get a sinking feeling in the pit of your stomach, like butterflies"); the other half were given arousal irrelevant expectations ("Your feet will feel numb, you may have an itching sensation over parts of your body, and you may get a slight headache").

Subjects who could attribute their arousal to the pill (expecting arousal side effects) showed increased tolerance for electric shock and reported their last shock as less painful than subjects who attributed their arousal to the shock (not expecting arousal side effects). These results were only found for subjects who were given low fear information about the shock. Subjects who were given high fear information showed fearful behavior regardless of attribution condition.

This notion of changing people's behavior by changing their attributions for arousal states has been examined by a number of investigators. Ross, Rodin, and Zimbardo (1969) found that subjects who expected their exposure to noise to cause arousal symptoms were able to spend more time working on a puzzle to be rewarded by money and less time working on a puzzle to avoid shock than subjects who were led to expect noise symptoms unrelated to arousal. Ross et al. suggest that the noise-attribution subjects could explain their fear of electric shock in terms of the noise (e.g., "Oh, my heart is racing, but I'm not afraid of the electric shock, that's just a reaction to the noise like the experimenter told me to expect."), and thus, believing themselves not to be afraid, could behave in a nonfearful fashion. Shock-attribution subjects on the other hand had no available explanation for their arousal, other than viewing it as fear of shock. Believing themselves to be afraid, they acted in a fearful fashion and spent their time trying to avoid getting shocked. Using a quite different paradigm, Girodo (1973) found similar results; his subjects, who were given arousal symptom side effect information consistent with arousal symptoms, were less anxious in their response to watching an arousing film.

The idea of reducing attributions to one's own emotional responses by providing information attributing arousal to external agents has even been applied to dissonance reduction. Zanna and Cooper (1974) report a study in which the typical forced-compliance situation (high choice versus low choice in behaving in a counter-attitudinal fashion) was conducted under various conditions of pill attribution. All subjects received a placebo: one-third were told the pill would make them tense, one-third that the pill would relax them, and one-third that there would be no side effects. Zanna and Cooper reasoned that dissonance arousal would be greatest when there was no available external agent to which to attribute arousal and least when there was such an external agent. Subjects who expect to be tense from the pill should show least dissonance reduction, those who expect to be relaxed should show most dissonance reduction, and those with no prior expectations should show moderate amounts of dissonance reduction. Their findings supported these hypotheses.

Thus the evidence indicates that emotional arousal of states such as fear, anxiety, and dissonance can be influenced by the person's causal attributions. Emotional arousal and its subsequent behaviors will occur when the person attributes his physiological arousal to his own emotional response; attributions to an external agent preclude a perceived emotional response. The Zanna and Cooper study further indicates that if arousal occurs when one expects *not* to be aroused, perceived emotional response and subsequent behavior are intensified.

Another study on the same general theme was conducted by Dienstbier and Munster (1971); this time the experimental focus was on the socially undesirable behavior of cheating. These investigators found that cheating was increased for subjects who had received pill-attributions consistent with physiological arousal. It was suggested that those subjects who expected to be aroused by the pill they had taken attributed their physiological arousal to the pill when placed in a situation conducive to cheating; they did not, apparently, attribute their arousal to conflict, or fear, or guilt about cheating. By reducing perceptions of emotional responses that would mitigate against cheating, cheating was increased. Subjects who had taken the pill but received side effect information irrelevant to physiological arousal could attribute their arousal to conflict, fear or guilt, and with such attributions, cheating was reduced.

While these studies are surely interesting to the clinician, such interest should be heightened by two pill-attribution studies that bear directly on clinical concerns. One common clinical occurrence is that clients receive medication designed to reduce their psychological distress or to control undesirable behaviors. A study by Davison and Valins (1969) addressed itself to the pyschological impact of believing that one's behavior is influenced by a drug. Subjects in this experiment received a series of electric shocks and set individual thresholds for pain and tolerance. Then, all subjects ingested a pill (in fact, a placebo) and underwent a second series of shocks. During this second series, intensities were reduced while the number of shocks was increased, so that subjects thought they were reaching higher levels of shock, although, in fact, they received exactly the same amount as in the first trial.

All subjects at this point believed tha the "drug" had affected their tolerance for shock. After this, one-half of the subjects were told that the drug was a placebo; the other half continued to believe the drug was real. In a third series of shocks, it was found that the subjects who knew the drug was a placebo tolerated more shock and found it less painful than subjects who believed the drug was real. Davison and Valins suggested that their experiment demonstrates one of the undesirable effects that can be obtained by using medication. A client who perceives that his behavior changes, but attributes this change to the medication, does not feel responsible for the behavior change, does not "own" the change in a psychological sense, and thus is not likely to maintain the change once the medication is stopped. On the other hand, clients who view their behavior change as caused by themselves do psychologically "own" this behavior change and should maintain it.

A study by Storms and Nisbett (1970) on pill-attribution effects is also highly relevant to clinical situations in that it deals with a problem frequently found among clinical populations. Storms and

Nisbett solicited volunteers who had insomnia. All of these subjects were given a pill (again, a placebo) to be taken at bedtime. One-half of them were told that the pill contained an arousing medication, and the other-half that the pill contained a relaxing medication. It was found that the subjects who received the supposed arousing pill slept better than their preexperimental levels and those who received the supposed relaxing pill slept worse. Storms and Nisbett suggested that insomnia may be caused, at least partially, by the fear of not being able to sleep. Subjects who took the arousing pill could expect to be aroused, not worry about any signs of arousal such as ruminations or restlessness, and thus go to sleep. Subjects who took the relaxing pill, however, expected to be relaxed. If any signs of restlessness occurred, such signs being highly likely for insomniacs, they might feel, "Oh, I'm really restless tonight; even the pill didn't stop it," and thus worry more and not go to sleep.

This study is extremely intriguing because it suggests that if clients receive a medication that they expect to "help" them, and the medication doesn't work as they had expected, they may become worse. Recall that Zanna and Cooper (1974) obtained a similar finding, and Snyder, Schulz, and Jones (1974) also have found evidence supporting this kind of "negative placebo effect."

The other inference from the Storms and Nisbett study is more complex. Some problems may be increased by the client's focusing on them and worrying about them. In these cases, it may help for the therapist to "take control of the client's symptoms" (to use Haley's term; see pp. 24-25) and for the therapist to cause the symptoms either through directions to the client to participate in the symptom or through physiological agents. The client is then free to not worry about his symptoms happening; they're going to happen and he expects them to happen. In some situations, this may allow for reduction in symptomatic behavior.

Perhaps at this point a little sorting out would be helpful. The literature cited in this section has an unfortunate tendency to become a somewhat chaotic melange of pill-attributions, shock-attributions, self-attributions, and so on. Fortunately, there seems to be some discernible order in all of this. To begin, we can separate the literature into two categories of clinical relevance (this categorization is based on a paper by Valins and Nisbett, 1971): (1) the cases in which an intrinsic attribution is desirable, and (2) the cases in which an extrinsic attribution is desirable. These two categories will be discussed in turn.

If a therapist is to use "attribution therapy" (as it has been called by Ross, Rodin, & Zimbardo, 1969) with his clients, he cannot assume that either "internalization" or "projection" is a priori to be preferred. He must instead ask himself what his goal is with each client. One way to ask this question is for the therapist to inquire, "Under what circumstances do I want this client to attribute his physiological arousal or, indeed, any kind of behavior, to himself and/or to his emotional reactions, rather than to environmental events?" The therapist can then determine when he wishes the client to make attributions to intrinsic sources, be they self-controlled behaviors or spontaneous emotional responses. The literature reviewed in this section suggests that there are several occasions during which such intrinsic attributions may be appropriate.

One occasion is when desirable behavior change has taken place. Following Davison and Valins (1969), behavior change is more likely to be maintained or increased when the person believes he has caused the original change than when this change is attributed to an outside agent, such as a medication. This principle suggests that clinicians must be careful in their utilization of medication. Whenever it does become necessary to administer medication, the therapist should always stress how important the client's own role is in any behavior change that occurs when he is on the medication. The placebo effect of having a client believe he is taking a powerful drug may be useful in the short term, but if all change is attributed to the drug, therapeutic progress may disappear when the medication is terminated.

Another occasion that seems appropriate for intrinsic attributions is when the therapist desires the client to experience his arousal as a spontaneous emotional response to environmental stimuli. Whether this desire is related to wanting the client to experience guilt so as not to behave in an antisocial fashion, or pleasure so as to behave in a prosocial fashion, or discomfort so as to reduce dissonance, the therapist should, in these situations, work to avoid any causal attributions to extrinsic entities other than those directly involved in the client's emotional response. The goal is for the client to believe, for example, "I feel guilty about cheating," rather than "The pill/weather/therapist makes me feel uncomfortable."

The "negative placebo effect" found by Zanna and Cooper (1974), Storms and Nisbett (1970), and Snyder, Schulz, and Jones (1974) represents a method of fostering intrinsic attributions that may or may not be desirable depending on the client's therapeutic goals. It is clearly undesirable in cases where the client expects a procedure to help him, feels the same as before, and thus, by contrast, perceives himself as being worse off than he thought he was—"I must really be in bad shape if that didn't help me." On the other hand, if the therapeutic goal would be facilitated by having the client have a strong emotional experience, this experience can be heightened by offering him an inert procedure that is supposed to make him feel some way (e.g., relaxation). When the client does not in fact feel the way the procedure was supposedly designed to make him feel, his original state or emotional experience (e.g., anxiety) should be exaggerated ("I must really be anxious if that didn't relax me").

The next question the attribution therapist would ask himself is the converse of the previous one, "Under what circumstances do I *not* want this client to attribute his physiological arousal or, indeed, any kind of behavior, to himself and/or to his emotional reactions?" In other words, when is an extrinsic attribution desirable? The studies by Nisbett and Schachter (1966), Ross, Rodin, and Zimbardo (1969), and Girodo (1973) suggest that when a therapist anticipates a client's experiencing deleterious emotional arousal, it may reduce undesirable behavioral consequences of this arousal if the physiological arousal can be accounted for in other terms. This is similar to, but critically distinct from, the cognitive desensitization procedure discussed earlier. In cognitive desensitization, the therapist attempts to convince the client that he is not aroused. In attribution therapy, the therapist attempts to convince the client that he is aroused for other reasons. In the studies cited, a pill has been used as the extrinsic reason, but other reasons could be used: the weather ("You always feel restless on rainy days"), other concerns ("Really, you're just worried about your job"), other people ("It's just that Joe was there").

In addition, it has been noted in the discussion of the study by Storms and Nisbett (1970) that extrinsic attributions for the creation of symptomatic behavior may be useful in some circumstances. If symptomatic behavior seems to be increased by the client's worrying over its occurrence, it may help, at least for an initial period, for the therapist to reduce the client's tension and anxiety by having him believe that some external force (e.g., medication or therapeutic procedure) will ensure that the symptomatic behavior will in fact take place. This approach has the benefit of allowing the client to avoid obsessive ruminations about whether or not the symptomatic behavior will occur; he can assume that it will and that control over it has been taken out of his hands. For clients whose ruminating is, in fact, the basis of their problem, this may result in a decrement in the symptom and in increased general well-being as their anxiety lessens.

Used in the above ways, attribution therapy represents a causal sleight-of-hand. The client's attention is directed to or away from himself and his own emotional responses, and onto or away from extrinsic causal agents that differ from the environmental events directly involved in his emotional response. In many cases, attribution therapy simply allows the therapist to direct the client's attention to whatever he (the therapist) believes is actually responsible for the client's arousal. In other cases, the therapist may choose to attempt to convince the client that a particular agent or event is responsible, even though the therapist does not necessarily believe this to be accurate. Fostering inaccurate perceptions is an uncomfortable therapeutic maneuver, but one that may be necessary if either a lack or an excess of emotional responsiveness is grossly interfering with the client's functioning. If an inaccurate perception can promote beneficial change, the therapist can utilize this procedure and retain the option of correcting the inaccuracy when new, desirable behaviors have become fully established.

In addition to the categories of intrinsic and extrinsic attributions, there is a third category of attributional therapy noted by Valins and Nisbett: the therapeutic change of abnormal attributions into normal ones. Neale (cited in Valins and Nisbett, 1971) convinced a client who feared he was homosexual that his behavior, in fact, reflected his inaccurate judgment about the size of his own penis, and that his lack of satisfactory intercourse and his interest in the size of other men's penises followed from this judgment. After teaching the client the laws of optics, that is, that the apparent size of objects viewed from above is diminished, and showing him that his penis was of normal size, the client's concerns about his homosexuality decreased and his emotional status improved.

In another case report, Davison (1966) worked with a 44-year-old male who was diagnosed as schizophrenic. Davison reported that this man complained of "pressure points" over his right eye that he said were caused by a "spirit." Davison taught this man that these pressure points varied with his (the client's) tension: increasing when he was tense and decreasing when he was relaxed. Given this new attribution, the client began to call his pressure points "sensations" and stopped referring to them as being caused by a "spirit." According to Davison, the client was quite relieved to have a normal explanation for the pressure points.

These case studies illustrate the simplest, and probably most easily acceptable, use of attribution therapy. The therapies used by Neale and Davison consisted of their giving to their clients information that they (the therapists) truly regarded as more accurate than the suppositions adopted by the clients. The importance of providing clients with accurate information is accepted by all clinicians, but it seems so simple that it may be forgotten. The reports by Neale and Davison and the theoretical underpinning provided by attribution theory (i.e., that people's attributions about causes influence their behavior) serve to remind clinicians that some clients may be helped by telling or showing them the "true" causes for their behavior or sensations.

The value of the more complex attribution procedures is less easily assessed. There remains a real question as to whether redirection of attributions will be effective with people who have strong internal sensations and a long history of "knowing" the cause of these sensations. Remember that the original Nisbett and Schachter effect was found only for low fear subjects. As noted in the section on cognitive desensitization, people seen in clinical practice tend to be in the high fear condition, and the emotional states that are of concern to them are relatively strong and inflexible. It is unlikely, for instance, that a long-time plane phobic could be convinced that the arousal he felt was due to being with strangers on the plane; the plane phobic knows it's the plane that causes all those fearful sensations. On the other hand, attribution therapy may be effective when the client is faced with new and somewhat ambiguous situations, such as taking medication or engaging in new behaviors. It may be in these novel circumstances that the therapist can have the most influence on the client's attributions.

THERAPEUTIC UTILIZATION
OF SELF-OBSERVATION

Stemming from Bem's theory of self-perception, there have been several studies demonstrating the effect of observing one's own behavior on subsequent behavior. Bandler, Madaras, and Bem (1968) reported that subjects who were told to press a button to stop shock (and who did so) rated shock as more uncomfortable than subjects who were told not press the shock-escape button (and who didn't) or subjects who pressed what they thought was a "reaction time" button, which stopped shock half of the time and didn't stop it the other half. Bandler et al. proposed that subjects who saw themselves pressing a button to stop shock (even though they had been instructed to do this) inferred that their pressing meant that they were bothered by the shock.

Kopel and Arkowtiz (1974) also produced a change in subjects' responses to shock by manipulating subjects' behavior and their observation of it. Subjects who were told to role-play being upset showed decreases in pain and tolerance thresholds, while subjects who were told to role-play being calm showed increases. Using a different type of behavioral manipulation, Laird (1974) induced subjects to arrange their faces in "smiles" or "frowns" without subjects attaching any emotional meaning to these facial positions (direct manipulation of facial muscles was utilized). Subjects who "smiled" reported themselves as happier and more amused by a cartoon than subjects who "frowned."

172 THEORIES OF ATTRIBUTION

These studies indicate that nonmotivated and nonemotional behavior can serve as the basis for people's inferences about their motivational and emotional states. The familiar problem exists, however, that these effects are probably limited under conditions of high emotional response. Indeed, G. O. Klemp and H. Leventhal (1972) found that the Bandler et al. results only held for subjects who had a high tolerance for shock and, presumably, a low fear of shock.

Given these limitations, these studies may most clearly support the clinician's use of role-playing techniques in therapy. They suggest that particularly when the client tries out novel behaviors for which he may not know the appropriate emotional response, the clinician can influence the client's response to the new behavior by having the client role-play the desired emotion. These emotions will, in turn, influence subsequent, related behavior.

Self-Observation in Conjunction with Observing a Model

A study by Kiesler, Nisbett, and Zanna (1969) indicates that sometimes people will adopt the causal attribution provided by a model as the attribution for their own behavior. Kiesler et al. got subjects to agree to argue against pollution. These subjects then heard a confederate state that he was going to argue for promoting auto safety either because he believed in it or because the experiment was scientifically valuable. Subjects who heard the first reason indicated later on a questionnaire that they believed more in fighting pollution than subjects who heard the second reason or than subjects who heard the believing confederate but who were not committed to arguing against pollution.

Again, it would seem that this study has maximum clinical relevance for times when clients are engaging in novel behaviors. They may agree to engage in such behaviors for vague and ill-formulated reasons. The therapist can refer to himself or to others he has known and suggest that he and/or these others when they engaged in the behaviors under consideration did so for X reason (e.g., they really felt assertive, they believed in being assertive, etc.). By such modeling, the therapist can direct the client's attention toward and, hopefully, get him to accept the attitude that would favor continued participation in the new behavior.

Self-Observation Effects over Time

Lepper (1973) argued that the effects of self-observation are durable and long-lasting. Lepper performed a replication of the Aronson and Carlsmith (1963) forbidden toy experiment in which children refrained from playing with a toy after receiving either a mild or a severe threat. This study has traditionally been interpreted as a demonstration of the effects of cognitive dissonance (see p. 94). Lepper, however, investigated this paradigm in terms of self-observation. He reasoned that the children who see themselves refrain from playing with the toy in conjunction with a mild threat can infer that they are capable of self-control. On the other hand, children who see themselves refrain under strong threat conditions cannot draw this conclusion, but can deduce that they need strong external restraints to resist temptation. If the observation of their own behavior in the toy situation leads to these self-beliefs, these self-beliefs should affect their behavior in other situations. This is what Lepper found. Three weeks later, subjects who had complied with the mild threat showed more resistance to cheating than subjects who had complied with the strong threat.

Note that Lepper's study cannot be taken as refuting dissonance interpretations of the Aronson and Carlsmith paradigm. Dissonance theorists could argue that the self-belief of self-control was created to reduce dissonance and would thus find Lepper's results perfectly consistent with dissonance theory. Both dissonance and attribution theorists expect self-beliefs to influence behavior; the issue in dispute is the origin of the self-beliefs, that is, whether they arise as a means of reducing dissonance or are inferred from observed behavior.

Whatever the origin of these self-beliefs, clinicians should find it interesting and important that once created, these self-beliefs affected behavior that occurred later and in a quite different setting. The Lepper experiment shows that behavior that occurs at time 1 and setting 1 can, through the creation of an intervening self-belief, influence behavior at time 2 and in setting 2. Both the dissonance literature and the attribution literature suggest ways to create new self-beliefs, opinions, attitudes, and so forth. The Lepper study suggests that the creation of these new views can have long-term and wide-ranging effects.

Instrinsic Motivation
versus Extrinsic Reward

In terms of Bem's analysis of self-perception processes, a person is more likely to believe that a behavior reflects his "true," internal motivations if this behavior does not occur in the presence of extrinsic rewards. While at a theoretical level this has provided an alternative explanation of some dissonance phenomena, at a practical level the consequences of Bem's position are the same as the consequences of following dissonance theory: the less the external justification for a behavior, the more likely the person will be to continue to engage in that behavior or similar behaviors. In dissonance terms, this would happen because the person has reduced dissonance by changing his attitude to conform with his behavior, and this attitude would produce further similar behavior. In self-perception terms, this would happen because the person perceives his unrewarded behavior as occurring because of an internal motivation, and this perceived internal motivation would lead to similar future behaviors. Dissonance theory and self-perception theory also agree that overjustification for a behavior may lead to a decrement in that behavior—either because no attitude is formed to promote it or because no internal motivation that would support it is perceived.

A study by Lepper, Greene, and Nisbett (1973) illustrates the effect of overjustification. Working with children, Lepper et al. selected a task in which all of the subjects originally showed considerable interest. Some of the children were told that they would receive a reward for engaging in the task; they expected the reward and then received it after they engaged in the task. Other children did not expect to receive a reward after the task, but, in fact, they did. In the third condition, children neither expected nor received a reward after engaging in the task. It was found that given a chance at a later period to engage in the task with no reward being offered, the children who both expected and received a reward showed less interest in the task than the other children. It is suggested that the children who expected and received the reward regarded their behavior as occurring because of the reward, while the other children regarded their behavior as occurring because of their own intrinsic interest. For those who attributed their earlier behavior to the reward, subsequent behavior in the absence of a reward was decreased. For those who attributed their earlier behavior to their intrinsic interest, subsequent behavior was maintained. Deci (1971, 1972) has also found a decrease in intrinsic motivation as a consequence of expected financial rewards.

While many conceptual and methodological issues remain unresolved in the investigation of intrinsic versus extrinsic motivation (see the critique by Calder & Staw, 1975, and the reply by Deci, Cascio, & Krusell, 1975), the basic proposition that expecting a reward for a behavior can decrease its frequency of occurrence has clinical implications entirely consistent with implications drawn earlier from dissonance theory. When a person decides to engage in a behavior and expects to be rewarded for it, the short-term goal of having the person behave in a certain way may be realized, but the long-term goal of continued behavioral engagement may be jeopardized.

As was done with dissonance theory, it should be pointed out that inducements may be necessary in order to facilitate the client's initial engagement in a desirable behavior. Even in the first stage, however, it would seem wise to keep such inducements at the minimal level necessary to elicit performance. After initial engagement in the behavior, rewards should be kept absolutely minimal in order to ensure that through whatever process, be it dissonance or self-perception, the person will continue to engage in the behavior in the face of changing, and frequently unrewarding, real-world circumstances.

SUMMARY

This chapter has explored clinical applications derived from two areas of investigations in attribution. First, a discussion was presented of the attributional effects relevant to emotional experience. Emphasis was placed on cognitive desensitization, in which people are convinced that they are not aroused, thus reducing emotional experience, and on the therapeutic use of redirecting attributions, in which people are convinced about the source of their arousal, thus changing emotional experience. With regard to the redirection of attributions, three areas of therapeutic endeavor were noted: promoting intrinsic attributions, promoting extrinsic attributions, and changing abnormal attributions into normal ones. Studies were examined that suggest that the observation of one's own behavior can influence one's subsequent behavior. It was pointed out that self-observation effects may provide support for utilizing role-playing procedures in therapy.

CHAPTER
TEN

CLINICAL APPLICATIONS OF ATTRIBUTION THEORIES

II Social processes in attribution, attributional effects of success and failure, the influence of information presentation, and individual differences in attribution

In this chapter a variety of attributional effects will be examined. The primary focus will be on attributional processes that involve the person's interaction with other people. Additional topics that will be covered include the attributional effects of success and failure, and the influence of information presentation. A brief section on individual differences will be provided at the end of the chapter.

SOCIAL PROCESSES IN ATTRIBUTION

Evaluations of Other People

The other person's responsibility. In evaluating another person, one important dimension concerns the person's responsibility for the outcomes he obtains. One line of research undertaken by attribution theorists has been to investigate how people evaluate the responsibility of another person who suffers a negative outcome. The original formulation of this process suggested that people would desire to attribute blame to the victim of a misfortune so as to reduce the feeling that the misfortune could occur to them. It was hypothesized that by believing that the other person could have prevented the unfortunate occurrence, people can reassure themselves that they would be more careful and thus could prevent any similar accident from happening to them. This sort of attribution hypothesis should sound quite familiar to clinicians. It closely resembles Murray's notions (1938/1962) about complementary projection, in which the state opposite to that which one feels is projected onto others. In this case, a person's own security is promoted by maintaining his belief in his own carefulness and projecting carelessness onto others.

As it turns out, the evidence from the attribution literature that such a tendency exists is quite ambiguous. The complementary projection hypothesis was confirmed by Walster (1966), by Shaw and Skolnick (1971) for males but not females, and by Stokols and Schopler (1973). However, in a 1967 study Walster failed to replicate her own findings, and Shaver (1970) reports an extensive but unsuccessful attempt to replicate. Thus, at this time there is very little in the attribution literature to support the hypothesis that people use complementary projection in the evaluation of other people's responsibility for their misfortunes.

Interestingly enough, however, Shaver (1970) has provided evidence of an attribution process that seems to resemble Murray's notion of supplementary projection. Shaver has suggested that especially when observing others similar to themselves, people may attribute blame for the misfortune to chance rather than to the victims' responsibility. This attribution allows the person to believe that if he were involved in such an accident, others would be as understanding with him and not blame him; maybe people actually do "do unto others as they would have them do unto them"! At any rate, Shaver's suggestion and the supportive evidence he has obtained are consistent with the idea of supplementary projection, where one projects the same feelings one has onto other people. By projecting "it wasn't my fault" onto others and acting in accordance with these projected feelings, the person may be able to believe that people would treat him similarly if he were involved in a misfortune.[1]

Evaluations of others. The research in conjunction with papers on "just world theory" by Lerner (e.g., Lerner, 1971; Lerner & Matthews, 1967; Lerner & Simmons, 1966) has stimulated

---

[1] It should be noted that in most considerations of projection as a psychodynamic defense it is postulated that the person denies his own feelings. The attribution hypotheses discussed above do not focus on nor investigate such denials. They do emphasize, however, that these attributions of blame or chance serve a defensive purpose for the person allowing him to anticipate good outcomes or good treatment for himself.

considerable interest in observers' evaluations of people who suffer misfortune. Regardless of whether we hold such people responsible for these outcomes, there is still the question of how favorably we regard them. It may be that by examining studies on this issue, clinicians can gain some understanding of how to increase compassion toward other people. Compassion is certainly an important prosocial behavior, and it is not atypical that some clients in therapy would benefit from having more compassion for other people. Since the work on evaluation of victims of misfortune has stemmed from a variety of theoretical interests, attribution being one among many, we will first consider some studies of evaluations of victims that do not stem directly from theories of attribution and then conclude this section by examining a more strictly attributional approach to the issue.

The principal finding in a series of interrelated but independently conducted studies has been that as the psychological distance between observer and victim is decreased, evaluations of the victim become increasingly positive. One can decrease this psychological distance by instructing people to empathize with the victim ("Imagine yourself in the person's place") as in a study by D. Aderman, S. S. Brehm, and L. Katz (1974), by having the person anticipate a similar experience to that of the victim as in studies by Chaikin and Darley (1973) and Sorrentino and Boutilier (1974), or by having the observer expect to interact with the victim as in a study by Stokols and Schopler (1973).

The first two approaches can easily be utilized by any therapist who desires to increase his client's compassion for other people who have incurred unfortunate outcomes. The therapist can instruct the client to empathize with the other person or can point out similarities between the person's experience and past or potential experiences of the client. The third approach may be somewhat more difficult for the therapist to implement, but suggests that if the client believes that he may interact with the unfortunate other, he may have more compassionate regard for him. The therapist may be able to assist by helping arrange for this interaction to occur or, more simply, by encouraging the client to think about or imagine interacting with the other person at some time.

In a recent study by Godfrey and Lowe (1975) an attributional analysis of the evaluation of victims was conducted. These investigators hypothesized that in studies where devaluation of a victim has been found consistently (such as in the studies by Lerner), the victim has been seen as having been coerced into negative outcome behavior, is seen as weak and yielding, and is thus devalued. In contrast, Godfrey and Lowe suggest that if the victim were presented as engaging in the negative outcome behavior for "good reasons" that reflected his own beliefs, the victim would not be derogated. Godfrey and Lowe view the case of "giving in" as eliciting attributions of extrinsic motivation, while they see the case of self-causation as stimulating attributions of intrinsic motivation. These hypotheses were supported by the results of their study, in which observers negatively evaluated victims who appeared extrinsically motivated and positively evaluated victims who appeared intrinsically motivated.

Godfrey and Lowe thus appear to believe that observers are much more likely to derogate a person if he appears weak than if he appears foolish. According to their formulation, the person who chooses a behavior that results in unpleasantness would not be devalued, while a person who was pressured to choose that behavior and "gave in" to it would be derogated. Clearly, this formulation has its limits. It is unlikely that an observer would derogate someone who engaged in negative outcome behavior as a result of being forced to do it by having a gun held to his head. However, there may be situations, such as that produced experimentally by Godfrey and Lowe, where compassionate regard is reduced due to the observer's inferring that the unfortunate other has given in, is weak, and is thus not to be respected. Therapists confronted with this specific situation with clients might use the Godfrey and Lowe paradigm and highlight the intrinsic motivational forces that contributed to the other person's behavior.

Dispositional Attributions

Recall that several of the attribution theorists dealt with making dispositional attributions to the person, although none in such detail as E. E. Jones and K. E. Davis (1965). Two postulates of the Jones and Davis model have received experimental validation. First, choice increases dispositional attributions (E. E. Jones & Harris, 1967; E. E. Jones, Worchel, Goethals, & Grumet, 1971; Snyder & E. E. Jones, 1974; Costanzo, Grumet, & S. S. Brehm, 1974). Second, if a chosen behavior cannot be explained on grounds of universal desirability (in this case, social norms in the experience at hand), dispositional attribution is increased (E. E. Jones, Davis, & Gergen, 1961).

These findings are amenable to prescriptive clinical statements. If a therapist wishes to decrease a client's general tendency to view others in dispositional terms and to not attend to situational variables that influence others, or to decrease the strength of a particular dispositional attribution made by the client, the therapist should emphasize that other people do not always freely choose their behavior and that sometimes their behavior reveals little about themselves other than that they conform to social norms and/or that they like pleasant things. Thus to decrease dispositional attributions, the lack of choice in engaging in, and the universal desirability of, a behavior of the observed other(s) are emphasized.

There may be some circumstances where it is desirable to increase the client's dispositional attributions. Some clients may repeatedly obtain negative outcomes for themselves because they fail to take into account the dispositional attributes of some other person. In this case, the other person's free choice and those nonuniversally desirable aspects of his behavior would be emphasized by the therapist in discussions with the client.

On a more general level, if the therapist considers the Jones and Davis model of correspondent inference to be not only a calculus for how observers operate, but also an accurate logic to apply in objectively inferring dispositional characteristics, the therapist can teach the client the Jones and Davis formula. This might be quite helpful for clients who appear to be making erratic and unreliable dispositional attributions, and who, in acting on such attributions (e.g., "He's mean," "She's nervous"), run into trouble in their social interactions. The therapist can point out to the client that he needs to observe how much choice the other person had in his behavior, to see what noncommon elements one finds between chosen and rejected alternatives, and to determine whether the chosen behavior can be accounted for in general terms (universal desirability) or if it reveals something unique about the person. The test of this therapeutic procedure is if the client, after learning the Jones and Davis rules, shows increased accuracy in his dispositional attributions.

The Actor-Observer Difference and How to Change It

The hypothesis of Jones and Nisbett that actors and observers typically make different attributions has been reviewed earlier. The major empirical support for the existence of such differences comes from a study by Nisbett, Caputo, Legant, and Marecek (1973). Nisbett et al. found that observers assumed that actors would behave in the future in ways similar to the ways that they had witnessed; actors did not make this assumption of behavioral continuity. Further, when asked to describe the reasons for their friends' choices, subjects gave many more dispositional properties as causes than when they described the reasons for their own behavior. As observers, subjects tended to make dispositional attributions, whereas, as actors, they tended to make situational attributions. Finally, subjects ascribed more personality traits to other people than to themselves.

Given the general tendency for such actor-observer differences, is there any way to reduce such differences? This question is similar to our earlier exploration of ways in which therapists can affect the dispositional attributions made by their clients. In that instance, it was suggested that the Jones and Davis model could be used to increase or decrease the probability that a client will attribute dispositions to other people. The present discussion will focus on those ways in which the general tendency of observers to make dispositional attributions can be affected; it is assumed that such a general tendency would hold even for observers who use the Jones and Davis model. In addition, ways of affecting self-attributions will be discussed.

Storms (1973) has suggested that by changing viewing perspectives, actor-observer differences can be changed. Storms employed video-tape equipment to give actors and observers different visual perspectives on a dyadic interaction. He found that when actors looked at the person with whom they were interacting and observers looked at the actor, observers made more dispositional attributions than actors. On the other hand, when actors viewed a video tape where the camera focused on them and observers viewed the other person in the interaction, actors made more dispositional attributions to themselves than observers.

Thus, the literal point of view seems to be critical. Actors usually see the environment, and observers usually focus on the acting person who stands out from the environment as figure against ground. Under these typical circumstances, observers make more dispositional attributions. When the actor can view himself, however, and the observer focuses on the background environment, the difference is reversed. Another way in which the actor-observer differences might be decreased has been suggested by E. E. Jones and R. E. Nisbett (1971), who stated that empathic observers should be less prone to making dispositional attributions than nonempathic, objective observers.

The study by Storms and the suggestion by Jones and Nisbett provide the therapist with several techniques to use in affecting dispositional attributions. Consider the following cases: (1) a client fails to see the underlying continuity in his own behavior (paucity of self-attributed dispositions), (2) a client sees too much continuity in his own behavior and fails to take environmental circumstances into account as affecting his behavior, (3) a client makes too many dispositional attributions to others, (4) a client makes too few attributions to others. Combining this discussion with the earlier one on the Jones and Davis model, the following therapeutic strategies could be suggested for each case.

1. *Too few self-attributed dispositions.* The therapist could video-tape the client during therapy, with the camera focused on the client, and then play the tape back for the client to view. While the client watches, the therapist could point out the continuity in the client's behavior. This procedure should increase the number of dispositional attributions that the client makes to himself.

2. *Too many self-attributed dispositions.* The therapist could tape therapy sessions, this time focusing the camera on himself or, in the case of group or family therapy, on other group or family members. While the client watches this tape, the therapist can point out how the client's behavior was affected by the behavior of the other person/people. This procedure should decrease the number of dispositional attributions that the client makes to himself and increase the client's appreciation of the role of the social environment in determining his behavior.

3. *Too many dispositional attributions to others.* The therapist has a variety of strategies available for this situation. He can use the Jones and Davis model (emphasize lack of choice, not enough or too many noncommon effects between decision alternatives, and the universal desirability of the chosen course of action); have the client view a tape of someone to whom he makes too many dispositional attributions, with the camera focused on the (social) environment; and/or have the client empathize with the person to whom he attributes too many dispositional traits. These procedures should reduce the client's tendency to see excessive continuity in others' behavior and to be insufficiently sensitive to environmental effects.

4. *Too few dispositional attributions to others.* For this class of clients, the obverse of the above strategies would apply. The therapist can use the Jones and Davis model (emphasize choice, appropriate number of noncommon effects and nonuniversal desirability of chosen alternative); have the client view a tape of someone to whom he attributes too few dispositional traits, with the camera focused on the person; and/or instruct the client not to empathize ("Don't imagine how you would feel"). These procedures should maximize dispositional attributions to others.

While these techniques are, in principle, usable in virtually any therapeutic context, they may be most powerful in group or family therapy. In such therapies the attributions of dispositions can become a major topic: "You think I do things just because I'm a bad person; you don't realize how other things affect me," or "You never give me credit for being the sort of person I am; you're always saying I did that because I had to." By a skillful and timely use of the above procedures, the therapist can open up alternative perspectives to his clients. He can do this because he wishes them to adopt one perspective instead of another, or he can use these procedures to demonstrate to his clients the relativity of all such dispositional and/or situational attributions in order that they may become less dogmatic about why other people or they themselves engage in specified behaviors.

Attributions of Emotion to Others

Much of the work on attribution of emotion has dealt with the ways in which people attribute emotions to themselves. A complementary line of research is the study of the attribution of emotion to others. In investigating this issue, Schiffenbauer (1974) found that aroused subjects were more likely to attribute emotions to others than were non-aroused subjects, and that the attributed emotions tended to be similar in hedonic quality (i.e., pleasant versus unpleasant) to their own arousal.

The results of this study suggest a projective process of emotional arousal that will, no doubt, be consistent with clinical experience. There are two levels of projection involved. First, there is a contrast between the aroused and non-aroused state. People who are not aroused will tend to perceive relatively little emotional expression in those about them; people who are aroused, however, will more likely perceive others as being emotionally aroused. Second, there is the type of arousal. A person experiencing a pleasant emotion will tend to see that same emotion and other positive emotions in others; a person experiencing an unpleasant emotion will tend to see that same emotion and other negative emotions in others.[2]

If the attribution of emotions is at least partially a projective state of affairs, this has some direct implications for clinical procedures. Again there are two levels to consider. If a therapist is concerned about the quantitative side of a client's attributions of emotions to others, he could increase arousal in order to increase emotional attributions or decrease arousal in order to decrease attributions. Usually, however, therapists are concerned about the specific, qualitative aspect of a client's emotional attributions. If a client is perceiving an excessive amount of positive or negative emotion in others, it may be because this reflects his own present emotional state. For specific inappropriate attributions to just a few other people, the therapist may be able to present compelling counter-evidence (e.g., showing a husband who thinks that his wife is unhappy that the wife smiles all the time), but for more general, pervasive tendencies to see others in a good mood or a bad one, the

---

[2] This type of projection would be deemed "suplementary projection," according to Murray's distinction.

therapist will find it difficult or at least very time-consuming to muster sufficient counterevidence, and the person's own felt emotion may continue to determine these tendencies.

When confronted with the above dilemma, the therapist may want to consider various strategies for effecting at least a temporary change in the client's emotional experience. This may not be easy, but it is possible that emotional changes of even short duration coupled with simultaneous consideration of other people to whom misattributions have been made will act to break the lock of seeing everyone else in the same fashion. Any emotional change technique can be used in this procedure, from reminding the client of times when he felt differently to explicit role-playing of the desired emotion. The critical element if attributions are to be changed is that when a different emotion has been induced, no matter for how short a period, the client should be asked directly to describe the emotional state he ascribes to each of the people to whom he has misattributed his own chronic emotional state. If a temporary change of the client's own mood can lead to different emotional attributions to others, the client's perceived social support for his chronic emotional state may be decreased and more substantial emotional change for the client himself may become possible.

Determinants of the Self-Attribution of Having Influenced Another Person

In the article from which the title of this section comes, Schopler and Layton (1972) explored the behaviors of another person that facilitate our perception that we have influenced him. One of their findings parallels studies of teacher attributions that will be discussed in a later section: we are more likely to infer that we have influenced another when that other person has succeeded than when he has failed. The second finding provides some empirical support for Kelley's principle of covariance (see pp. 150–152). Schopler and Layton found that perceived influence is increased when the target person behaves in an unexpected way. Thus the principle of covariance: the person who usually behaves in X way when we are absent, behaves in Y way when we are present, and we infer from this that our influence led to this behavior change.

These findings can be applied to two levels of the clinical process. First, a therapist may wish to increase or decrease the client's perception of his interpersonal influence. Pointing out that another person behaved in some new, unusual, or successful fashion following interaction with the client would help to increase the client's perception of his own influence. The opposite tactic, emphasizing the other person's continued, typical, or unsuccessful behavior after interaction with the client may assist in decreasing the client's self-attributions of interpersonal influence.

The second level of the clinical process to which the Schopler and Layton findings apply is therapists' self-attributions of influence. Therapists need to be aware that there are general trends to attribute interpersonal influence to oneself when the client acts in new, unusual, or successful ways. Sometimes such attributions may be appropriate and indicate that the therapy is having an effect. Other times, and this is critical when considering therapists' self-attributions of influence, these attributions may be inappropriate. The client's new or successful behavior may be a consequence of events totally independent of therapeutic interactions. When examining the effects of their influence, it behooves therapists to be aware of the trends found by Schopler and Layton and to know that they can be misled by such trends. Therapist-attributions of influence can be made only after carefully exploring other events in the client's life that may have been responsible for new or successful behaviors seen during the course of therapy.

Attributions and Dependency

Schopler and Matthews (1965) have explored the relationship among attributions, dependency, and help-giving. Their results indicated that a powerful person who perceives another's dependence on him as caused by external, environmental factors will be more helpful to that other person than if the other's dependence is perceived as caused by internal, personal factors. In accounting for their results, Schopler and Matthews proposed that the person perceived as showing internally determined dependence does not arouse the norm of social responsibility because he is seen as responsible for his own fate; the person with externally caused dependence, on the other hand, may be seen as at the mercy of the environment and does arouse the social responsibility norm. It should be noted that Schopler and Matthews' results would also be predicted from reactance theory. In reactance theory terms, externally caused dependency would have fewer future implications of threatening the help-giver's freedom than the internally caused dependency. It is relatively easy to help someone out in "bad times"; it may be more difficult to help someone out who seems a needy person in general and may require continued help.

The study by Schopler and Matthews may be of assistance to clinicians attempting to increase their clients' prosocial behavior. It suggests that clients may be able to be more helpful to other people if the therapist has emphasized the role of external factors in the plight of the others. If, to the contrary, a therapist wishes to reduce his client's help-giving, an emphasis on the internal, personal causes of the other person's dependency may facilitate this.[3]

The Schopler and Matthews study is another examination of attributions that has relevance for therapists' responses to their clients. It was pointed out in Chapters Two and Three on reactance theory that therapists may have opportunities to help out their clients above and beyond normal therapeutic procedure; examples given included helping to get the client a job, getting the client out of academic obligations, and dealing with bureaucratic systems on the client's behalf. Looking at this situation in light of the Schopler and Matthews study, therapists may find that they too are more helpful to clients whose dependency they view as stemming from environmental factors than to those who are seen as dependent because of their own personality traits. Of course, if such differential responses represent considered judgments by the therapist, there is no problem. A problem exists only if therapists are unaware of the cause of their differential helpfulness and if these unconsidered responses are not beneficial to their clients. Social psychological principles can almost always cut two ways: they can help the therapist understand and change client behavior; they can also help the therapist understand his own behavior and change it if it is not in the client's best interests.

SUCCESS AND FAILURE

Attribution theorists have been greatly interested in the processes by which one comes to attribute abilities to others and to oneself. Much of this work has focused on the effects of success and failure on attributions of related abilities such as intelligence and skill. This section will not provide a detailed review of this extensive and

---

[3] These results appear somewhat at odds with the Godfrey and Lowe (1975) study cited earlier (pp. 179–180). To clarify this discrepancy, note that Godfrey and Lowe focused on evaluation of an unfortunate other, while Schopler and Matthews focused on help-giving. The two behaviors may have different antecedents, although one would think they would be positively correlated. More psychologically meaningful, perhaps, is the different evaluative quality the different investigators attached to their forms of external and internal factors. Godfrey and Lowe portrayed their victim as "giving in" to external forces; Schopler and Matthew presented a victim "at the mercy" of these forces. It may be that perceiving another person as "giving in" would reduce positive evaluations and help-giving, while perceiving another as "at the mercy" of the environment would increase positive evaluations and help-giving. In terms of making an intrinsic attribution, the intrinsic factors were also portrayed quite differently. Godfrey and Lowe presented a strong person making her own decisions, while Schopler and Matthews operationalized intrinsic factors in the form of a chronically needy person. It may be that the positive portrayal of the strong person would increase positive evaluations and help-giving, while the negative depiction of the needy person would decrease both of these responses.

complex literature. Instead, brief mention will be made of a variety of distinct approaches to this issue and then a more detailed examination will be carried out for clinically relevant findings.

Achievement Motivation

Weiner has proposed a theory of achievement motivation based on attributional considerations. This theory has been explicated in a number of studies (e.g., Weiner & Kukla, 1970; Weiner, Heckhausen, Meyer, & Cook, 1972; Rest, Nierenberg, Weiner, & Heckhausen, 1973; McMahan, 1973) as well as in a summary paper (Weiner, Frieze, Kukla, Reed, Rest, & Rosenbaum, 1971) and recent book (Weiner, 1972). We will not examine this theory here, since much of its focus is to map out general principles of ability attribution and is not directly relevant to clinical practice. The interested reader is referred to the sources just cited.

Attribution by Teachers

Teachers are confronted daily with students who succeeed and students who fail. What are their attributions of causality? The original investigations were somewhat dismaying to those of us who teach: Johnson, Feigenbaum, and Weiby (1964) reported that when college subjects (females taking educational psychology courses) were asked to teach children in a controlled situation (the experimenters controlling the children's success and failure), they attributed responsibility for the students' success to themselves and responsibility for the students' failure to the students. This self-serving pattern of attributions was replicated by Beckman (1970), who also found that observers did not make such teacher-gratifying responses.

Fortunately (for the teachers and the students), a recent study by Ross, Bierbrauer, and Polly (1974) has indicated that the situation may not be quite so bleak. These investigators found that their subjects rated teacher factors as more important for a student's failure and student factors as more important for a student's success. This pattern of results was most pronounced for subjects who actually were professional teachers. Thus, it may be that experience in teaching fosters a more humble attitude toward student success and a more responsible one toward student failure.

These results are presented for appraisal by clinicians because of one major assumption: therapists, whatever else they may be, are also teachers. As such, they need to be on the alert for self-serving attributions such as that found in the Johnson et al. and Beckman studies. Hopefully, in therapy too, experience may provide some wisdom.

Defensive Attribution

It was noted earlier that people may seek to comfort or reassure themselves by the attributions they make to other people. In accordance with this principle, it has been found that people take increasing credit for increasing success (Streufert & Streufert, 1969), that more causality is attributed to internal sources for success than for failure (Fitch, 1970), and that after people have failed, they attribute causality to external factors and see themselves as less motivated and the task as less important than people who succeed (Wortman, Costanzo, & Witt, 1973). These self-protective maneuvers are probably visible on a daily basis to clinicians and are noted only to make the point that self-defense of this sort is a general process that occurs in the normal population.

Changing Attributions About Success and Failure: Patterns of Success and Failure

Therapy is a process concerned with change, not with static properties, and there are a few studies that may give therapists some insight about changing their clients' attributions concerning success and failure. Let us first consider the evidence on observers' attributions of intelligence to others. E. E. Jones, Rock, Shaver, Goethals, and Ward (1968) found that observers attributed more intelligence to performers with a descending success rate (early successes; later failures) than to performers with an ascending success rate (early failures; later successes). This finding was refined in a study by Thompson (1972) in which she found that the Jones et al. results applied only to competitive observers, not to observers in cooperative conditions.

Thus for people engaged in cooperative give-and-take with another person, the other person's pattern of success and failure seems not to be terribly important in attributions of intelligence. For people in competitive situations, however, the pattern may be critical. In clinical practice, the application of these findings is straightforward. When a therapist is working with a client who has, for whatever reason, a competitive orientation toward another person and who attributes excessive intellectual abilities (or any kind of relevant skill) to this person, the therapist can moderate such attributions by pointing out the early instances where the person failed or at least failed to perform to perfection. If, on the other hand, the competitive client is underestimating the intelligence or skill of the other person, the therapist's emphasis on the early successes of this person should be effective in raising the client's evaluation.

If the pattern of success and failure is not terribly influential in cooperative settings, it may be that when cooperating with another person success and failure per se are (within limits) not especially important, but that other, more dispositional attributes are. Beckman (1970) found that students with an ascending success rate were seen as more *motivated* than students with a descending success rate. Thus for clients who are in a cooperative venture with another person and who are making inaccurate or harmful attributions to that person, the following approaches may be helpful. Therapists can draw the client's attention to more recent successes of the other person in order to increase the client's attributions of motivation; conversely, therapists can emphasize the more recent failures of the person to decrease attributions of motivation. It is presumed that within a cooperative setting, increased attributions of motivation will induce increased liking of and respect for the other person.

This discussion has focused on observers' attributions, but what about self-attributions as they relate to success and failure? Jones et al. also examined self-attributions as a function of patterns of success and failure. They found that for self-attributions, ascending success led to more confidence than descending success. Thus, we would expect a client's estimate of his ability to be raised by an emphasis on his recent successes and lowered by an emphasis on his recent failures.

Risk-Taking

Further suggestions about affecting attributions concerned with success and failure come from a study by Jellison, Riskind, and Broll (1972). They found that on a skill task (but not on a chance task), people who take high risks are perceived as higher in ability than those who take low risks. Again, a simple procedure is indicated. To raise a client's assessment of another person's ability vis-à-vis a certain skilled endeavor, the therapist can emphasize the risks (financial, personal, social, or whatever) that the other person took in engaging in the task; to lower the client's estimate, these risks can be minimized.

The Effects of Anticipated Performance

It was noted earlier that decreasing the psychological distance between observer and victim may increase the observer's compassion for the victim. A similar factor may affect one's estimates of one's own abilities. Wortman, Costanzo, and Witt (1973) found that subjects who anticipated future performance on an observed task attributed less ability on this task to themselves than subjects who did not so anticipate. Thus, decreasing the psychological distance between the observer and the task seems to have a sobering effect on the observer's estimate of his own abilities on this task. It is easy to think of oneself as a great potential chessplayer; it's harder to feel so confident when one actually expects to have to play. Clinically, a procedure of arranging for a client to perform the relevant task, or at least stimulating him to begin to think in terms of performing it, may assist in reducing unrealistically high self-estimates of abilities.

INFORMATION PRESENTATION
EFFECTS ON ATTRIBUTIONS

The sections on clinical applications have focused primarily on deriving from the empirical literature suggested methods by which therapists can affect various attributions made by their clients. These applications have usually been specific as to content (e.g., attributions of emotions, attributions of intrinsic motivation, self-attributions of influence, etc.). There are, however, several studies on attributional processes that address more general issues of how types of information presentation can affect attributions. The techniques derived from these studies can be useful in many of the more specific strategies described earlier.

First, let us consider the situation where the therapist is providing information to the client in such a way as to influence the client's attributions. In this case, both therapist and client are observing behavior (of others or of the client) and are making interpretations of the causes for that behavior. What circumstances will allow the therapist's information to have the most powerful effect? The results from a study by Himmelfarb (1972) suggest that information about attributions will have more effect if it comes from multiple sources than if it comes from a single source. In addition, Himmelfarb found that information that was consistent through a variety of behavior observation situations was given more weight in making attributions.

Thus, when the therapist is attempting to change client attributions, he should support his information and interpretations with references to other people who agree with his point of view or, if in group therapy, he should have these others speak for themselves. If information comes only from the therapist, the client can disregard it as reflecting the therapist's own egocentric perspective, but if that information is supported by a social consensus, the client may consider revising his perspective.

Himmelfarb's second finding would seem to apply most to cases of dispositional attributions. If a therapist believes that the client is failing to make a necessary dispositional attribution, he might have the client observe the other person in a variety of situations, with the dispositional attribution in mind. Himmelfarb's study suggests that if the other person behaves in the same way throughout a number of environmental situations and the client observes this, the client will be more likely to make a dispositional attribution to the one constant in these situations—the other person.

Of course this procedure could also be used to test out a dispositional attribution. If the client, or the therapist, is unsure whether a dispositional attribution is appropriate to another person with whom the client typically interacts in only one kind of situation, the client could test this attribution by arranging to be with or at least to observe the other person in other situations. If the other person behaves similarly across different situations, the client would tend to follow Kelley's covariance principle and attribute the behavior to the entity (in this case, the person), but if the other person changes his behavior across situations, the client needs to examine carefully the characteristics of the situation in which he usually interacts with the other person. Different behavior in different situations suggests environmental rather than dispositional causation, and the client, being part of the environment for the other person, may find that it is his (the client's) behavior that is inducing the other's behavior in their usual interactions. If so, and if the client wants to change the other's behavior, the client may have to change his own behavior first.

A study by Geothals (1972) focused on the characteristics of another person that had the most influence on one's own attributions. Goethals' findings can be separated into three parts. First, he found that agreement with one's attributions increased one's confidence in these attributions more than disagreement. This seems only a logical derivation from Kelley's notions of consensual validation. A somewhat more interesting finding was that similar persons had a greater effect on one's confidence about one's attributions than did dissimilar others. Agreement by a similar other increased confidence, while disagreement decreased confidence.

Goethals' third finding was that considering agreement only, a dissimilar other increased confidence more than a similar other when both the subject and the other had the same information; when the two people had different information, however, the agreement of a similar other increased confidence more than the agreement of a dissimilar other. This finding was later clarified in a study by Goethals and Nelson (1973). It was found that agreement by a dissimilar other was more effective when a belief about some event was concerned, but that agreement by a similar other was more effective when a value was concerned. This distinction would seem to parallel the earlier findings by Goethals. Beliefs or opinions are based on an assessment of the real world. When others, who are usually very different from us, view a set of facts and agree with our conclusion, our confidence in our conclusion is greatly increased. It is possible for people to have the same information on which to base beliefs. But it may be impossible for others to have the same information on which to base values. Values represent the cumulative product of our experiences. We are, if anything, disturbed when a dissimilar other agrees with our values; he couldn't have the same information, how could he draw the same conclusion? We are relieved and confident when a similar other agrees with our values; he has confirmed our cumulative experience.

These findings translate into a set of applications based on the relationship between the characteristics of the therapist and those of the client. When the therapist seeks to decrease the client's confidence in his attributions (presumably about either others or himself), the similar (on variables such as sex, race, socioeconomic class, attitudes, etc.) therapist who disagrees will be most effective. When the goal is increased attributional confidence, however, a more complex set of relationships obtains. Sometimes the therapist and the client will be dealing with beliefs or opinions. At these times, Goethals' data suggest that the therapist who is different or who can at least point out some differences between himself and the client will be the most effective in increasing the client's attributional confidence. On other occasions, however, when the client and the therapist are focusing on values, a similar therapist will be most effective.

Another style of information presentation that can affect attributions involves the method of observation. Using video-tape stimulus materials, Newtson (1973) found that subjects made more dispositional attributions and were more confident in their judgments when they were instructed to segment the observed behavior into fine units. Although the exact reasons for this effect are unclear, it seems important that therapists be aware of this effect. Whether the material under observation consists of video tapes of others or oneself, or of *in vivo* observations of others, the therapist who instructs his client to observe carefully by looking at small units of behavior may be predisposing the client to make strong, dispositional attributions. If this is desirable, such instructions would be highly appropriate, but if this is undesirable, such instructions should be avoided.

Furthermore, Newtson's findings may have a highly significant message for therapists. A therapist looks very closely at a client's behavior, dividing it into what may appear to lay observers to be minute units. Clinical obsessiveness is known, by experience, to the profession and, by rumor at least, to the general public. Newtson's study suggests that this division of the client's behavior into fine units may lead to the clinician's making more dispositional attributions (read "diagnostic labeling") and to being more confident about these attributions (read "clinical authority"). This process may account for the oft-lamented tendency of clinical practitioners to see pathology everywhere. Looking closely may simply lead to more dispositional attributions, and the ones clinicians have at hand are terms denoting psychopathology. To guard against this tendency, one needs to know that it exists. It may also be helpful to take environmental circumstances into very serious consideration when assessing a client's functioning. Behavior therapists have done this and it seems to have reduced dispositional attributions on their part!

INDIVIDUAL DIFFERENCES

Although the attribution literature has paid some attention to individual differences, few such differences investigated thus far are of significant interest to clinicians. Most of the individual differences examined have been those of high versus low achievement motivation and high versus low self-esteem. It has been found, for example, that people with high achievement motivation tend to attribute success or failure to themselves more than people with a lower achievement orientation (Kukla, 1972), that high achievers seek help less than low achievers (Tessler & Schwartz, 1972), and that people with low self-esteem attribute the causal locus for failure more to internal sources within themselves than do people with high self-esteem (Fitch, 1970).

These findings are useful for mapping out the interconnections between general attribution processes and general personality orientations. They are not terribly helpful in the clinical setting. Thus, rather than being able to consult an empirical literature that provides specific strategies geared to personality types, the clinician interested in the therapeutic use of attribution processes will have to rely on his own ingenuity in applying to specific clients the general principles enunciated in this chapter.

A NOTE ON THE CLIENT'S FREEDOM AND THE THERAPEUTIC TEACHING OF SOCIAL PSYCHOLOGY

A recurring theme of this book has been the client's perceived freedom. For reactance theory, threats to perceived freedom can create boomerang effects, pushing the client toward the opposite response from that advocated by the therapist. For dissonance theory, perceived freedom was necessary to induce behavior-consistent attitude change. And now, in these chapters on attribution theories, perceived freedom has been dissected into instances in which attributions to internal sources may be desirable and in which such attributions may be undesirable.

This division seems critical for clinical activity. For most clinical efforts, it is probably helpful for the client to perceive his own freedom and to take the responsibility for his own actions. This coincides with general humanistic values of a free, responsible person and with specific strategies designed to produce attitude and behavior change that have been discussed in this book. Much of the discussion of attributional effects has also stressed the desirability of having the client believe himself to cause his own outcomes. Attribution theories, however, can also serve to alert the clinician that there are times when attributions to external sources can be helpful to the client.

Another theme that has appeared already, but perhaps is most appropriately emphasized for these chapters, is that of teaching the client social psychology. Most of the clinical applications that have been suggested in this book have presumed that the therapist has certain goals for the client and that he can utilize social psychological principles in obtaining these goals. From time to time, however, it has been noted that a quite effective therapeutic activity may be to teach the client certain tenets of social psychology and by teaching, to thus equip the client to use these tenets in pursuit of his own goals.

This teaching approach may be most relevant to the theories of attribution. Most theories of attribution provide both an attempt to predict how human beings behave and a logical calculus of rational attributional behavior. For clients who display significant attributional difficulties, making seemingly inaccurate or at least unreliable attributions of causality to themselves or to others, the most efficient and effective therapeutic strategy may be to teach them principles of attribution such as the Jones and Davis model and the Kelley principle of covariance. These principles may allow them to re-order their attributions into a more coherent, reliable, and accurate perspective on themselves and the world.

SUMMARY

This chapter has discussed a variety of clinical applications that can be derived from theories of attribution. A number of social processes in attribution were examined, including evaluations of other people, dispositional attributions, the actor-observer difference, attributions of emotion to others, determinants of having influenced another person, and attributions of dependency. A brief presentation of the literature was offered on attributions concerning success and failure, with the emphasis on how therapists can alter their clients' attributions in this area. Information presentation effects on attribution were explored, and the paucity of findings on individual differences in attributional styles was noted. The concluding topic reiterated what attribution theories have to say about the client's feeling of freedom and responsibility in therapy, and suggested that teaching clients the principles of attribution theories may be of therapeutic utility.

SUGGESTED SOURCES

Jones, E. E., Kanouse, D. E., Kelley, H. H., Nisbett, R. E., Valins, S., & Weiner, B. *Attribution: Perceiving the causes of behavior.* Morristown, N.J.: General Learning Press, 1972.

Shaver, K. *An introduction to attribution processes.* Cambridge, Mass.: Winthrop, 1975.

PART FOUR

ADDITIONAL THEORIES

CHAPTER ELEVEN

ADDITIONAL THEORIES OF INTEREST

Although the reactance, dissonance, and attribution theories discussed here represent some of the more influential theories and larger empirical literatures to be found in experimental social psychology, there are, of course, numerous other theories, models, and hypotheses of importance in the field. This book does not attempt to cover all of these theoretical positions. The reader interested in gaining a broader perspective on social psychology is referred to any of the many social psychology textbooks that survey the field (e.g., Berkowitz, 1975; E. E. Jones & Gerard, 1967; Middlebrook, 1974; Secord & Backman, 1974).

A few other theories, however, are of particular interest to the author and seem relevant to clinical endeavors. These theories will be briefly described and applied to clinical work in this chapter. As has been the policy throughout this book, selected reviews will be presented to highlight aspects of the theories and findings that may be useful to clinicians.

COMMITMENT

Robert White (1964) on the commitment required of the client in psychoanalysis:

> Standard psychoanalysis takes a very long time. Treatment is usually scheduled to take place for one hour a day, five days a week. In spite of

this rigorous schedule, it is rare for a psychoanalysis to be completed in less than one year, it is common for the treatment to last two or three years, and in some cases . . . five or more years. (p. 296)

Kiesler and his colleagues (Kiesler, 1971) have presented a conceptual framework and many empirical investigations of the psychological effects of commitment. Kiesler defines commitment as "the pledging or binding of the individual to behavioral acts" (p. 30). He notes two major assumptions concerning commitment. First, he assumes that there will be a tendency for attitudes to be consistent with behavioral commitments. This assumption is virtually identical to the assumption made about the function of commitment by dissonance theorists. Kiesler's second assumption is that the effect of commitment is to make an act less changeable.

For the purposes of this chapter, Kiesler's second assumption will constitute the major focus. It is presumed that his first assumption does not differ significantly from commitment effects investigated under the dissonance rubric, and these effects have been discussed earlier in some detail (see pp. 90-91). Thus, rather than look at what happens when a person commits himself to a counterattitudinal act, we will examine Kiesler's research on what happens when a person commits himself to an act consistent with his prior beliefs. This topic would be of interest in clinical situations in which the therapeutic goal is to strengthen an already existing attitude or behavior. Note, therefore, that our discussion of commitment will not examine strategies of behavior/attitude change, but rather strategies of behavior/attitude maintenance.

Kiesler notes and indeed has utilized in his experiments a number of methods by which commitment is effected. Commitment is deemed to increase as the act becomes more explicit (more public, more unambiguous), as the importance of the act increases, as the degree of irrevocability increases, as the number of acts performed by the person increases (as psychoanalysis seems to have discovered long ago), and as the degree of volition about the act increases. This multiple definition of operational forms of commitment should be quite helpful to the clinician. There seems to be a rather wide variety of techniques that feed into the same psychological state, and the practitioner is free to use whichever one best suits the specific clinical circumstances.

Clinical Applications

Resistance to change. One strong effect of behavioral commitment is that both the act itself and the attitude associated with it are made more resistant to change. Kiesler and Sakumura (1966) report a study in which public commitment to an attitudinal position (one already held by the subjects) made that attitude more resistant to later counterattitudinal communications. In addition, Kiesler and Mathog (in Kiesler, 1971) conducted a study in which subjects who engaged in a behavior a number of times were less likely to want to change their behavior when such change was advocated than were subjects who had engaged in the behavior only a few times.

These studies, each using a different method of effecting commitment, illustrate Kiesler's assumption that commitment renders the act/attitude less changeable. No matter what our opinions or acts, it is almost inevitable that we will encounter a situation where change in these opinions or acts is advocated. There are times in clinical practice when it is critical that such suggestions or demands for change *not* be met. Perhaps the most typical example would be where a clinician and client have worked for some time to enable the client to engage in new, highly desirable behaviors. When the client begins performing these behaviors in the real world, it is always possible that he will meet criticism or counterpropositions.

To guard the new behavior from being susceptible to these influences, the clinician is well advised to have the client become highly committed to the new behavior: make it public, do it a number of times, and so on. Elegantly enough, this strategy of increasing commitment should stabilize the behavior no matter whether the client regards the behavior as counterattitudinal or as consistent with his existing attitudes. In the counterattitudinal case, dissonance principles would dictate the use of high commitment; in the consistent case, Kiesler's model of and findings on commitment indicate the value of high commitment.

Increasing the behavior. While attitudes and behavioral choices have been shown to be made more resistant to change by commitment, a study by Kiesler, Mathog, Pool, and Howenstine (in Kiesler, 1971) suggests that commitment can create a more positive and dramatic effect. Not only did these investigators find that commitment to an attitude decreased susceptibility to a later attack on that attitude, but that willingness to engage in behaviors related to the attitude was increased by the combination of commitment and attack. Thus, commitment to an attitude does not increase the extremity of that attitude (Kiesler & Sakumura, 1966); it makes it more resistant to attack. The Kiesler, Mathog, Pool, and Howenstine study suggests, however, that when the commitment is followed by an attack and then by an opportunity to engage in attitudinally consistent behaviors, the willingness to engage in these behaviors is increased.[1]

These results provide a powerful indicator of the importance of having the client be committed to desirable behaviors. First, given high commitment, resistance to attack is strengthened. Second, given high commitment and attack, willingness to engage, and presumably engagement itself, will be increased. Thus, not only can commitment guard against undesirable influences, it can make those undesirable influences work to maintain desirable behaviors.

It was suggested earlier that attacks on one's behavior and/or opinions are likely to occur naturally. If, however, such attacks do not occur, the therapist might wish to consider exposing a client who is highly committed to a therapeutically desirable behavior to an attack on that behavior or on the attitude underlying it. This attack should not affect the attitude directly, but it should have the beneficial effect of increasing the client's tendencies to engage in the behavior.

Forewarning. In the discussion of dissonance theory, considerable attention was paid to circumstances under which it is appropriate to indicate possible negative or positive consequences of the behavioral commitment (pp. 101-104). Kiesler too has addressed this notion of forewarning, but in a more limited sense. The clinical situation of interest is when a therapist is quite sure that someone in the client's environment will attack his (the client's) desirable attitude or behavior. It is, of course, not at all infrequent that clients make changes in therapy that are then greeted with less than total enthusiasm by significant others in their environment who may be threatened by the clients' changes or at least find adjusting to these changes difficult. Given this situation, it would be important to know when to forewarn the client about these possible attacks and when not to forewarn him.

Studies by Jones and Kiesler (in Kiesler, 1971) suggest that forewarning may decrease attitude change in the direction of the attack when the person is committed, but may increase this change when the person is not committed. This increase is attributed to the person's anticipatory face-saving in the light of anticipated attack; in some circumstances, it may also reflect the person's desire to avoid the attack by not engaging in the behavior that presumably would stimulate the attack. Thus with a highly committed client, fore-warning him about possible attacks against his attitude/behavior

---

[1] A reactance theory analysis of this phenomenon would suggest that commitment has established the person's freedom to engage in the behavior and that the attack threatens this freedom. Increased attractiveness of and engagement in the behavior, and in other similar ones, would then be predicted by reactance theory.

would strengthen these attitudes/behaviors and reduce their suscept-ibility to attack.[2] For noncommitted clients, however, such fore-warning may have the adverse effect of decreasing the client's confidence in the desirable attitude/behavior and may create pressures for him to disavow the desirable attitudes or behaviors.

When the therapist is quite sure that the client will be exposed to attack on his new behaviors or beliefs, the therapist may feel that it is unrealistic, and thus perhaps necessarily nontherapeutic, not to warn even uncommitted clients of probable attack. Furthermore, the therapist would, of course, be concerned that the attack, expected or not, might be successful in influencing the client to make undesirable changes. These problems can be solved by having the client become committed to the behavior. By inducing commitment, by whatever method, forewarning becomes a positive strategy (increasing the strength of the desirable attitude/behavior) and the client's resistance in the face of actual attack is increased.

Conclusion

Although this discussion of Kiesler's model of commitment has been quite limited (see Kiesler, 1971, for a fuller presentation), it should have been sufficient to alert the clinician to the dual usefulness of commitment. Commitment can be used as part of dissonance strategies; however, it can also be used as part of strategies designed to strengthen behaviors that are consistent with existing attitudes. Therapy is often a behavior-change enterprise, but at times it is also a behavior-maintenance enterprise, particularly when the behavior to be maintained is the product of the therapeutic endeavor.

OBJECTIVE SELF AWARENESS

St. Augustine on his consideration of himself before conversion:

> But Thou, O Lord, . . . didst turn me towards myself, taking me from behind my back, where I had placed myself while unwilling to exercise self-scrutiny; and Thou didst set me face to face with myself, that I might

---

[2] It should be noted that this proposition is entirely consistent with dissonance principles. Earlier (p. 103), alerting the client to possible negative consequences was advocated for those clients who had committed themselves to counterattitudinal behavior. It has been found that such foreseen negative consequences increase dissonance and increase attitude change in the direction consistent with the behavior. Kiesler's discussion suggests that even under situations where dissonance would not apply, i.e., the behavior is consistent with the existing attitude, the desired attitude (in this case, the existing one) will be strengthened when a committed client foresees possible negative consequences to his behavior.

behold how foul I was, and how crooked and sordid, bespotted and
ulcerous. And I beheld and loathed myself; and whither to fly from myself
I discovered not. And if I sought to turn my gaze away from
myself . . . Thou again opposedst me unto myself, and thrustedst me
before my own eyes, that I might discover my iniquity, and hate it. I had
known it, but acted as though I knew it not, —winked at it, and forgot it.
(quoted in Kaplan, 1964)

St. Augustine is describing a very intense experience of self awareness. While, fortunately, not all considerations of the self are so
painful nor, indeed, so pathological, one's view of oneself has
traditionally been an important topic of psychological inquiry. Many
"self theorists" have formulated theories of personality and approaches to clinical practice based on their conceptions of self
awareness (see Wylie, 1968, and Hall & Lindzey, 1957, for reviews of
these conceptions). The theory of objective self awareness brings to
this traditional area of interest a provocative theoretical perspective
that should allow for both rigorous empirical examination and the
derivation of therapeutic strategies.

The Theory

The theory of objective self awareness postulates two, dichoto-
mous states of self awareness. It is hypothesized (Duval & Wicklund,
1972) that there are two different ways in which we can be aware of
ourselves: as a subject, "the feeling of being the source of forces
directed outward" (p. 3), and as an object, "when attention is
directed inward and the individual's consciousness is directed upon
himself" (p. 2). Subjective and objective self awareness are seen as
discontinuous, mutually exclusive states of consciousness that can,
however, alternate rapidly. Presumably, one is always *either* objectively or subjectively aware.

According to Duval and Wicklund, a person's state of self
awareness is determined by the stimuli in his environment. Subjective
self awareness is stimulated by activity in the environment. The
person engaged in action, by necessity, focuses his attention on the
environment and is aware of himself only as the source of his actions.
Objective self awareness is created by stimuli that lead the person to
focus on himself. There are two classes of such stimuli: inanimate
objects and other people. Inanimate objects that elicit objective self
awareness are those that remind the person "of his status as an object
in the world" (Duval & Wicklund, p. 7), such as cameras, tape
recordings of the person's own voice, and mirrors. Other people are
capable of eliciting self awareness when the person knows of their
attention. A person would *not* be stimulated to objective self
awareness in the presence of another person who was known *not* to

be attending (e.g., who was asleep). Thus, in terms of the Duval and Wicklund formulation, one takes oneself as an object when one is aware that another is taking oneself as an object.

During objective self awareness, it is postulated that the person becomes aware of discrepancies from internally held standards. Initially it was believed (Duval & Wicklund, 1972) that such discrepancies were always negative, that is, involving a failure to meet a standard. In his most recent theoretical statement, Wicklund (1975) has proposed that there should be a general tendency for discrepancies to be negative, but that a recent success experience can trigger awareness of a positive discrepancy, that is, exceeding one's standards. This positive discrepancy should, however, be relatively short-lived, given the tendency for people to readjust their aspirations to a higher level after a success.

With awareness of a negative discrepancy, the person should experience negative affect and should be motivated (1) to avoid being objectively self aware so as to avoid awareness of the discrepancy or (2) if he is unable to avoid the state of objective self awareness, to reduce the discrepancy. Given a positive discrepancy, the person should experience positive affect and may be motivated to remain in the state of objective self awareness and maintain the discrepancy.[3]

The quote from St. Augustine represents an extreme case of objective self awareness. St. Augustine is describing how he examined himself, took himself as an object, "exercise[d] self-scrutiny." Throughout the passage, there is a repeated concern with *looking* at oneself: "face to face with myself," "turn my gaze away from myself," "thrustedst me before my own eyes," and "winked at it." This observation of himself was apparently brought on by his awareness of God's awareness of him. St. Augustine's state of objective self awareness was obviously one of severe negative discrepancy. He felt his self-examination revealed himself to be a terrible person. He "sought to turn [his] gaze away from [himself]," but found this was not possible. As we know, he never did manage to avoid this state of objective self awareness, but ended up, instead, reducing the negative discrepancy by converting to Christianity.

In a state of subjective self awareness, the person is not aware of the discrepancies between his standards and his performance. His focus would be on the environment and on the effects of his actions. Thus far there has been little theoretical work on the motivational aspects of subjective self awareness. At present, subjective self

---

[3]The latter statement concerning motivation has not been explicitly hypothesized by either Duval and Wicklund (1972) or Wicklund (1975), but would certainly appear to be a logical possibility.

awareness stands primarily as an alternative to objective self awareness, an alternative that becomes attractive when the state of objective self awareness is unattractive. One way to avoid being objectively self aware would be to engage in vigorous physical activity in an attempt to become subjectively self aware.

Clinical Applications

Self-evaluation. The most direct application of objective self awareness to the clinical setting concerns the effect of self awareness on the person's feelings about himself. Ickes, Wicklund, and Ferris (1973) found that people who heard their own tape-recorded voice gave themselves lower self-esteem ratings than did subjects who heard another person's voice. In addition, it was found that self-esteem was enhanced by the presence of a mirror and positive feedback, while it was diminished by the presence of a mirror and negative feedback. Thus in the absence of feedback concerning the self, objective self awareness appears to decrease self-esteem. In the presence of feedback, however, objective self awareness tends to act as an intensifying factor: increasing positive self-regard after positive feedback and decreasing positive self-regard after negative feedback.

These findings may be exceedingly interesting for the clinical setting. It is likely that psychotherapy, at least in its initial stages, has the effect of making people objectively self aware: they are asked to focus on themselves, their feelings, their problems, and they sit in a small room with another person who directs his attention exclusively on them. This setting, then, may in and of itself evoke objective self awareness and, in the absence of feedback, a negative evaluation. In this way, one of the main initial effects of psychotherapy may be make to the person feel worse about himself.

To reduce this trend, the therapist has two alternatives. First, he can give the client direct positive feedback—complimenting the client, saying good things about him, pointing out his abilities, and so on. Such feedback should lead to significantly increased self-esteem. The second approach would be to help the client avoid objective self awareness by having him engage in physical activity, thus promoting subjective self awareness. It is interesting that this suggestion is consistent with the behavior of many therapists who work with adolescents and children. Such therapists frequently conduct therapy outside the confines of the office—in the playground, in "activity groups," on walks. The theory of objective self awareness would predict that such changes in setting should reduce objective self awareness, stimulate subjective self awareness, and elicit more positive self-regard. This strategy should apply to all clients, not only to age groups that may be made most uncomfortable by "self-consciousness."

In addition, the finding by Ickes et al. that negative feedback and exposure to stimuli eliciting objective self awareness result in decreased self-esteem suggests that criticism or negative feedback during therapy must be carefully administered. If the therapy setting does, indeed, induce objective self awareness, the potential for extremely negative self-evaluation is great.

Avoidance. It was noted that if a person becomes aware of negative discrepancies during objective self awareness, he will be motivated to avoid the objective state. Duval, Wicklund, and Fine (in Duval & Wicklund, 1972), and Gibbons and Wicklund (in Wicklund, 1975) have found that subjects spend less time in the presence of objective self awareness stimuli (respectively, a mirror and a tape-recording of the subject's own voice) when they have received negative feedback.

Thus, if it is assumed that therapy can stimulate objective self awareness, then negative feedback received during therapy may well motivate clients to avoid therapy. Furthermore, if negative discrepancies are salient during objective self awareness unless positive feedback is provided, then even without negative feedback, clients may be motivated to avoid therapy as a means of avoiding the negative state it induces. Positive feedback to the client during therapy would mitigate these avoidance tendencies and might even produce tendencies to remain in therapy.[4]

Self-distraction. Liebling, Seiler, and Shaver (1974) found that smoking was increased by having subjects wait alone in a room with a mirror. Wicklund (1975) has suggested that this effect is due to subjects' trying to provide distractions for themselves in an attempt to avoid objective self awareness. Thus, if leaving therapy is not viable for the client, he may engage in self-distraction activities to reduce the discomfort stemming from awareness of negative discrepancies. Therapists should probably facilitate such self-distractions, since if they are unavailable, the client may engage in the more direct avoidance tactic of avoiding the therapeutic sessions.

---

[4] This suggestion may seem at odds with the suggestion in the dissonance chapter that clients need to expend effort in therapy and that justifications should be minimal. As general principles, the two suggestions do conflict. As specific strategies, however, the two can be combined. The therapist can deliver positive feedback on those aspects of the client's behavior that are not the focus of dissonance techniques. This feedback can help to maintain positive self-esteem and to reduce avoidance tendencies. On specific attitudes and behaviors that are the focus of dissonance techniques, however, the use of positive feedback should be governed by the principles enunciated earlier (see pp. 129–130).

Wicklund (1975) has proposed that this distraction behavior may account for the nervous habits frequently observed in people speaking in public. Certainly public speaking would be a condition of high objective self awareness: the audience is attending and probably evaluating and the speaker should be acutely aware of himself. By engaging in nervous habits such as smoking, pacing, arm-waving, and the like, the speaker may facilitate a reduction in objective self awareness and an increase in subjective self awareness. This change in state of awareness should be beneficial to the speaker in two ways. One, he should feel better about himself since he is not attending to negative discrepancies between his standards about performance and his actual performance and, two, his performance should improve since there is evidence that extreme states of objective self awareness can lead to performance decrements (Liebling & Shaver, 1973).

Thus, it may be helpful for clients with severe speech anxiety to know that increased physical movement (or smoking, or any other self-distraction behavior) may reduce objective self awareness, and this may reduce their anxiety and benefit their performance. Such clients could be instructed to try out this strategy by purposefully engaging in as much physical activity as possible while speaking.

Test validity. Wicklund (1975) reports an experiment by Pryor, Gibbons, and Wicklund that should be of interest to clinicians who use self-report measures in their assessment of clients. The investigators found that a simple, face-valid measure of sociability correlated more highly with overt social behavior when subjects filled out the sociability measure in the presence of a mirror. Wicklund suggests that during objective self awareness, people will be aware of discrepancies between their behavior and their self-reporting tendencies and should attempt to reduce this discrepancy by having their self-report more accurately reflect their behavior. The study by Pryor et al., while only a suggestive beginning, does support this reasoning and may indicate that assessment procedures would benefit from stimulating objective self awareness. Presumably, this benefit would only apply to assessment devices that require accuracy of self-report and are relatively face-valid, although it might be interesting to examine the effect of objective self awareness on more indirect measures such as projective tests.

Attribution. Since the state of objective self awareness indicates, by definition, a focus on the self and the state of subjective self awareness indicates, by definition, a focus away from the self, self-attributions should be affected by these states. Duval and Wicklund (1973) found that objective self awareness conditions increased attributions of responsibility to the self for both positive and negative events. Wicklund and Duval (in Duval & Wicklund,

1972) found that subjective self awareness (elicited by physical activity such as gripping a hand grip and rotating a turntable) decreased self-attributions of blame.

These findings indicate the general conditions under which one's sense of responsibility will be increased and those under which one's sense of responsibility will be decreased. They provide an explanatory device for attribution findings such as those of Storms, whose study (1973) was discussed in the chapter on attribution processes (see p. 182). In terms of objective self awareness, Storms's subjects who watched a video tape of themselves were made objectively self aware, and this led to increased attributions to the self.

Therapists wishing to utilize objective self awareness in relation to self-attributions can do so in a straightforward manner. If increased self-attributions of causality and responsilibity are desired, the client should be made objectively self aware. If decreased self-attributions are desired, the client should be made subjectively self aware. Since the latter state may be difficult to attain within traditional therapeutic settings, the therapist may have to rearrange the therapeutic setting so that physical activity is facilitated. It should be noted, however, that the goal of increased self-attributions may have its drawbacks. While relatively easy to obtain (through tape recordings, video tapes, mirrors, etc.), the state of objective self awareness may, as noted, lead to negative self-evaluations and avoidance tendencies and so should probably be used sparingly.

Aggression. Recall that it is hypothesized that objective self awareness makes the person more aware of discrepancies between standards and behavior and leads to attempts to reduce these discrepancies if avoidance is not possible. Two studies on the relationship between aggression and objective self awareness have illustrated this theoretical point quite vividly. Scheier, Fenigstein, and Buss (1974) found that subjects reduced aggression under conditions stimulating objective self awarenesss. This would be the expected result, assuming that most subjects view aggression as a "bad" thing and have standards prohibiting it. Carver (1974), however, showed that when subjects were given the standard that aggression was the correct behavior (in this case, they were instructed that a high level of electric shock would facilitate the victim's learning), objective self awareness increased aggression.

Thus, for therapists who consider using objective self awareness to assist clients with aggression problems, it is critical for the therapist to understand the client's standard on aggression. If the client views aggression as "wrong," objective self awareness should decrease aggression; if the client views aggression as "good," or at least as

"OK," objective self awareness should increase aggression. Indeed, for clients who view aggression as permissible and who correspondingly display too much aggression, the therapist may wish to teach the client how to avoid stimulating objective self awareness in potentially aggressive situations. This avoidance could be accomplished by having the client avoid stimuli such as mirrors, having him avoid being with other people or at least in front of a potential audience, and having him engage in (nonaggressive) physical activity.

Cognitive dissonance. Some readers may have been reminded of cognitive dissonance when statements about objective self awareness and discrepancy reduction were made. After all, discrepancy reduction between attitudes and behavior is exactly what the forced-compliance situation in dissonance theory is all about. This relationship has not escaped investigators in the field. Wicklund and Duval (1971) found that subjects under objective self awareness conditions changed their attitudes in the direction of the counter-attitudinal behavior more than subjects who were not under objective self awareness conditions. This general tendency for discrepancy reduction is important for the theory of objective self awareness, but due to Wicklund and Duval's failure to manipulate such variables as choice and justification, its meaning for dissonance theory is ambiguous. Insko, Worchel, Songer, and Arnold (1973) did conduct a study focusing more clearly on dissonance processes, and they found that under conditions of maximal dissonance (high choice and high effort), objective self awareness increased attitude change in the direction of the counterattitudinal behavior.

Thus, for therapists who wish to utilize dissonance strategies, it would appear that objective self awareness facilitates dissonance effects. However, this suggestion is made in the context of the possible overall negative effects of objective self awareness and the need to monitor such effects carefully.

Conclusion

Even for such a recent theory as that of objective self awareness, the present coverage has been far from exhaustive. Hopefully, however, this presentation has indicated to clinicians the potential of this theory for clinical work. Its usefulness should be twofold: it should allow for specific techniques to obtain specific effects, and it should help the clinician to explain certain general aspects of client behavior such as negative self-regard and avoidance of therapy.

Furthermore, the theory of objective self awareness is a particularly good example of the advantage of social psychological theorizing for clinical endeavors. Therapists and theorists (from Freud to Rogers) have discussed the self, but much of this discussion has been vague, speculative, and unamenable to empirical investigation. The theory of objective self awareness is stated and operationalized in such a way that empirical examination is facilitated. Clinicians utilizing this theory have the distinct advantage of working from principles that have been formulated clearly and tested empirically.

SELF-EXPRESSIVE DECISION-MAKING

R. D. Laing (1965) on the experience of schizophrenia:

> Despite the fear of losing her self, all her efforts to "recapture reality" involved not being her self.... She saw that her life had become a systematic attempt to destroy her own identity and to become nobody. She avoided everything whereby she could be specifically defined as an actual person. (pp. 153, 156)

Eric Hoffer (1951) on the fanatical style of life:

> We cannot be sure that we have something worth living for unless we are ready to die for it. (p. 24)

The theories presented thus far have ranged from well-established theoretical perspectives such as that of dissonance theory to more recently developed theories such as that of objective self awareness. While this range correlates highly with the amount of empirical literature available, the older theories having a larger literature than the newer ones, all the theories discussed have substantial empirical support. This empirical support has formed the basis for clinical application of the theories.

In this final theoretical section, a theory will be presented that is quite new and, as of the moment, has little empirical foundation. Thus we enter into a highly speculative realm. Accordingly, specific clinical applications will be offered sparingly. If empirical support of the present model is forthcoming, it should be possible to derive, with greater confidence, a greater number of clinical strategies. At the moment, it is hoped that this presentation will provide, at least, an example of how social psychological theories can be formulated in order to guide experimental investigation and, at most, a source of provocative ideas for the clinician to consider.

The Theory

How does a person tell other people what kind of person he is? This would seem a rather basic question for psychology, and yet there is surprisingly little information with which to answer it. In

1959, Goffman discussed this issue in his book *The Presentation of Self in Everyday Life,* but Goffman's focus was limited primarily to nonverbal methods of self-presentation, and his observations, while cogent and interesting, were not supported by experimental validation. Other investigators have suggested a variety of goals of self-presentation (e.g., ingratiation—E. E. Jones, 1964; consistency—Tedeschi, Schlenker, & Bonoma, 1971; desirable outcomes in a mental institution—Braginsky, Braginsky, & Ring, 1969) as well as possible variables affecting self-presentation (interaction goals and personalistic feedback—Gergen, 1965), but there exists no general, theoretical formulation of the principles of self-presentation.

In addition, there is the question of how a person convinces himself that he is one sort of person rather than another. From both a Bemian (1967) and dissonance perspective, it would seem that our behavior influences how we think of ourselves. Again, however, there is no theoretical framework that seeks to explicate the determinants of self-convincing behavior nor the variety of effects such behavior might have.

The theory of self-expressive decision-making proposes that both of these processes, telling others who we are and convincing ourselves, can be brought under the same theoretical rubric. The basic assumption of the theory is that people "know," although they are not necessarily able to articulate, that freely made choices provide the best information to others and to ourselves about our individual dispositions. This assumption represents an extension of the E. E. Jones and K. E. Davis (1965) model of correspondent inference, which, as discussed earlier (pp. 148–150), postulates that observers can most confidently infer the dispositional traits of an actor when they see that actor make a free choice. This postulate has been confirmed in a number of studies with both adults and children (Costanzo, Grumet, & Brehm, 1974; E. E. Jones & Harris, 1967; E. E. Jones, Worchel, Goethals, & Grumet, 1971; Snyder & E. E. Jones, 1974).

As was noted in the earlier examination of the Jones and Davis model, the importance of choice seems to be twofold. First, one would hesitate to infer anything about the person who performs a behavior in accordance with the directions of someone who points a gun at him. The person has no free choice and, while we as observers may be able to infer something about the gunman by his directions, we can infer very little about the victim by his compliance, other than that he values his life. In addition, a free choice between decision alternatives allows the person to choose one alternative and reject another. In terms of information, we get two bits for the price of one. Thus, from both a psychological and an informational perspective, free choice among decision alternatives seem to be a potent source of information about the characteristics of the person.

Now, if observers use this strategy in assessing other people, it would seem reasonable that actors might use the same strategy in impressing observers. That is, if an actor desires to impress someone that he (the actor) is one type of person rather than another, the best arena for such an expression might be a freely made decision. Furthermore, it would seem that free choices would be most powerful in convincing ourselves about ourselves. If we make a decision because we're forced to, we can dismiss this information. If, however, we make a free decision, we can conclude that we decided what we did because we "wanted to," and we "wanted to" because that's the kind of person we are. This hypothesis about self-convincing is quite consistent with Bem's notions about "tacting" (see pp. 152–153) and with dissonance principles about the circumstances under which behaviors have implications for our attitudes (see pp. 91–96). Free decisions that serve the function of expressing ourselves to others or of convincing ourselves about ourselves will be termed self-expressive decisions.

Considering the universe of possible free decisions, only some decisions will be utilized for self-expression. Several dimensions would seem to be involved in predicting whether any one specific decision will be a self-expressive one. Some decisions appear clearly related to dispositions, while others appear virtually not at all related. Choosing whether or not to cheat on a test seems unequivocally related to a person's honesty, while choosing whether to eat a pear or an apple seems unrelated to any particular dispositional trait. The first type of decision, a self-relevant decision, thus may almost always be self-expressive, in that the person and observers would tend to infer something from the decision about the person's characteristics, in this case his honesty. The second decision, a self-irrelevant decision, may almost never be self-expressive.

Between these two extremes of clearly relevant and clearly irrelevant decisions, there will be a variety of actions (e.g., choosing a foreign rather than a domestic car, choosing which movie to see, etc.) that may or may not be used in self-expressive decision-making. These types of decisions can be used for self-expression if the person *desires* to convey information about himself to others and/or if he *desires* to obtain information about himself for himself. People who are thus motivated to express themselves should do so on self-relevant decisions, but they may also do so on decisions that are not so clearly related to personal characteristics. Thus in some cases, it will be the decision itself, its meaning, that determines whether it will be used for self-expression. In other cases, it will be the person's motivation that determines this.

From this framework, two predictions follow. (1) If a decision is perceived as relevant to a self-belief, the decision alternative that is consistent with the belief will be chosen. (2) If the person is motivated to express himself (to others or to himself), the decision alternative that is consistent with the desired inference or belief about the self will be chosen. The first prediction assumes that people have beliefs about themselves and, given an obviously self-relevant decision in the absence of any particular motivation, they will tend to choose the alternative that is consistent with their self-beliefs. When motivation enters the scene, however, things become more complicated. The person who is motivated to impress others or to convince himself that he is a certain type of person may be so motivated because he really is that way or because he wants others or himself to believe that he is that way. Thus, under motivated conditions, the person may choose alternatives consistent with a preexistent self-belief *or* with a desired view of himself.

There are some other important differences between the motivated self-expresser and the nonmotivated one. First, a motivated self-expresser may be particularly sensitive to the self-expressive potentials of decisions and may thus perceive self-expressive aspects in decisions that ordinarily would not be seen as particularly relevant to the self. Furthermore, such a person may tend to seek out opportunities to express himself. From either this change in perspective or this seeking out, the motivated person should make more self-expressive decisions than the nonmotivated person.

The hypothesis that the motivated person will make more self-expressive decisions than the nonmotivated person assumes that there are a large number of decisions available to the motivated person. But what if the number of potential self-expressive decisions is limited? Would the motivated person behave differently from the nonmotivated one on a limited number of self-expressive decisions? It would seem possible that even with a limited number of self-expressive decisions, the motivated person would express himself differently from the nonmotivated person. First, the motivated person can make more extreme self-expressive decisions. For example, the nonmotivated person who believes himself to be honest may pay $25.00 of unnecessary taxes, that he could avoid, just to express his honesty; the motivated person may pay $50.00.

Second, the motivated person can choose the decision alternatives that not only are consistent with his self-belief (or desired self-impression), but that also have nothing else to recommend them. E. E. Jones and K. E. Davis (1965) have noted that if a person chooses something that is universally desirable, we learn very little about him from that choice—"everybody" would choose that. But if a person chooses something that is not universally desirable, we can infer particular characteristics of the person from the choice. Similarly, if a person desires to express himself through a decision, he will be more impressive if his chosen alternative is, for example, hedonically negative but consistent with his existing or desired picture of himself. It is assumed that the person's willingness to tolerate unpleasant alternatives increases as a function of his motivation to express himself effectively. Ordinarily, people will probably compromise between expressing themselves and having a pleasant decision alternative; under conditions of high motivation, however, the person may find the self-expressive power of the decision alternative more important than its hedonic quality.

Having considered the consequences of motivated self-expression, we need to examine its determinants. In some cases where the aim is to impress others, the motivation may stem from the desire to obtain a specific goal such as a job or desirable living accommodations. Apart from such specific goals, however, there is a general category of events that should increase the person's motivation to express the sort of person he is. That general category consists of threats to a person's self-beliefs or self-presentations. Other people may tell us that we're not the kind of person we think we are or that we're not the person we want them to think we are. In either case, we should become motivated to express ourselves through decisions.

It is also possible for a person to threaten himself by acting in a manner that is inconsistent with established and important beliefs about the self. This too should lead to increased motivation to utilize self-expressive decision-making. It should be noted that of these two types of threats the most powerful should be when other people tell us we're not the person we think we are. Not only would this increase the motivation to convince others of the way we really are, but it may generate self-doubt and increase the motivation to convince ourselves. Thus, a person may be motivated to self-express to others, to self-express to himself, or to engage in self-expressive decision-making so as to both impress others and convince himself.

This discussion of the increase in motivation for self-expression as a result of threat has assumed that the threat is not directly related to prior self-expression. It has been assumed that the person has certain beliefs and desires about the self and is confronted with a threat to these beliefs or desires. In these cases, threat should act to increase motivation, and this increased motivation should be reflected in increased strength of self-expressive decision-making (i.e., increased frequency, extremity, or non-universal desirability of self-expressive decisions). But what if we consider the more complex situation where a person has already made a self-expressive decision and is then met with the response of other people? How would threat act in these cases?

There should be three possible responses of other people to a person's self-expressive decision. First, other people could respond with the appropriate inference. Under these conditions, there would be no threat, no increase in motivation, and thus no increased strength of self-expressive decision-making. For example, the person who makes what he considers to be a decision denoting his honest character and is termed "honest" by others has been successful in his self-expressive decision-making. This type of response to self-expressive decisions will be called congruent. There are, however, responses that other people could make that would not be consistent with the person's self-expression. This inconsistency could result from some peculiar characteristics of the other people that lead them to make noncongruent inferences. Or it could result from the person's inability to understand the inferences people usually make from specific decisions, and thus he makes decisions that fail to express the characteristics he wishes to impress upon others. In any case, it appears that two types of inconsistent response are possible.

The first would be an oppositional response. For example, the person makes what he considers to be a decision conveying his honesty and is termed "a crook" by others. The person confronted with such a response should feel that the other people involved have made an error, but that it is a correctable one. After all, the right dimension was involved, but the wrong inference was drawn. Given an oppositional response, the person should increase the strength of his self-expressive decision-making in an effort to correct the social environment's error.

The second type of inconsistent response presents more difficulties to the person. Suppose the person makes that "honest" decision and then is termed "artistic" by others. The observers' response is completely unrelated to the person's self-expressive decision. It too is an error, but it is not clear how the person could correct it. Under these circumstances, the person should decrease the strength of his self-expressive decision-making. The person should feel unable to figure out how to correct this type of uncorrelated error and, rather than run the risk of a multitude of inferential errors that may eventually threaten his own view of himself, he should make fewer and fewer self-expressive decisions, at least in this particular social environment.

These predictions of no change in strength of self-expressive decision-making after congruent responses, increased strength after oppositional responses, and decreased strength after uncorrelated responses have been confirmed in a study by myself and F. Bryant (in press). This experiment was conducted under the theoretical rubric we have been discussing. Subsequently, however, I have considered a detailed discussion of the relationship between reactance (J. W. Brehm, 1966) and learned helplessness (Seligman, 1974) by Wortman and J. W. Brehm (1975) and some revisions in these notions seem called for.

In their paper, Wortman and Brehm suggest that there is a curvilinear relationship between the amount of threat to a person's control over his environment and the person's response. When confronted with small or moderate amounts of such threats, the person may respond with restorative, reactance-like behavior designed to reestablish control. When, however, the person is confronted with extreme amounts of freedom-restricting behavior on the part of the social or asocial environment, the person may respond by "giving up" and appearing helpless as he fails to attempt to reassert control.

Applying this curvilinear model to the above propositions about self-expressive decision-making, it may be that both oppositional and uncorrelated responses to self-expressive decision-making lead to the same pattern by the self-expresser in subsequent decisions, but that the different types of threat are differentially powerful in moving the person along the continuum from reassertion to giving up. Thus, oppositional responses may also lead to giving up, decreasing the strength of self-expressive decisions, but only after the person has made many restorative efforts that have failed. Conversely, uncorrelated responses may initially trigger a restorative response, increased strength of self-expressive decisions, but after only a few restorative attempts the person may begin to decrease his self-expressive decision-making.

Thus it may be that the subsequent self-expressive behavior of a person who has made a self-expressive decision and is then confronted with an inconsistent response from other people will be determined by both the type of response from others (oppositional versus uncorrelated) and the number of such responses. It would seem attractive as a general proposition that inconsistent responses by others act as a threat and lead to increased motivation and increased strength of self-expressive decision-making. After repeated failures to change the inconsistent responses of others into consistent ones, motivation to self-express would be decreased with resultant decreased strength of self-expressive decision-making. This decrease in motivation might arise both because the situation is viewed as hopeless and because the person wishes to avoid cumulative inconsistent responses that might significantly threaten his own view of himself. Looking at the process of threat and self-expressive decision-making in this manner, the type of threat would be important as an indication of how likely it is that the person might be able to correct the inconsistent response. It would be assumed that the more likely it is that the response might be corrected, the more attempts the person will make to correct it before concluding that it cannot be corrected.

Possible Clinical Relevance

The theory of self-expressive decision-making takes a clear perspective on human functioning. It suggests that people are concerned with both their own and other people's understanding about what kind of people they are. This suggestion is, of course, not unusual from a clinical standpoint. Many clients, from adolescents to the middle-aged, have deep concerns about their own identity, and all of us at one time or another desire to let someone else know what kind of person we are.

Given this general perspective, the theory as it now stands focuses on possible errors in the self-expressive decision-making process. It is this focus on errors that makes the theory interesting, at least to its author, and that may give it clinical utility. If a person's self-expressive decision-making were to go well, we would probably take little notice of it. It is when this process goes badly that its manifestations are most noticeable.

For instance, a person could use inappropriate decisions, that is, self-irrelevant decisions, to express himself. This use could occur because the person is unaware of the inferences people usually make about such decisions or because the person has had self-beliefs threatened and is using every possible decision to express himself. Self-expression through self-irrelevant decisions could start a rather vicious circle. Other people would be unable to respond congruently to such self-expressive decision-making because they would not perceive the connection between the decision and a dispositional characteristic of the person. Met with inconsistent responses, the person would become more motivated and might make extreme decisions or decisions that are unpleasant except for their (to the person) self-expressive meaning. Social difficulties might ensue, since the person's behavior would look increasingly odd and, if the person continued to utilize inappropriate decisions, congruent responses would still not occur. After a while, the person might stop making self-expressive decisions in order to avoid further inconsistent responses from others. At this point, the person would be unable to solicit social confirmation of his identity and might become quite confused and uncertain about himself. As quoted in the beginning of this section, R. D. Laing (1965) has described this kind of failure to assert the self in an effort, usually futile, to protect oneself.

As another example, consider that the person may be relatively accurate in his choice of self-expressive decisions, but that he may reside in an environment that is deviant in its interpretations of such decisions. Again, we would have the above pattern of increased restorative efforts, continued difficulties in obtaining a congruent response, and eventual withdrawal from self-expression. Even when the social environment was not entirely deviant, the person's self-expressive decision-making might become impaired. This sort of environment might give just enough consistent responses to maintain the person's restorative efforts. The person would escape the social isolation of giving up on self-expressive decision-making, but as a function of his highly motivated state, he might utilize inappropriate decisions, be very extreme in his decisions, and choose hedonically negative alternatives. All of these behaviors would result in his appearing deviant, probably cause him considerable social difficulties, and leave him continually anxious about who he is and who other people think he is. Perhaps Eric Hoffer's "true believer" (1951), who can find certainty only in extremity, can be viewed as an example of someone caught in this self-expressive trap.

These examples are composites, drawn for dramatizing the problems that might result from difficulties in the process of self-expressive decision-making. Clients might show a full composite or they might show only bits and pieces. Whatever the exact specifications of client behavior, certain therapeutic principles seem to be implied.

There are three primary sources of error that need to be considered. First, the person may lack adequate information. Any given person may assume that any given decision conveys a specific disposition on his part, when, in fact, other people do not see it that way. They may make a different dispositional attribution from the decision or no dispositional attribution at all (i.e., making a situational or entity attribution in the terms of the attribution theories). In this case, the helpful approach would be quite simple and would consist of providing normative information about the relationship between specific decisions and the specific dispositions they convey. Such informational problems may be especially likely to occur when people are interacting within an unfamiliar cultural situation.

The second source of error in the self-expressive decision-making process may reside in particular other people. The client may be making perfectly reasonable and accurate self-expressive decisions, but the other people with whom he interacts most frequently, or who are most important to him, may make peculiar inferences from his behavior. In this case, possible alternatives consist of persuading the client to become involved with people who make more congruent inferences, helping him to expect and tolerate and not be much affected by peculiar responses, and/or helping the other people of concern learn to make more congruent inferences about the client from his self-expressive decisions.

The third source of error is undoubtedly the most complex. The client may himself be confused as to what kind of person he is and may be making erratic and confusing self-expressive decisions. He may be saying to himself and others that he is one type of person at one time and another type of person at another time. This may bewilder other people, may make it impossible for them to socially confirm any set of characteristics for the client, and may thus increase the client's personal confusion. There is no easy answer to such a problem. The client needs to sort out the various views of himself that he has and to begin, at least tentatively, to make his self-expressive decisions from some coherent set of self-beliefs. This may be quite difficult and take considerable time and effort on the part of both the client and the therapist.

What may take less time and be comforting, although not "curative" in and of itself, is for the therapist to point out to the client that his confusion is the source of others people's confusion. This could be demonstrated by having the client engage in some self-expressive decision-making designed to convey a specific disposition to others. He need not actually believe himself to be this way; it would be important simply for him to discover that if his self-expressive decision-making is clear and unambiguous, his self-beliefs as presented will be confirmed by others. This does not, of course, solve the problem of the client's settling on who he is, but it does indicate to the client that when he's ready, he can get others to think of him the way he thinks of himself.

Conclusion

Many other clinical situations could be described to which the theory of self-expressive decision-making would be relevant. This seems inappropriate, however, in light of the highly speculative nature of such suggestions at this time. Much research is needed on the basic propositions of the theory and their possible application to clinical endeavors. Hopefully, the present discussion will stimulate continued theoretical development and refinement and, most critically, some of the needed research.

SUMMARY

This chapter has briefly examined three social psychological theories. In the presentation of the theory of commitment, the usefulness of commitment for therapeutic strategies of behavior/ attitude maintenance was emphasized. Commitment was shown to increase the resistance to change of already existing attitudes and attitudinally consistent behaviors. It also was found to interact with attempts at counterattitudinal persuasion such that the likelihood of attitudinally consistent behavior was increased. Finally, the relationship between commitment and forewarning of possible negative consequences to the committed behavior was discussed.

The second section of this chapter dealt with the theory of objective self awareness. The theory was applied to various topics of clinical interest, including clients' self-evaluations, tendencies to avoid therapy, self-distracting behavior, assessment validity, and aggression. Aspects of the theory that pertain to other previously discussed theories in social psychology, such as cognitive dissonance and attribution, were also considered.

The final section presented the theory of self-expressive decision-making. The theory assumes that people are concerned with expressing themselves to other people and to themselves. Possible difficulties in the self-expressive process were explored and possible therapeutic approaches to such difficulties were offered.

SUGGESTED SOURCES

Commitment

Kiesler, C. A. *The psychology of commitment.* New York: Academic Press, 1971.

Objective Self Awareness

Duval, S., & Wicklund, R. A. *A theory of objective self awareness.* New York: Academic Press, 1972.

Wicklund, R. A. Objective self awareness. In L. Berkowitz (Ed.), *Advances in experimental social psychology* (Vol. 9). New York: Academic Press, 1975.

Self-Expressive Decision-Making

At present, discussion in this chapter represents the fullest explication of the theory of self-expressive decision-making in print.

The reader is referred to S. S. Brehm and F. Bryant (in press) to examine the present empirical support for the theory.

The following reference may be of interest to readers who wish to explore the relationship between amount of threat to control and restorative versus withdrawal responses.

Wortman, C., & Brehm, J. W. Responses to uncontrollable outcomes: An integration of reactance and the learned helplessness model. In L. Berkowitz (Ed.), *Advances in experimental social psychology* (Vol. 9). New York: Academic Press, 1975.

PART FIVE

CONCLUSION

CHAPTER
TWELVE

CONCLUSION

A variety of social psychological theories and applications of these theories and their related findings to the practice of clinical psychology have now been presented. Many general issues have been raised by the preceding discussions, general issues that by and large have been deferred for examination until this concluding chapter. Now that we have established a context of specific theory and specific application, explication of at least some of these general issues appears appropriate.

SOCIAL ENGINEERING

Implicit throughout this book has been a particular view of the clinical enterprise. In this section, an effort will be made to be more explicit about this view and its general implications for clinical work.

Clinical psychology is, of course, seen as many different things by many different people. To some, its purpose and meaning are encompassed by the word "testing." To others, it is exemplified by therapeutic practices such as a "nondirective" therapist's allowing a person's "free" and "natural" self-expression to develop. To still others, it's the guy with the M&M's, or more ominously, the clockwork-orange type ready to subjugate the individual to the mores of the "establishment."

This book is based on the belief that clinical psychology is a form of social engineering. The psychologist is viewed as an engineer to whom people come with certain problems that they are unable to remedy on their own. From this perspective, the psychologist's job is to find out what the nature and specifications of the "problem" are, to devise a method of solving the problem, and to implement this solution. Methods for problem-solving are deemed to flow from the understanding of basic theoretical principles concerning psychological processes.

Thus, the first step for the psychologist-as-social-engineer is to assess the nature of the client's difficulty. A wide variety of assessment devices are available for these purposes, including behavioral observation, client report, and personality inventories. Whatever assessment technique is used, the criterion for its continued use should be its ability to provide information that helps the clinician formulate a therapeutic strategy.

The next step in the social engineering approach to clinical work is for the clinician to devise a therapeutic strategy designed to remedy or at least ameliorate the now defined problem. This is where the knowledge of theory becomes so important. Ideally, the therapist-cum-social-engineer should be familiar with a wide range of theoretical perspectives and able to apply them—"tailor them"—to the specific client's specific problem. Obviously some therapists will know some theories better than others, and this restriction in knowledge may well restrict their clinical activity to certain kinds of clients with certain kinds of problems. Specialization should be perfectly functional as long as the therapist recognizes that he is specialized and does not assume that a limited repertoire is capable of being used with an unlimited variety of clients and problems.

Implementing a proposed solution may, of course, uncover unexpected difficulties. Some solutions won't work with some clients. Some solutions that looked great on paper, fail miserably in reality. Some solutions create unexpected effects that are not desirable. The therapist-engineer must be prepared to deal with such events and to literally "go back to the drawing board." Again, grounding in theory is critical. The therapist's theoretical analysis of the problem and its solution may be accurate, but his operationalization of the solution may fail. In this case, a good understanding of the theory can allow for changes in the operations without necessarily changing the analysis of the problem; almost all the theoretical conceptual variables that have been discussed in this book have multiple ways of being put into practice. On the other hand, if it is the analysis that is in error and not the implementation, the therapist with a good theoretical background should be able to reanalyze the situation in light of the new variables that he may have discovered. Again, almost all the theories discussed in this book allow for the complex interplay of several variables. In statistical terms, life is not always a main effect, it can be full of interactions.

Finally, the therapist-engineer should be prepared and equipped to evaluate his effectiveness. This is a somewhat complicated point and should be made clear. Evaluation in this sense does not mean investigation of the specific causes of specific effects. For example, the therapist-engineer may build several theoretical variables into his therapeutic strategy, such as a dissonance strategy *and* an attribution strategy. It is not up to the therapist to conduct research to determine which of the two theories best accounts for his results. It *is* the responsibility of the therapist to keep track of the client's behavior as a function of his (the therapist's) therapeutic endeavors. If the client's behavior does not change in the desired direction, it is necessary to go back to the drawing board. If desired change does occur, the therapist may wish to switch from change-inducing strategies to change-maintenance strategies and/or to go on to work with other problems.

This view of the therapist as a social engineer shares some aspects of the perspectives taken by previous approaches to clinical psychology. The closest resemblance is between this view and that of behavior therapists. In both, the clinical enterprise is seen as an interplay between theory and individual application.

> Thus guided by a general principle, the therapist has to rely on improvisation and inventiveness as demanded by the clinical situation. (Davison & Neale, 1974, p. 512)

Indeed, most behavior therapists would probably endorse the notion of the therapist-as-social-engineer who works on assessment, analysis, implementation, and evaluation. The major difference between the view of behavior therapists and the present one is that this book has stressed principles derived from social psychology, while behavior therapists have traditionally relied on principles derived from experimental psychology, especially the work on animal and human learning. Therapists working from within a social psychological framework may, indeed, utilize many behavior therapy techniques. Typically, however, they would interpret the effects of such techniques in social psychological terms rather than in terms of learning theory.

The relationship between the proposed therapist-as-engineer model and the psychoanalytic model of clinical practice is not as close. These models do share an emphasis on theory as well as an emphasis on cognitive and emotional factors, both psychoanalysis and social psychology presuming there's something "in the black box." In addition, both models promote whatever behavior, or lack of it, on the part of the therapist that will help solve the client's problem, although from the social engineering perspective, problems will tend to be defined in more limited and behavioral terms than they would be defined by orthodox psychoanalysis, for example, excessive aggression toward others versus anal-expulsive stage fixation. The major difference between the psychoanalytic and the engineering model consists in their differential approaches to empirical evidence. For the psychoanalyst, the most important evidence for his theory is clinical evidence, specific data from case studies. For the engineer, the most important evidence for his theory is evidence obtained in basic research that in large part takes place in the laboratory. In terms of evidence for their theory's clinical utility, both the psychoanalyst and the social engineer would emphasize clinical data, although the social engineer would require more experimental procedures than are used in the case study method, which is acceptable to and preferred by the psychoanalyst.

Finally, we might consider the relationship between the engineering model and the growth-oriented or humanistic model espoused by such theorists as Rogers, May, Perls, and Maslow. The hallmark of the varying humanistic approaches lies in their emphasis on the client's spontaneous growth and experience. This, of course, is radically different from the planned and calculated approach to therapy that has been advocated in this book. Depending on one's perspective, this difference can be sharpened or blurred. Certainly, the therapist-engineer needs to take into account specific, individual characteristics of his client; the need for individual "tailoring" has been stressed repeatedly. A planned approach to therapy does not mean treating all clients the same; it strongly emphasizes the need to fit the therapy to the client. Moreover, the therapist-engineer would not reject any of the techniques used by humanistic psychologists. He'll use whatever technique works with whatever client, though he may understand its working in theoretical terms that differ from those employed by the technique's inventor.

But these similarities should not obscure the fundamental difference between the humanistic and social engineering models: the former emphasizes spontaneous experience; the latter emphasizes planned problem-solving. Perhaps the best example of this difference concerns the client's sense of volition. The humanistic model stresses the need for the client *to be free* because this is morally right, philosophically sound, and consistent with the basic nature of man. The social engineer using dissonance, reactance, or attribution theories would stress the need for the client *to feel free* because his specific therapeutic interventions could only be successful given this sense of volition.

Thus, to return to the previous examples of how clinical psychology may be viewed, the psychologist-as-social-engineer can partake of all three. He can utilize tests for assessment of the problem at hand, he can engage in what appears to be "nondirective therapy," and he can use M&M's. The exact techniques that one utilizes do not define the essence of the social engineering approach. This definition is provided by an orientation that views the therapist's job as specifying problems, analyzing them in accordance with a set of theoretical premises, and proceeding to implement interventions designed to remedy or ameliorate these problems.

ETHICAL ISSUES

The therapist-as-engineer shares another similarity with the earlier examples of possible views of clinical psychology. He is confronted with the same clockwork-orange ethical dilemmas as the behavior therapist. Who decides what is "desirable" or "therapeutic"? Doesn't the therapist risk imposing his values and beliefs on the client? In order to answer these questions, a number of factors need to be carefully considered.

First, let us focus on clients who come to therapy voluntarily. Most people who come to therapy come because they have problems they have been unable to cope with satisfactorily on their own. Therapy is expensive, time-consuming, and still somewhat stigmatized; for many people, coming to therapy is the last resort in the face of severe difficulties. The exception to this general rule is found in people who seek growth experiences or enriched understanding of themselves; for these people, they desire a general revitalization that does not seek to solve immediate problems but that may, if successful, prevent problems from developing later.

It should be said at once that a social engineering approach to the latter type of client is inappropriate. Approaches emphasizing growth, spontaneity, or insight are probably much more appropriate for such desires for enrichment. The author would add to this that teaching these people general psychological principles in order to enlarge their understanding of themselves and others would also be appropriate. The therapeutic goal with such clients would be to provide them with information and experiences for them to use as they desire. Attempts to influence should be minimal, and ethical dilemmas should, accordingly, be infrequent.

On the other hand, it would seem that for the former type of client, people with problems that propel them into therapy to seek relief, growth-oriented and insight therapies are inappropriate. These people have a problem and want something done. Now, it may turn out that their problem can be remedied by providing them with objective information. In this case, the information is simply provided, no particular influence attempts are initiated, and ethical issues are virtually nonexistent. In many cases, however, providing information will not be sufficient. The therapist may decide after assessing the client's situation that new feelings, new attitudes, or new behaviors are necessary and that the client will not develop these on his own. Thus, influence by the therapist would be called for if the problem is to be solved, and ethical dilemmas begin to appear in abundance.

The most satisfying way of dealing with the ethical issues of control and influence is to negotiate a contract with the client. In making up the contract, the therapist and the client discuss the goals of therapy. Both can suggest goals and both can argue against certain goals, but the final contract should be a joint product. During the discussion of the contract, the therapist should refrain from calculated influence attempts and simply state his opinions and beliefs freely and openly. Acceptance of the contract is based on the client's agreeing that the proposed goals are desirable for him, the therapist's believing that he has the necessary skills to help the client achieve the proposed goals, and the therapist's feeling comfortable about working with the client on these goals. If the client finds the goals proposed unacceptable, no contract can be negotiated. If the therapist believes himself unable to help the client achieve these goals, he should recommend another therapist to the client. And, finally, if the therapist feels uncomfortable with the goals desired by the client, he should state this and again refer the client elsewhere. Contracts that are successfully negotiated should be as specific as possible about the behaviors, feelings, attitudes, and so forth that constitute the therapeutic goal.

Once a contract has been accepted by both therapist and client, the issue of who decides what is "desirable" has been settled. The client has decided this. There remain, however, other ethical difficulties concerning the procedures to be used to obtain the contractual goals. In this regard, behavior therapists who use learning principles appear to have a certain ethical edge over the therapist who uses social psychology. Most learning techniques are not harmed by and, indeed, may benefit from the client's knowing exactly what will happen. One does not keep it a secret from the client that, for example, relaxation is to be paired with exposure to anxiety-producing stimuli in order to desensitize the client. On the other hand, explaining cognitive dissonance principles prior to utilizing dissonance in creating new attitudes would probably reduce, if not completely destroy, the effectiveness of the dissonance strategy.

Thus, it would seem that behavior therapists can obtain prior consent for both the therapeutic goals and the techniques utilized to achieve these goals, while therapists relying on social psychological techniques can obtain prior consent only for the goals.

This distinction suggests that if nondeceptive techniques can be utilized effectively, they are to be preferred over techniques that require a certain amount of deception in order for them to work. This seems straightforward and yet, even with this distinction, there are complications. Suppose, for instance, that a therapist accepted dissonance and attribution notions that minimal reward is most effective. Such a therapist could reveal to a client that he is going to utilize rewards in order to "reinforce" the client's behavior and to increase this behavior in accordance with the client's stated desire in the therapeutic contract. But does this therapist also note that he will use *minimal* rewards because they are most effective? Stating this could arouse reactance and might hinder the reward program's effectiveness.

Furthermore, even if the therapist does not accept social psychological principles and believes himself to be totally nondeceptive, is the "prior consent" he obtains truly "informed"? How much knowledge, for example, of the principles of learning does the client need to have to grant informed consent? Does the therapist need to show the client all the literature on the principles involved and on the techniques and then have the client choose whether or not to let the therapist utilize the technique? Such complications are, of course, greatest when the therapist believes that *only* a relatively deceptive technique will be effective. Here the ethical dilemma is most crucial: which is more "unethical," to deceive a client or to refuse to utilize techniques that will alleviate his problem?

My personal opinion is that truly informed consent is virtually impossible to obtain. If one believes that truly informed consent is necessary, then psychologists will probably be limited to working with other psychologists, just as physicians would be limited to working with other physicians (and presumably only those who shared their speciality area), and just as auto mechanics would only repair the cars of other auto mechanics. The reason we pay "experts" for their "expertise" is precisely that we are *not* experts. Given a lack of expertise, one cannot give truly informed prior consent.

Based on these assumptions, the author would opt for using whatever therapeutic techniques, deceptive or not, that would be most effective in meeting the goals of the contract. The client should, of course, be informed of this decision. Therapists can tell their clients that they will be as open and honest with them as possible, but that from time to time they will use their "expertise" in ways that clients might not understand. It can also be stated that one important aspect of the therapeutic endeavor consists of the therapist using his trained judgment to make decisions about how to help the client achieve his goals. Most clients will probably not find this at all disconcerting; after all, it is just that expertise and trained judgment for which they are paying.

This reliance on expert knowledge and trained judgment makes the training clinical psychologists receive very important. A discussion of training as it would apply to the social engineering model is given below. Peer review would also be important in this orientation to clinical practice. If clients cannot give informed prior consent, then informed inspection of a therapist's work by other experts in his field becomes critical. Some of these issues will be discussed in the section below on therapist accountability.

The last topic in the present section is undoubtedly the most difficult. Thus far we have restricted the discussion to clients who come voluntarily for therapy. What about those who do not come voluntarily? What about children brought by their parents, psychotic patients committed by their families or official agencies, prisoners in prisons? Now we are truly in clockwork-orange territory.

The first efforts in such situations should be to try to find areas of mutual agreement that can be put into a therapeutic contract. The therapist will have to use his judgment about whether the client is agreeing freely to the contract stipulations or is being coerced by others into agreeing. If some areas of true agreement can be mapped out, therapy will proceed as with more voluntary clients.

But what about clients who do not desire any kind of therapy? One may be able to help such clients by helping those around them. Children may be unwilling, but their parents may consent to therapy. In therapy, the parents can negotiate a contract concerning their desire to get along better with the child, and the therapist can work to obtain new parental behavior, attitudes, feelings, and so forth that would facilitate this. The same approach could be taken with families of psychotics and staffs of institutions. Through this kind of approach, the client might indeed be influenced without his consent, but this influence would not be "therapy" for him; it would be the influence from others that occurs daily in any case.

But let's take the most difficult situation. What if the client and the therapist cannot carve out a mutually acceptable contract and the client's behavior continues unaffected despite work with significant others in his environment? Should direct influence attempts be initiated? Does a child have the right to refuse his parents' desires that his behavior be changed? Does a person who is psychotic have the right to remain psychotic? Does a prisoner have the right to refuse to be rehabilitated? What are the rights of parents and society? These are exceedingly difficult questions that need to be discussed and examined by members of the society, both "experts" and laymen. I do not presume to know the answers, but the questions need to be stated and debated. At present, clinicians who work with involuntary clients must confront these questions and devise their own answers, but these temporary, individual answers must occur in the context of a continuing debate within the profession and within the society.

ETHICAL ISSUES–THE OTHER SIDE

While there are critical ethical dilemmas arising out of a social engineering approach to clinical practice, there are also ethical problems associated with other approaches. First, it is "unethical" to provide the client with a therapy whose effectiveness either for the clinical technique itself or for the theoretical principles underlying the technique has been not proved. If a psychologist is going to function as a religious leader or philosopher rather than as a scientist, he should inform his clients of this. Some of his clients may be more enamored of scientific method than he is and wish a different kind of therapy and therapist.

Second, if the therapist's goal differs from the client's goal, the client should be aware of this. Some therapists, for example, may value "understanding" while their clients want a change in their behavior. To simply assume that understanding will lead to behavior change is not satisfactory; the client must be informed that the goal of therapy is understanding because that is what the therapist views as an appropriate goal. Having been informed, the client is free to work for understanding or to go elsewhere for behavior change.

Third, any kind of therapy runs the risk of imposing the therapist's values on the client, just as any kind of human interaction runs the risk of one person influencing the other. Therapists are especially likely to influence their clients, given the power position of the therapist vis-à-vis the client. After all, clients seek out and pay therapists, nor the other way around.

Indeed, in many ways a social engineering approach to clinical practice results in increased client freedom. Contracts are negotiated, options are discussed, and goals are mutually agreed upon. The engineer will have little difficulty explaining his orientation to clients. He is an expert whose job is to help the client obtain his (the client's) goals through the use of his (the therapist's) knowledge and skill as based on the best scientific information currently available. Most important, the therapist-engineer will be vividly aware of his potential to influence the client, since this influence forms part of his repertoire of therapeutic techniques. It can be argued that the most ethical clinician will be the one who is most aware of his influence on his clients. For the therapist-as-social-engineer, ethical dilemmas will not be hidden by philosophical or cultish assumptions, the dilemmas will be right there staring him in the face, which is right where they should be for any therapist.

THERAPIST ACCOUNTABILITY

Perhaps the greatest contribution that the therapist-as-social-engineer approach can make to clinical practice is to increase therapist accountability. Prior to the advent of behavior therapy, therapist accountability was abysmally low. If clients did not benefit from the therapist's interventions, it was the client's fault—he was "resisting" or "defending" or whatever. Since the goal was "personality change," therapists felt free to have therapy last for years and years. No time limits were set for therapeutic endeavors. In addition, therapeutic success meant whatever the therapist deemed it to mean, since no one could measure to anyone else's satisfaction that elusive goal of "personality change."

Behavior therapy brought about great changes in these procedures. Specified and thus measureable goals were set. Success or failure could be reliably judged. Very short therapies proved to be quite effective. And, critically, therapists began to assume more of the responsibility for therapeutic failures. This book supports these changes and, in fact, calls for more. Therapy should not be conducted in such a way that it is to the therapist's financial advantage for therapy to take a long time. Time-limited contracts should be set, with the therapist estimating the length of time therapy will take. If after this time, therapy has not been successful, the client should be reimbursed. Therapists should be paid for success, not failure. Of course, if success is to be the criterion for payment, then success must be clearly defined. Goals must be concrete, specific, and observable. I have little doubt that if therapists knew they would be paid only for documentable success, they would have no difficulty in defining specific therapeutic goals.

Beyond this revision in the contingency system for therapists, greater peer review is badly needed. Therapists must be accountable to their colleagues as well as to their clients. If professional records are kept of surgical operations, they can be kept of psychotherapy as well. These records should show the therapist's assessment of the problem, his interventions and the outcome of these interventions, and the amount of time the therapy took. Such records should be examined periodically by a peer review board and evaluated in terms of other clinicians' performance in the field.

Baseline expectations will need to be set such that clinicians will not be penalized for working with clients who require more time and occasion more failures. But this should not be terribly difficult. Most everyone would agree, for instance, that schizophrenic clients are more difficult to work with than clients with airplane phobias. The review boards in most cases will serve as a stimulus to clinicians to do the best job they can, but the boards should have the power to suspend clinicians who have an inordinate number of therapeutic failures or take an inordinate amount of clients' time and money.

The side benefits of increased professional responsibility might be enormous. Therapists might be more motivated to be effective, they might do a better job in keeping up with recent developments in the field as a method of increasing their effectiveness, they might strive for better assessment procedures to facilitate more adequate interventions, they might work harder at treatment evaluation in order to ensure their utilization of the most effective techniques, and research on diagnosis and prognosis might be greatly facilitated. Even without such side benefits, however, increased therapist accountability seems to be ethically imperative.

TRAINING

From a variety of standpoints, the social engineering approach to clinical practice is concerned with training. For the practicing clinician, three kinds of training experiences would seem vital. First, the clinician needs an adequate understanding of theoretical principles such as those of social psychological processes and/or human learning. Second, the clinician needs supervised experience in working with clients. Third, the clinician needs to be able to evaluate treatment programs. Most important, these three elements need to be tied together in a such way that the student being trained gains experience in translating theoretical principles into practical applications, actually implementing such applications and then evaluating the success or failure of his clinical procedures.

Note that this model of training does not mention the clinician's need to be able to conduct basic theoretical research. The omission of such a qualification is not accidental. After over a quarter of a century of the Boulder model of the clinician-cum-scientist-cum-teacher, it is possible to evaluate the effectiveness of this model; in general, it appears to have been a failure. Despite the vaunted combination approach, most clinicians don't do basic research, and most academicians don't do much clinical work. We have found that our profession is not composed of Supermen and Superwomen who can be all things at all times. All too often, clinical programs have turned out students who are neither clinicians, nor scientists, nor teachers, but are some undistinguished, ambivalent blend.

The elegance of a social engineering approach to clinical practice is that it doesn't require all things of all people. Some people will want to be clinicians. There should be good programs for them that emphasize the three elements of theoretical knowledge, supervised experience, and evaluation skills. Some research training is necessary but it should be the kind of research useful in clinical practice—that is, evaluation research. As for basic research, clinicians need not do it, but they should be able to critically evaluate the theoretical and empirical literature and use this literature as a base from which to derive therapeutic techniques. Indeed, the clinician who adopts the social engineering model will frequently be more informed than his academic colleagues. In academic life, people's interests tend to narrow. As a clinician, one should be broadly read and broadly informed.

On the other hand, some people will want to do basic research. They should be provided with programs designed to equip them to do this most effectively—that is, research-oriented doctoral programs. If their interests are in clinical phenomena, they will need clinical experience, but this can be gained primarily after the doctoral program. And then, of course, some people will want to do everything. There really are people, if only a few, who can be scientists, practitioners, and teachers. The social engineering model would not make it impossible for people to become true exemplars of the Boulder model, but it would emphasize that in order to fulfill the tripartite role, one must master two different (and full-time) programs: the clinical program and the research program.

There are, of course, many practical problems associated with this view of training. Would clinical students receive a Ph.D or some other degree? If "some other degree," would this handicap them in pursuing their profession—that is, would it result in lower pay and lower prestige? How could one ensure that clinical students are exposed to accurate presentations of the state of psychological knowledge rather than the *Reader's Digest* presentation so prevalent in psychiatry? All of these difficulties would have to be worked out, and one doesn't want to underestimate how long it would take or how hard it would be to do this.

The objective, however, of restructuring of clinical training should be clear and eminently worth the effort: we should be able to train good, competent clinicians. I would suggest that the training programs created in the image of the Boulder model have not obtained this objective and that training based on a social engineering approach might be more effective. Clinical training as envisioned from a social engineering perspective would not be a retreat to mindless technology, but a creative endeavor requiring students to use existing psychological theory in novel and ingenious ways within the framework of providing a service to other people. If we adopt a social engineering approach to clinical training, we will not be lowering our level of aspiration for our clinical students; we will be raising it.

THE ROLE OF BASIC RESEARCH

Perhaps because of the Boulder model and the irrelevance of much a present-day clinical training to clinical activity after graduation, basic research and the clinical enterprise have often seemed to be antithetical and conflicting enterprises. They do conflict, of course, if one is expected to be very good at both of them and it takes all one's time to be good at one. They also conflict if basic research training is imposed on people who will never use it. Within the social engineering model of therapy, however, they do not conflict.

This entire book has rested upon a critical assumption. It has presumed that practical application depends on theoretical understanding. In this view, basic research is absolutely necessary for clinical practice. We need carefully controlled investigations of theoretical relationships. We need the framework of theory in order to operate as clinicians. But the clinician does not have to do this research himself. He does, as noted above, have to keep himself informed about it. In order to build a bridge, one does not have to conduct basic research on the effects of stress and tension; one does, however, have to know the principles of stress and tension to be sure the bridge will stay up. The basic researcher, on the other hand, does not have to go out and build bridges in order to prove his value to society. His role is to seek theoretical understanding that may be useful in a variety of practical applications.

Thus, the social engineering model of clinical practice would see basic researchers and clinicians as existing in a productive, symbiotic relationship. One maps out general principles; the other applies them to the real world. One is not better than the other; they simply are involved in different enterprises.

CONCLUSION

It is very difficult to conclude a book that may have raised more questions that it has answered. Much of this book has been speculative and, toward the end, downright opinionated. Research is badly needed on the suggested applications of social psychological theory. The theories themselves need further refinement. The issues of ethics and training need to be examined and debated much more. The whole concept of the therapist as a social engineer needs careful consideration. But whatever the final resolution of any of these aspects of the book, it is hoped that the reader has been stimulated by this presentation. We can all profit from giving more thought to the premises assumed and the procedures utilized in clinical practice.

SUGGESTED SOURCE

The following book is highly recommended for an extended examination of the possible relationship between basic research and practical application. It deals primarily with industrial problems, rather than clinical ones, but the approach is consistent with the social engineering model advocated here.

Varella, J. A. *Psychological solutions to social problems.* New York: Academic Press, 1971.

REFERENCES

Adams, J. S. Toward an understanding of inequity. *Journal of Abnormal and Social Psychology,* 1963, *67,* 422–436.

Adams, J. S. Inequity in social exchange. In L. Berkowitz (Ed.), *Advances in experimental social psychology* (Vol. 2). New York: Academic Press, 1965.

Aderman, D., Brehm, S. S., & Katz, L. Empathic observation of an innocent victim: The just world revisited. *Journal of Personality and Social Psychology,* 1974, *29,* 342–347.

Adorno, T., Frenkel-Brunswik, E., Levinson, D. J., & Sanford, R. N. *The authoritarian personality.* New York: Harper, 1950.

Amsel, A. Frustration, persistence and regression. In H. D. Kimmel (Ed.), *Experimental psychopathology.* New York: Academic Press, 1971.

Andreoli, V., Worchel, S., & Folger, R. Implied threat to behavioral freedom. *Journal of Personality and Social Psychology,* 1974, *30,* 765–771.

Aronson, E. Dissonance theory: Progress and problems. In R. P. Abelson, E. Aronson, W. J. McGuire, T. M. Newcomb, M. J. Rosenberg, & P. H. Tannenbaum (Eds.), *Theories of cognitive consistency: A sourcebook.* Chicago: Rand McNally, 1968.

Aronson, E., & Carlsmith, J. M. Performance expectancy as a determinant of actual performance. *Journal of Abnormal and Social Psychology,* 1962, *65,* 178–182.

Aronson, E., & Carlsmith, J. M. Effect of severity of threat on the valuation of forbidden behavior. *Journal of Abnormal and Social Psychology,* 1963, *66,* 584–588.

Aronson, E., & Mettee, D. Dishonest behavior as a function of differential levels of induced self-esteem. *Journal of Personality and Social Psychology,* 1968, *9,* 121–127.

Aronson, E., & Mills, J. The effect of severity of initiation on liking for a group. *Journal of Abnormal and Social Psychology,* 1959, *59,* 177–181.

Aronson, E., Turner, J. A., & Carlsmith, J. M. Communicator credibility and communication discrepancy as determinants of opinion change. *Journal of Abnormal and Social Psychology,* 1963, *67,* 31–36.

Arrowood, A. J., Wood, L., & Ross, L. Dissonance, self-perception and the perception of others: A study in *cognitive* cognitive dissonance. *Journal of Experimental Social Psychology,* 1970, *6,* 304–315.

Bandler, R., Madaras, G., & Bem, D. Self-observation as a source of pain perception. *Journal of Personality and Social Psychology,* 1968, *9,* 205–209.

Bandura, A. *Principles of behavior modification.* New York: Holt, Rinehart and Winston, 1969.

Bandura, A., & Walters, R. H. *Social learning and personality development.* New York: Holt, Rinehart and Winston, 1963.

Barefoot, J., & Straub, R. Opportunity for information search and the effect of false heart-rate feedback. *Journal of Personality and Social Psychology,* 1971, *17,* 154–157.

Beck, A. T. *Depression: Clinical, experimental and theoretical aspects.* New York: Harper & Row, 1967.

Beckman, L. Effects of students' performance on teachers' and observers' attributions of causality. *Journal of Educational Psychology,* 1970, *61,* 76–82.

Beijk, J. Expectancy, performance and self-concept. *Acta Psychologia,* 1966, *25,* 381–388.

Bem, D. J. An experimental analysis of self-persuasion. *Journal of Experimental Social Psychology,* 1965, *1,* 199–218.

Bem, D. J. Self-perception: An alternative interpretation of cognitive dissonance phenomena. *Psychological Review,* 1967, *74,* 183–200.

Bem, D. J. The epistemological status of interpersonal simulation: A reply to Jones, Linder, Kiesler, Zanna and Brehm. *Journal of Experimental Social Psychology,* 1968, *4,* 270–274.

Bem, D. J. Self-perception theory. In L. Berkowitz (Ed.), *Advances in experimental social psychology* (Vol. 6). New York: Academic Press, 1972.

Bem, D. J., & McConnell, H. K. Testing the self-perception explanation of dissonance phenomena: On the saliency of pre-manipulation attitudes. *Journal of Personality and Social Psychology,* 1970, *14,* 23–31.

Bergin, A. The effect of dissonant persuasive communications upon changes in self-referring attitudes. *Journal of Personality,* 1962, *30,* 423–438.

Berkowitz, L. The judgmental process in personality functioning. *Psychological Review,* 1960, *67,* 130–142.

Berkowitz, L. *A survey of social psychology*. Hinsdale, Ill.: The Dryden Press, 1975.

Bettelheim, B., & Janowitz, M. *Dynamics of prejudice*. New York: Harper, 1950.

Bishop, F. V. The anal character: A rebel in the dissonance family. *Journal of Personality and Social Psychology*, 1967, *6*, 23–36.

Bochner, S., & Insko, C. A. Communication discrepancy, source credibility and opinion change. *Journal of Personality and Social Psychology*, 1966, *4*, 614–621.

Bogart, K., Loeb, A., & Rutman, I. Behavioral consequences of cognitive dissonance. Paper presented at the meeting of the Eastern Psychological Association, 1969.

Borkovec, T. D., & Glasgow, R. E. Boundary conditions of false heartrate feedback effects on avoidance behavior: A resolution of discrepant results. *Behavior Research and Therapy*, 1973, *11*, 171–177.

Bowers, K. An attributional analysis of operant conditioning: Paradoxical effects of reinforcement on the endurance of behavior change. Paper presented at the 79th annual meeting of the American Psychological Association, 1971.

Braginsky, B. M., Braginsky, D. D., & Ring, K. *Methods of madness*. New York: Holt, Rinehart and Winston, 1969.

Bramel, D. A dissonance theory approach to defensive projection. *Journal of Abnormal and Social Psychology*, 1962, *64*, 121–129.

Bramel, D. Selection of a target for defensive projection. *Journal of Abnormal and Social Psychology*, 1963, *66*, 318–324.

Brehm, J. W. Post-decision changes in the desirability of alternatives. *Journal of Abnormal and Social Psychology*, 1956, *52*, 384–389.

Brehm, J. W. Increasing dissonance by a *fait accompli*. *Journal of Abnormal and Social Psychology*, 1959, *58*, 379–382.

Brehm, J. W. Attitudinal consequences of commitment to unpleasant behavior. *Journal of Abnormal and Social Psychology*, 1960, *60*, 379–383.

Brehm, J. W. Motivational effects of cognitive dissonance. In M. R. Jones (Ed.), *Nebraska symposium on motivation*. Lincoln, Neb.: University of Nebraska Press, 1962.

Brehm, J. W. *A theory of psychological reactance*. New York: Academic Press, 1966.

Brehm, J. W., & Cohen, A. R. Choice and chance deprivation as determinants of cognitive dissonance. *Journal of Abnormal and Social Psychology*, 1959, *58*, 383–387. (a)

Brehm, J. W., & Cohen, A. R. Re-evaluation of choice alternatives as a function of their number and qualitative similarity. *Journal of Abnormal and Social Psychology*, 1959, *58*, 373–378. (b)

Brehm, J. W., & Cohen, A. R. *Explorations in cognitive dissonance.* New York: Wiley, 1962.

Brehm, J. W., & Cole, A. H. Effect of a favor which reduces freedom. *Journal of Personality and Social Psychology,* 1966, *3,* 420–426.

Brehm, J. W., & Jones, R. A. The effect on dissonance of surprise consequences. *Journal of Experimental Social Psychology,* 1970, *6,* 420–431.

Brehm, J. W., & Mann, M. The effect of importance of freedom and attraction to group members on influence produced by group pressure. *Journal of Personality and Social Psychology,* 1975, *31,* 816–824.

Brehm, J. W., & Rosen, E. Attractiveness of old alternatives when a new attractive alternative is introduced. *Journal of Personality and Social Psychology,* 1971, *20,* 261–266.

Brehm, J. W., & Sensenig, J. Social influence as a function of attempted and implied usurpation of choice. *Journal of Personality and Social Psychology,* 1966, *4,* 703–707.

Brehm, J. W., Stires, L. K., Sensenig, J., & Shaban, J. The attractiveness of an eliminated choice alternative. *Journal of Experimental Social Psychology,* 1966, *2,* 301–313.

Brehm, J. W., & Wicklund, R. A. Regret and dissonance reduction as a function of postdecision salience of dissonant information. *Journal of Personality and Social Psychology,* 1970, *14,* 1–7.

Brehm, M. L., Back, K. W., & Bogdonoff, M. D. A physiological effect of cognitive dissonance under stress and deprivation. *Journal of Abnormal and Social Psychology,* 1964, *69,* 303–310.

Brehm, S. S., & Bryant, F. Effects of feedback on self-expressive decision-making. *Journal of Personality,* in press.

Brock, T. C. Cognitive restructuring and attitude change. *Journal of Abnormal and Social Psychology,* 1962, *64,* 264–271.

Brock, T. C. Communicator-recipient similarity and decision change. *Journal of Personality and Social Psychology,* 1965, *1,* 650–654.

Brock, T. C. Relative efficacy of volition and justification in arousing dissonance. *Journal of Personality,* 1968, *36,* 49–66.

Brock, T. C., & Blackwood, J. E. Dissonance reduction, social comparison and modification of others' opinions. *Journal of Abnormal and Social Psychology,* 1962, *65,* 319–324.

Brock, T. C., & Buss, A. Dissonance, aggression and evaluation of pain. *Journal of Abnormal and Social Psychology,* 1962, *65,* 197–202.

Brock, T. C., & Buss, A. Effects of justification for aggression and communication with the victim on post-aggression dissonance. *Journal of Abnormal and Social Psychology,* 1964, *68,* 403–412.

Brock, T. C., Edelman, S., Edwards, D., & Schuck, J. Seven studies of performance expectancy as a determinant of actual performance. *Journal of Experimental Social Psychology,* 1965, *1,* 295–310.

Brock, T. C., & Grant, L. D. Dissonance, awareness and motivation. *Journal of Abnormal and Social Psychology,* 1963, *67,* 53–60.

Buss, A., & Brock, T. C. Repression and guilt in relation to aggression. *Journal of Abnormal and Social Psychology,* 1963, *66,* 345–350.

Calder, B. J., Ross, J., & Insko, C. A. Attitude change and attitude attribution: Effects of incentive, choice and consequences in the Festinger and Carlsmith paradigm. *Journal of Personality and Social Psychology,* 1973, *25,* 84–99.

Calder, B. J., & Staw, B. M. Interaction of intrinsic and extrinsic motivation: Some methodological notes. *Journal of Personality and Social Psychology,* 1975, *31,* 76–80.

Carlsmith, J. M., & Aronson, E. Some hedonic consequences of the confirmation and disconfirmation of expectancies. *Journal of Abnormal and Social Psychology,* 1963, *66,* 151–156.

Carlsmith, J. M., Collins, B. E., & Helmreich, R. L. Studies in forced compliance: I. The effect of pressure for compliance on attitude change produced by face-to-face role playing and anonymous essay writing. *Journal of Personality and Social Psychology,* 1966, *4,* 1–13.

Carson, R. C. *Interaction concepts of personality.* Chicago: Aldine, 1969.

Carver, C. S. Facilitation of physical aggression through objective self awareness. *Journal of Experimental Social Psychology,* 1974, *10,* 365–370.

Chaikin, A., & Darley, J. Victim or perpetrator? Defensive attribution of responsibility and the need for order and justice. *Journal of Personality and Social Psychology,* 1973, *25,* 268–275.

Chase, T. C. Attitude change in the advocate as a function of attitude change in the audience and being seen by the audience as sincere: A clarification of the effect of "reward" for counterattitudinal advocacy. Unpublished doctoral dissertation, University of Texas, 1970.   .

Cherulnik, P. D., & Citrin, M. M. Individual difference in psychological reactance: The interaction between locus of control and mode of elimination of freedom. *Journal of Personality and Social Psychology,* 1974, *29,* 398–404.

Christie, R., & Geis, F. L. *Studies in Machiavellianism.* New York: Academic Press, 1970.

Cialdini, R. B. Attitudinal advocacy in the verbal conditioner. *Journal of Personality and Social Psychology,* 1971, *17,* 350–358.

Cohen, A. R. Communication discrepancy and attitude change: A dissonance theory approach. *Journal of Personality,* 1959, *27,* 386–396.

Cohen, A. R. A dissonance analysis of the boomerang effect. *Journal of Personality,* 1962, *30,* 75–88.

Cohen, A. R., Brehm, J. W., & Fleming, W. H. Attitude change and justification for compliance. *Journal of Abnormal and Social Psychology,* 1958, *56,* 276–278.

Cohen, A. R., Greenbaum, C. W., & Mansson, H. H. Commitment to social deprivation and verbal conditioning. *Journal of Abnormal and Social Psychology,* 1963, *67,* 410–422.

Cohen, A. R., Terry, H. I., & Jones, C. B. Attitudinal effects of choice in exposure to counter-propaganda. *Journal of Abnormal and Social Psychology,* 1959, *58,* 388–391.

Collins, B. E., & Hoyt, M. F. Personal responsibility-for-consequences: An integration and extension of the "forced compliance" literature. *Journal of Experimental Social Psychology,* 1972, *8,* 558–593.

Conger, J. C., Conger, A. J., & Brehm, S. S. Fear level as a moderator of false feedback effects in snake phobics. *Journal of Consulting and Clinical Psychology,* in press.

Cooper, J. Personal responsibility and dissonance: The role of foreseen consequences. *Journal of Personality and Social Psychology,* 1971, *18,* 354–363.

Cooper, J., & Brehm, J. W. Prechoice awareness of relative deprivation as a determinant of cognitive dissonance. *Journal of Experimental Social Psychology,* 1971, *7,* 571–581.

Cooper, J., & Duncan, B. L. Cognitive dissonance as a function of self-esteem and logical inconsistency. *Journal of Personality,* 1971, *39,* 289–302.

Cooper, J., & Goethals, G. R. Unforeseen events and the elimination of cognitive dissonance. *Journal of Personality and Social Psychology,* 1974, *29,* 441–445.

Cooper, J., & Scalise, C. J. Dissonance produced by deviations from life styles: The interaction of Jungian typology and conformity. *Journal of Personality and Social Psychology,* 1974, *29,* 566–571.

Cooper, J., & Worchel, S. Role of undesired consequences in arousing cognitive dissonance. *Journal of Personality and Social Psychology,* 1970, *16,* 199–206.

Costanzo, P., Grumet, J., & Brehm, S. S. The effect of choice and source of constraint on children's attributions of preference. *Journal of Experimental Social Psychology,* 1974, *10,* 352–364.

Cottrell, N. Performance expectancy as a determinant of actual performance: A replication with a new design. *Journal of Personality and Social Psychology,* 1965, *2,* 685-691.

Crano, W. D., & Messé, L. A. When does dissonance fail? The time dimension in attitude measurement. *Journal of Personality,* 1970, *38,* 493-508.

Davis, K. E., & Jones, E. E. Changes in interpersonal perception as a means of reducing cognitive dissonance. *Journal of Abnormal and Social Psychology,* 1960, *61,* 402-410.

Davison, G. Differential relaxation and cognitive restructuring in therapy with a "paranoid schizophrenic" or "paranoid state." Paper presented at the 74th annual meeting of the American Psychological Association, 1966.

Davison, G., & Neale, J. M. *Abnormal psychology.* New York: Wiley, 1974.

Davison, G., & Valins, S. Maintenance of self-attributed and drug-attributed behavior change. *Journal of Personality and Social Psychology,* 1969, *11,* 25-33.

Deci, E. L. Effects of externally mediated rewards on intrinsic motivation. *Journal of Personality and Social Psychology,* 1971, *18,* 105-115.

Deci, E. L. Intrinsic motivation, extrinsic reinforcement and inequity. *Journal of Personality and Social Psychology,* 1972, *22,* 113-120.

Deci, E. L., Cascio, W. F., & Krusell, J. Cognitive evaluation theory and some comments on the Calder and Staw critique. *Journal of Personality and Social Psychology,* 1975, *31,* 81-85.

Dembroski, T. M., & Pennebaker, J. W. Reactions to severity and nature of threat among children of dissimilar socioeconomic levels. *Journal of Personality and Social Psychology,* 1975, *31,* 338-342.

DesLauriers, A. M., & Carlson, C. F. *Your child is asleep.* Homewood, Ill.: The Dorsey Press, 1969.

Deutsch, M., Krauss, R., & Rosenau, N. Dissonance or defensiveness? *Journal of Personality,* 1962, *30,* 16-28.

Dienstbier, R., & Munster, R. Cheating as a function of labeling natural arousal. *Journal of Personality and Social Psychology,* 1971, *17,* 208-213.

Duval, S., & Wicklund, R. A. *A theory of objective self-awareness.* New York: Academic Press, 1972.

Duval, S., & Wicklund, R. A. Effects of objective self awareness on attribution of causality. *Journal of Experimental Social Psychology,* 1973, *9,* 17-31.

Ellis, A. *Reason and emotion in psychotherapy.* New York: Lyle Stuart, 1962.

Epstein, R. The effect of commitment to social isolation on children's imitative behavior. *Journal of Personality and Social Psychology*, 1968, *9*, 90–95.

Fenichel, O. *The psychoanalytic theory of neurosis.* New York: Norton, 1945.

Festinger, L. *A theory of cognitive dissonance.* Stanford, Calif.: Stanford University Press, 1957.

Festinger, L. The psychological effects of insufficient reward. *American Psychologist*, 1961, *16*, 1–12.

Festinger, L. *Conflict, decision and dissonance.* Stanford, Calif.: Stanford University Press, 1964.

Festinger, L., & Bramel, D. The reactions of humans to cognitive dissonance. In A. Bachrach (Ed.), *The experimental foundations of clinical psychology.* New York: Basic Books, 1962.

Festinger, L., & Carlsmith, M. Cognitive consequences of forced compliance. *Journal of Abnormal and Social Psychology*, 1959, *58*, 203–210.

Festinger, L., Riecken, H. W., & Schachter, S. *When prophecy fails.* Minneapolis: University of Minnesota Press, 1956.

Firestone, I. Insulted and provoked: The effects of choice and provocation on hostility and aggression. Unpublished doctoral dissertation, New York University, 1966.

Fitch, G. Effects of self-esteem, perceived performance and choice on causal attributions. *Journal of Personality and Social Psychology*, 1970, *16*, 311–316.

Ford, D. H., & Urban, H. B. *Systems of psychotherapy.* New York: Wiley, 1963.

Frank, J. D. *Persuasion and healing* (Rev. ed.). Baltimore: The Johns Hopkins University Press, 1973.

Frankl, V. Paradoxical intention: A logotherapeutic technique. In V. Frankl (Ed.), *Psychotherapy and existentialism.* New York: Simon and Schuster, 1967.

Fraser, S. C., & Fuijitomi, I. Perceived prior compliance, psychological reactance and altruistic contributions. Paper presented at the 80th annual meeting of the American Psychological Association, 1972.

Freedman, J. L. Attitudinal effects of inadequate justification. *Journal of Personality*, 1963, *31*, 371–385.

Freedman, J. L. Long-term behavioral effects of cognitive dissonance. *Journal of Experimental Social Psychology*, 1965, *1*, 145–155.

Freedman, J., & Fraser, S. C. Compliance without pressure: The foot-in-the-door technique. *Journal of Personality and Social Psychology*, 1966, *4*, 195–202.

Freud, S. Analysis terminable and interminable (J. Riviere, trans.). *International Journal of Pyschoanalysis*, 1937, *18*, 373–405.

Freud, S. *Collected Papers* (Vol. III). London: Hogarth Press, 1946.

Fromm, E. *Escape from freedom*. New York: Farrar and Rinehart, 1941.

Gailon, A. K., & Watts, W. A. The time of measurement parameter in studies of dissonance reduction. *Journal of Personality*, 1967, *35*, 521–534.

Gaupp, L. A., Stern, R. M., & Galbraith, G. G. False heart-rate feedback and reciprocal inhibition by aversive relief in the treatment of snake avoidance behavior. *Behavior Therapy*, 1972, *3*, 7–20.

Gerard, H. B. Deviation, conformity and commitment. In I. D. Steiner & M. Fishbein (Eds.), *Current studies in social psychology*. New York: Holt, Rinehart and Winston, 1965.

Gerard, H. B. Choice difficulty, dissonance and the decision sequence. *Journal of Personality*, 1967, *35*, 91–108.

Gerard, H. B., & Matthewson, G. C. The effects of severity of initiation on liking for a group: A replication. *Journal of Experimental Social Psychology*, 1966, 2, 278–287.

Gergen, K. The effects of interaction goals and personalistic feedback on the presentation of self. *Journal of Personality and Social Psychology*, 1965, *1*, 413–424.

Girodo, M. Film-induced arousal, information search and the attribution process. *Journal of Personality and Social Psychology*, 1973, *25*, 357–360.

Glass, D. C. Changes in liking as a means of reducing cognitive discrepancies between self-esteem and aggression. *Journal of Personality*, 1964, *32*, 531–549.

Glass, D. C., Canavan, D., & Schiavo, S. Achievement motivation, dissonance and defensiveness. *Journal of Personality*, 1968, *36*, 474–492.

Godfrey, B. W., & Lowe, C. A. Devaluation of innocent victims: An attribution analysis within the just world paradigm. *Journal of Personality and Social Psychology*, 1975, *31*, 944–951.

Goethals, G. R. Consensus and modality in the attribution process: The role of similarity and information. *Journal of Personality and Social Psychology*, 1972, *21*, 84–92.

Goethals, G. R., & Cooper, J. Role of intention and postbehavioral consequence in the arousal of cognitive dissonance. *Journal of Personality and Social Psychology*, 1972, *23*, 293–301.

Goethals, G. R., & Nelson, R. E. Similarity in the influence process: The belief-value distinction. *Journal of Personality and Social Psychology,* 1973, *25,* 117–122.

Goffman, E. *The presentation of self in everyday life.* New York: Doubleday, 1959.

Goldstein, A. P., Heller, K., and Sechrest, L. B. *Psychotherapy and the psychology of behavior change.* New York: Wiley, 1966.

Goldstein, A. P., & Simonson, N. R. Social psychological approaches to psychotherapy research. In A. E. Bergin & S. L. Garfield (Eds.), *Handbook of psychotherapy and behavior change.* New York: Wiley, 1971.

Goodstadt, M. Helping and refusing to help: A test of balance and reactance theories. *Journal of Experimental Social Psychology,* 1971, *7,* 610–622.

Gordon, A., & Glass, D. C. Choice ambiguity, dissonance and defensiveness. *Journal of Personality,* 1970, *38,* 264–272.

Götz-Marchand, B., Götz, J., & Irle, M. Preference of dissonance reduction modes as a function of their order, familiarity and reversibility. *European Journal of Social Psychology,* 1974, *4,* 201–228.

Grabitz-Gniech, G. Some restrictive conditions for the occurrence of psychological reactance. *Journal of Personality and Social Psychology,* 1971, *19,* 188–196.

Green, D. Dissonance and self-perception analyses of "forced-compliance": When two theories make competing predictions. *Journal of Personality and Social Psychology,* 1974, *29,* 819–828.

Greenbaum, C. W. Effect of situational and personality variables on improvisation and attitude change. *Journal of Personality and Social Psychology,* 1966, *4,* 260–269.

Greenbaum, C. W., Cohn, A., & Krauss, R. M. Choice, negative information, and attractiveness of tasks. *Journal of Personality,* 1965, *33,* 46–59.

Grinker, J. The control of classical conditioning by cognitive manipulation. Unpublished doctoral dissertation, New York University, 1967.

Haak, N. Comments on the analytical situation. *International Journal of Psychoanalysis,* 1957, *38,* 183–195.

Haley, J. *Strategies of psychotherapy.* New York: Grune and Stratton, 1963.

Hall, C. S., & Lindzey, G. *Theories of personality.* New York: Wiley, 1957.

Hardyck, J. A., & Braden, M. Prophecy fails again. *Journal of Abnormal and Social Psychology,* 1962, *65,* 136–141.

Harvey, J., & Mills, J. Effect of a difficult opportunity to revoke a counterattitudinal action upon attitude change. *Journal of Personality and Social Psychology*, 1971, *18*, 201-209.

Harvey, O. J. Some situational and cognitive determinants of dissonance resolution. *Journal of Personality and Social Psychology*, 1965, *1*, 349-354.

Harvey, O. J., & Ware, R. Personality differences in dissonance resolution. *Journal of Personality and Social Psychology*, 1967, *7*, 227-230.

Hattem, J. V. A cognitive dissonance approach to psychotherapy. Unpublished manuscript. Los Angeles: Los Angeles County—University of Southern California Medical Center, Adult Psychiatric Outpatient Clinic, 1973.

Heider, F. Social perception and phenomenal causality. *Psychological Review*, 1944, *51*, 358-374.

Heider, F. *The psychology of interpersonal relations.* New York: Wiley, 1958.

Helmreich, R. L., & Collins, B. E. Studies in forced compliance: Commitment and magnitude of inducement to comply as determinants of opinion change. *Journal of Personality and Social Psychology*, 1968, *10*, 75-81.

Heslin, R., & Amo, M. F. A detailed test of the reinforcement-dissonance controversy in the counter-attitudinal advocacy situation. *Journal of Personality and Social Psychology*, 1972, *23*, 234-242.

Himmelfarb, S. Integration and attribution theories in personality impression formation. *Journal of Personality and Social Psychology*, 1972, *23*, 309-313.

Hoffer, E. *The true believer.* New York: Mentor, 1951.

Hokanson, J. E. The effects of frustration and anxiety on overt aggression. *Journal of Abnormal and Social Psychology*, 1961, *62*, 346-351.

Holmes, J. G., & Strickland, L. H. Choice freedom and confirmation of incentive expectancy as determinants of attitude change. *Journal of Personality and Social Psychology*, 1970, *14*, 39-45.

Horney, K. *New ways in psychoanalysis.* New York: Norton, 1939.

Hoyt, M. F., Henley, M. D., & Collins, B. E. Studies in forced compliance: The confluence of choice and consequences on attitude change. *Journal of Personality and Social Psychology*, 1972, *23*, 205-210.

Ickes, W. J., Wicklund, R. A., & Ferris, C. B. Objective self awareness and self esteem. *Journal of Experimental Social Psychology*, 1973, *9*, 202-209.

Insko, C. A., Worchel, S., Songer, E., & Arnold, S. E. Effort, objective self awareness, choice and dissonance. *Journal of Personality and Social Psychology,* 1973, *28,* 262–269.

Jellison, J. M., & Mills, J. Effect of public commitment upon opinions. *Journal of Experimental Social Psychology,* 1969, *5,* 340–346.

Jellison, J. M., Riskind, J., & Broll, L. Attribution of ability to others on skill and chance tasks as a function of level of risk. *Journal of Personality and Social Psychology,* 1972, *22,* 135–138.

Johnson, T. J., Feigenbaum, R., & Weiby, M. Some determinants and consequences of the teacher's perception of causation. *Journal of Educational Psychology,* 1964, *55,* 237–246.

Jones, E. E. *Ingratiation.* New York: Appleton-Century-Crofts, 1964.

Jones, E. E., & Davis, K. E. From acts to dispositions: The attribution process in person perception. In L. Berkowitz (Ed.), *Advances in experimental social psychology* (Vol. 2). New York: Academic Press, 1965.

Jones, E. E., Davis, K. E., & Gergen, K. J. Role playing variations and their informational value for person perception. *Journal of Abnormal and Social Psychology,* 1961, *63,* 302–310.

Jones, E. E., & Gerard, H. B. *Foundations of social psychology.* New York: Wiley, 1967.

Jones, E. E., & Harris, V. A. The attribution of attitudes. *Journal of Experimental Social Psychology,* 1967, *3,* 1–24.

Jones, E. E., & Nisbett, R. E. *The actor and the observer: Divergent perceptions of the causes of behavior.* Morristown, N. J.: General Learning Press, 1971.

Jones, E. E., Rock, L., Shaver, K., Goethals, G. R., & Ward, L. Pattern of performance and ability attribution: An unexpected primacy effect. *Journal of Personality and Social Psychology,* 1968, *10,* 317–340.

Jones, E. E., Worchel, S., Goethals, G. R., & Grumet, J. Prior expectancy and behavioral extremity as determinants of attitude attribution. *Journal of Experimental Social Psychology,* 1971, *7,* 59–80.

Jones, R. A. Volunteering to help: The effects of choice, dependence and anticipated dependence. *Journal of Personality and Social Psychology,* 1970, *14,* 121–129.

Jones, R. A., & Brehm, J. W. Attitudinal effects of communicator attractiveness when one chooses to listen. *Journal of Personality and Social Psychology,* 1967, *6,* 64–70.

Jones, R. A., & Brehm, J. W. Persuasiveness of one- and two-sided communications as a function of awareness there are two sides. *Journal of Experimental Social Psychology,* 1970, *6,* 47–56.

Jones, R. A., Linder, D. E., Kiesler, C. A., Zanna, M., & Brehm, J. W. Internal states or external stimuli: Observers' attitude judgments and the dissonance-theory-self-persuasion controversy. *Journal of Experimental Social Psychology,* 1968, *4,* 247-269.

Kanfer, F. H. Implications of conditioning techniques for interview therapy. *Journal of Counseling Psychology,* 1966, *13,* 171-177.

Kaplan, B. *The inner world of mental illness.* New York: Harper & Row, 1964.

Kelley, H. H. Attribution theory in social psychology. In D. Levine (Ed.), *Nebraska symposium on motivation.* Lincoln, Neb.: University of Nebraska Press, 1967.

Kelley, H. H. *Attribution in social interaction.* Morristown, N. J.: General Learning Press, 1971.

Kelley, H. H. *Causal schemata and the attribution process.* Morristown, N.J.: General Learning Press, 1972.

Kelley, H. H. The process of causal attribution. *American Psychologist,* 1973, *28,* 107-128.

Kelly, G. *The psychology of personal constructs* (Vols. 1 & 2). New York: Norton, 1955.

Kent, R. N., Wilson, G. T., & Nelson, R. Effect of false heartrate feedback on avoidance behavior: An investigation of "cognitive desensitization." *Behavior Therapy,* 1972, *3,* 1-6.

Kiesler, C. A. *The psychology of commitment.* New York: Academic Press, 1971.

Kiesler, C. A., Nisbett, R. E., & Zanna, M. On inferring one's beliefs from one's behavior. *Journal of Personality and Social Psychology,* 1969, *11,* 321-327.

Kiesler, C. A., & Sakumura, J. A test of a model for commitment. *Journal of Personality and Social Psychology,* 1966, *3,* 349-353.

Klemp, G. O., & Leventhal, H. Self-persuasion and fear reduction from escape behavior. In H. London & R. E. Nisbett (Eds.), *Cognitive alteration of feeling states.* Chicago: Aldine, 1972.

Kopel, S., & Arkowitz, H. Role-playing as a source of self-observation and behavior change. *Journal of Personality and Social Psychology,* 1974, *29,* 677-686.

Kruglanski, A. W., Alon, S., & Lewis, T. Retrospective misattribution and task enjoyment. *Journal of Experimental Social Psychology,* 1972, *8,* 493-501.

Kukla, A. Attributional determinants of achievement-related behavior. *Journal of Personality and Social Psychology,* 1972, *21,* 166-174.

Laing, R. D. *The divided self.* Baltimore: Penguin, 1965.

Laird, J. Self-attribution of emotion: The effects of expressive behavior on the quality of emotional experience. *Journal of Personality and Social Psychology,* 1974, *29,* 475–486.

Latané, B., & Darley, J. M. *The unresponsive bystander: Why doesn't he help?* New York: Appleton-Century-Crofts, 1970.

Lawrence, D. H., & Festinger. L. *Deterrents and reinforcement: The psychology of insufficient reward.* Stanford, Calif.: Stanford University Press, 1962.

Lazarus, A. A. *Behavior therapy and beyond.* New York: McGraw-Hill, 1971.

Leitenberg, H., Agras, W. S., Thompson, L. E., & Wright, D. E. Feedback in behavior modification: An experimental analysis in two phobic cases. *Journal of Applied Behavior Analysis,* 1968, *1,* 131–137.

Lepper, M. Dissonance, self-perception and honesty in children. *Journal of Personality and Social Psychology,* 1973, *25,* 65–79.

Lepper, M., Greene, D., & Nisbett, R. E. Undermining children's intrinsic interest with extrinsic rewards: A test of the overjustification hypothesis. *Journal of Personality and Social Psychology,* 1973, *28,* 129–137.

Lepper, M., Zanna, M., & Abelson, R. Cognitive irreversibility in a dissonance reduction situation. *Journal of Personality and Social Psychology,* 1970, *16,* 191–198.

Lerner, M. J. Observer's evaluation of a victim: Justice, guilt and veridical perception. *Journal of Personality and Social Psychology,* 1971, *20,* 127–135.

Lerner, M. J., & Matthews, G. Reactions to suffering of others under conditions of indirect responsibility. *Journal of Personality and Social Psychology,* 1967, *5,* 319–325.

Lerner, M. J., & Simmons, C. H. Observer's reaction to the "innocent victim": Compassion or rejection? *Journal of Personality and Social Psychology,* 1966, *4,* 203–210.

Leventhal, G. S. The distribution of rewards and resources in groups and organizations. In E. Walster & L. Berkowitz (Eds.), *Advances in experimental social psychology* (Vol. 9). New York: Academic Press, in press.

Levy, L. H. *Psychological interpretation.* New York: Holt, Rinehart and Winston, 1963.

Liebling, B. A., Seiler, M., & Shaver, P. Self-awareness and cigarette-smoking. *Journal of Experimental Social Psychology,* 1974, *10,* 325–332.

Liebling, B. A., & Shaver, P. Evaluation, self-awareness and task performance. *Journal of Experimental Social Psychology,* 1973, *9,* 297–306.

Linder, D. E., Cooper, J., & Jones, E. E. Decision freedom as a determinant of the role of incentive magnitude in attitude change. *Journal of Personality and Social Psychology,* 1967, *6,* 245–254.

Linder, D. E., Cooper, J., & Wicklund, R. A. Pre-exposure persuasion as a result of commitment to pre-exposure effort. *Journal of Experimental Social Psychology,* 1968, *4,* 470–482.

Linder, D. E., & Crane, K. A. Reactance theory analysis of predecisional cognitive processes. *Journal of Personality and Social Psychology,* 1970, *15,* 258–264.

Linder, D. E., & Worchel, S. Opinion change as a result of effortfully drawing a counterattitudinal conclusion. *Journal of Experimental Social Psychology,* 1970, *6,* 432–448.

Linder, D. E., Wortman, C. B., & Brehm, J. W. Temporal changes in predecision preferences among choice alternatives. *Journal of Personality and Social Psychology,* 1971, *19,* 282–284.

Lindner, R. *The fifty-minute hour.* Toronto: Clarke, Irwin, 1954.

Lindzey, G., & Aronson, E. (Eds.). *The handbook of social psychology* (2nd ed., 5 vols.). Reading, Mass.: Addison-Wesley, 1968.

London, P. The end of ideology in behavior modification. *American Psychologist,* 1972, *27,* 913–920.

Lowin, A., & Esptein, G. Does expectancy determine performance? *Journal of Experimental Social Psychology,* 1965, *1,* 248–255.

Macaulay, J., & Berkowitz, L. *Altruism and helping behavior.* New York: Academic Press, 1970.

Madsen, C. K., & Madsen, C. H. *Parents/children/discipline: A positive approach.* Boston: Allyn & Bacon, 1972.

Malewski, A. The influence of positive and negative self-evaluation on post-decisional dissonance. *Polish Sociological Bulletin,* 1967, *3–4,* 39–49.

Mansson, H. H. The cognitive control of thirst motivation: A dissonance approach. Unpublished doctoral dissertation, New York University, 1965.

Marecek, J., & Mettee, D. R. Avoidance of continued success as a function of self-esteem, level of esteem certainty and responsibility for success. *Journal of Personality and Social Psychology,* 1972, *22,* 98–107.

Marlowe, D., Frager, R., & Nuttall, R. Commitment to action taken as a consequence of cognitive dissonance. *Journal of Personality and Social Psychology,* 1965, *2,* 864–868.

McMahan, I. Relationships between causal attributions and expectancy of success. *Journal of Personality and Social Psychology,* 1973, *28,* 108–114.

Menninger, K. *Theory of psychoanalytic technique.* New York: Harper & Row, 1964.

Middlebrook, P. *Social psychology and modern life.* New York: Knopf, 1974.

Mills, J. Changes in moral attitudes following temptation. *Journal of Personality,* 1958, *26,* 517–531.

Moses, M., & Marcia, J. Performance decrement as a function of positive feedback: Self-defeating behavior. *Journal of Social Psychology,* 1969, *77,* 259–267.

Muir, W. K., *Prayer in the public schools.* Chicago: University of Chicago Press, 1967.

Murray, H. The effect of fear upon estimates of the maliciousness of other personalities. *Journal of Social Psychology,* 1933, *4,* 310–329.

Murray, H. *Explorations in personality.* New York: Wiley, 1962.

Nel, E., Helmreich, R. L., & Aronson, E. Opinion change in the advocate as a function of the persuasibility of his audience: A clarification of the meaning of dissonance. *Journal of Personality and Social Psychology,* 1969, *12,* 117–124.

Newtson, D. Attribution and the unit of perception of ongoing behavior. *Journal of Personality and Social Psychology,* 1973, *28,* 28–38.

Nezlek, J., & Brehm, J. W. Hostility as a function of the opportunity to counteraggress. *Journal of Personality,* 1975, *43,* 421–433.

Nisbett, R. E., Caputo, D., Legant, P., & Marecek, J. Behavior as seen by the actor and as seen by the observer. *Journal of Personality and Social Psychology,* 1973, *27,* 154–164.

Nisbett, R. E., & Schachter, S. Cognitive manipulation of pain. *Journal of Experimental Social Psychology,* 1966, *2,* 227–236.

Notz, W. W., Staw, B. M., & Cook, T. O. Attitude toward troop withdrawal from Indochina as a function of draft number: Dissonance or self-interest? *Journal of Personality and Social Psychology,* 1971, *20,* 118–126.

Osgood, C. E., & Tannenbaum, P. H. The principle of congruity in the prediction of attitude change. *Psychological Review,* 1955, *62,* 42–55.

Ostfeld, B., & Katz, P. A. The effect of threat severity in children of varying socioeconomic levels. *Developmental Psychology,* 1969, *1,* 205–210.

Pallak, M. S., & Heller, J. F. Interactive effects of commitment to future interaction and threat to attitudinal freedom. *Journal of Personality and Social Psychology,* 1971, *17,* 325–331.

Pallak, M. S., Sogin, S. R., & Van Zante, A. Bad decisions: The effect of volition, locus of causality and negative consequences on attitude change. *Journal of Personality and Social Psychology*, 1974, *30*, 217-227.

Paul, G. *Insight versus desensitization in psychotherapy*. Stanford, Calif.: Stanford University Press, 1966.

Pepitone, A., McCauley, C., & Hammond, P. Change in attractiveness of forbidden toys as a function of severity of threat. *Journal of Experimental Social Psychology*, 1967, *3*, 221-229.

Rabbie, J. M., Brehm, J. W., & Cohen, A. R. Verbalization and reactions to cognitive dissonance. *Journal of Personality*, 1959, *27*, 407-417.

Raven, B. R., & Fishbein, M. Acceptance of punishment and change in belief. *Journal of Abnormal and Social Psychology*, 1961, *63*, 411-416.

Rest, S., Nierenberg, R., Weiner, B., & Heckhausen, H. Further evidence concerning the effects of perceptions of effort and ability on achievement evaluation. *Journal of Personality and Social Psychology*, 1973, *28*, 187-191.

Rosen, G. M., Rosen, E., & Reid, J. B. Cognitive desensitization and avoidance behavior: A reevaluation. *Journal of Abnormal Psychology*, 1972, *80*, 176-182.

Rosen, S. Post-decision affinity for incompatible information. *Journal of Abnormal and Social Psychology*, 1961, *63*, 188-190.

Ross, L., Bierbrauer, R., & Polly, S. Attribution of educational outcomes by professional and nonprofessional instructors. *Journal of Personality and Social Psychology*, 1974, *29*, 609-618.

Ross, L., Rodin, J., & Zimbardo, P. G. Toward an attribution therapy: The reduction of fear through induced cognitive-emotional misattribution. *Journal of Personality and Social Psychology*, 1969, *12*, 279-288.

Ross, M., & Shulman, R. Increasing the salience of initial attitudes: Dissonance versus self-perception theory. *Journal of Personality and Social Psychology*, 1973, *28*, 138-144.

Rotter, J. B. Generalized expectancies for internal versus external control of reinforcement. *Psychological Monographs*, 1966, *80* (1, Whole No. 609).

Rutner, I. The effects of feedback and instructions on phobic behavior. *Behavior Therapy*, 1973, *4*, 338-348.

Sarnoff, I. *Testing Freudian concepts*. New York: Springer, 1971.

Schachter, S., & Singer, J. E. Cognitive, social and physiological determinants of emotional state. *Psychological Review*, 1962, *69*, 379-399.

Schachter, S., & Wheeler, L. Epinephrine, chlorpromazine and amusement. *Journal of Abnormal and Social Psychology*, 1962, *65*, 121–128.

Scheier, M. F., Fenigstein, A., & Buss, A. Self awareness and physical aggression. *Journal of Experimental Social Psychology*, 1974, *10*, 264–273.

Schiffenbauer, A. Effect of observer's emotional state on judgments of the emotional state of others. *Journal of Personality and Social Psychology*, 1974, *30*, 31–35.

Schlachet, P. J. The effect of dissonance arousal on the recall of failure stimuli. *Journal of Personality*, 1965, *33*, 443–461.

Schopler, J., & Layton, B. Determinants of the self-attribution of having influenced another person. *Journal of Personality and Social Psychology*, 1972, *22*, 326–332.

Schopler, J., & Matthews, M. The influence of the perceived causal locus of partner's dependence on the use of interpersonal power. *Journal of Personality and Social Psychology*, 1965, *2*, 609–612.

Schwartz, S. H. Elicitation of moral obligation and self-sacrificing behavior: An experimental study of volunteering to be a bone-marrow donor. *Journal of Personality and Social Psychology*, 1970, *15*, 283–293.

Secord, P., & Backman, C. *Social psychology.* New York: McGraw-Hill, 1974.

Seligman, M. E. P. Depression and learned helplessness. In R. J. Friedman & M. M. Katz (Eds.), *The psychology of depression.* Washington, D.C.: Hemisphere, 1974.

Shapiro, D. *Neurotic styles.* New York: Basic Books, 1965.

Shaver, K. Defensive attribution: Effects of severity and relevance on the responsibility assigned for an accident. *Journal of Personality and Social Psychology*, 1970, *14*, 101–113.

Shaver, K. *An introduction to attribution processes.* Cambridge, Mass.: Winthrop, 1975.

Shaw, J., & Skolnick, P. Attribution of responsibility for a happy accident. *Journal of Personality and Social Psychology*, 1971, *18*, 380–383.

Sherman, S. J. Attitudinal effects of unforeseen consequences. *Journal of Personality and Social Psychology*, 1970, *16*, 510–519. (a)

Sherman, S. J. Effects of choice and incentive on attitude change in a discrepant behavior situation. *Journal of Personality and Social Psychology*, 1970, *15*, 245–256. (b)

Silverman, I., & Marcantonio, C. Demand characteristics versus dissonance reduction as determinants of failure-seeking behavior. *Journal of Personality and Social Psychology*, 1965, *2*, 882–884.

Skinner, B. F., *Verbal behavior*. New York: Appleton-Century-Crofts, 1957.

Smith, E. E. The power of dissonance techniques to change attitudes. *Public Opinion Quarterly*, 1961, *25*, 626-639.

Snyder, Mark, & Ebbesen, E. Dissonance awareness: A test of dissonance theory versus self-perception theory. *Journal of Experimental Social Psychology*, 1972, *8*, 502-517.

Snyder, Melvin, & Jones, E. E. Attitude attribution when behavior is constrained. *Journal of Experimental Social Psychology*, 1974, *10*, 585-600.

Snyder, Melvin, Schulz, R., & Jones, E. E. Expectancy and apparent duration as determinants of fatigue. *Journal of Personality and Social Psychology*, 1974, *29*, 426-434.

Sorrentino, R., & Boutilier, R. Evaluation of a victim as a function of fate similarity/dissimilarity. *Journal of Experimental Social Psychology*, 1974, *10*, 84-93.

Steiner, I. D., & Rogers, E. D. Alternative responses to dissonance. *Journal of Abnormal Social Psychology*, 1963, *66*, 128-136.

Stokols, D., & Schopler, J. Reactions to victims under conditions of situational detachment: The effects of responsibility, severity and expected future interaction. *Journal of Personality and Social Psychology*, 1973, *25*, 199-209.

Storms, M. Videotape and the attribution process: Reversing actors' and observers' points of view. *Journal of Personality and Social Psychology*, 1973, *27*, 165-175.

Storms, M., & Nisbett, R. E. Insomnia and the attribution process. *Journal of Personality and Social Psychology*, 1970, *16*, 319-328.

Streufert, S., & Streufert, S. C. Effects of conceptual structure, failure and success on attribution of causality and interpersonal attitudes. *Journal of Personality and Social Psychology*, 1969, *11*, 138-147.

Sullivan, D. S., & Deiker, T. E. Subject-experimenter perceptions of ethical issues in human research. *American Psychologist*, 1973, *28*, 587-591.

Sushinsky, L. S., & Bootzin, R. R. Cognitive desensitization as a model of systematic desensitization. *Behavior Research and Therapy*, 1970, *8*, 29-34.

Tedeschi, J., Schlenker, B., & Bonoma, T. Cognitive dissonance: Private ratiocination or public spectacle? *American Psychologist*, 1971, *26*, 685-695.

Tessler, R., & Schwartz, S. Help-seeking, self-esteem and achievement motivation: An attributional analysis. *Journal of Personality and Social Psychology*, 1972, *21*, 318-326.

Thompson, D. Attributions of ability from patterns of performance under competitive and cooperative conditions. *Journal of Personality and Social Psychology,* 1972, *23,* 302–308.

Thoresen, C. E., & Mahoney, M. J. *Behavioral self-control.* New York: Holt, Rinehart and Winston, 1974.

Turner, E. A., & Wright, J. Effects of severity of threat and perceived availability on the attractiveness of objects. *Journal of Personality and Social Psychology,* 1965, *2,* 128–132.

Valins, S. Cognitive effects of false heart-rate feedback. *Journal of Personality and Social Psychology,* 1966, *4,* 400–408.

Valins, S., & Nisbett, R. E. *Attribution processes in the development and treatment of emotional disorders.* Morristown, N.J.: General Learning Press, 1971.

Valins, S., & Ray, A. Effects of cognitive desensitization on avoidance behavior. *Journal of Personality and Social Psychology,* 1967, *7,* 345–350.

Walster, E. Assignment of responsibility for an accident. *Journal of Personality and Social Psychology,* 1966, *3,* 73–79.

Walster, E. "Second-guessing" important events. *Human relations,* 1967, *20,* 239–250.

Ward, W., & Sandvold, K. Performance expectancy as a determinant of actual performance: A partial replication. *Journal of Abnormal and Social Psychology,* 1963, *67,* 293–295.

Waterman, A., & Ford, L. Performance expectancy as a determinant of actual performance: Dissonance reduction or differential recall? *Journal of Personality and Social Psychology,* 1965, *2,* 464–467.

Watts, W. A. Commitment under conditions of risk. *Journal of Personality and Social Psychology,* 1966, *3,* 507–515.

Weik, K. E. Reduction of cognitive dissonance through task enhancement and effort expenditure. *Journal of Abnormal and Social Psychology,* 1964, *68,* 533–539.

Weiner, B. *Theories of motivation.* Chicago: Markham Press, 1972.

Weiner, B., Frieze, I., Kukla, A., Reed, L., Rest, S., & Rosenbaum, R. *Perceiving the causes of success and failure.* Morristown, N.J.: General Learning Press, 1971.

Weiner, B., Heckhausen, H., Meyer, W.-U., & Cook, R. Causal ascriptions and achievement behavior: Conceptual analysis of effort and reanalysis of locus of control. *Journal of Personality and Social Psychology,* 1972, *21,* 239–248.

Weiner, B., & Kukla, A. An attributional analysis of achievement motivation. *Journal of Personality and Social Psychology,* 1970, *15,* 1–20.

White, R. H. *The abnormal personality* (3rd ed.). New York: Ronald Press, 1964.

Wicklund, R. A. *Freedom and reactance.* Hillsdale, N.J.: Lawrence Erlbaum Associates, 1974.

Wicklund, R. A. Discrepancy reduction or attempted distraction? A reply to Liebling, Seiler and Shaver. *Journal of Experimental Social Psychology,* 1975, *11,* 78–81.

Wicklund, R. A. Objective self awareness. In L. Berkowitz (Ed.), *Advances in experimental social psychology* (Vol. 8). New York: Academic Press, 1975.

Wicklund, R. A., & Brehm, J. W. Attitude change as a function of felt competence and threat to attitudinal freedom. *Journal of Experimental Social Psychology,* 1968, *4,* 64–75.

Wicklund, R. A., & Brehm, J. W. *Perspectives on cognitive dissonance.* Hillsdale, N.J.: Lawrence Eslbaum Associates, in press.

Wicklund, R. A., Cooper, J., & Linder, D. E. Effects of expected effort on attitude change prior to exposure. *Journal of Experimental Social Psychology,* 1967, *3,* 416–428.

Wicklund, R. A., & Duval, S. Opinion change and performance facilitation as a result of objective self-awareness. *Journal of Experimental Social Psychology,* 1971, *7,* 319–342.

Wicklund, R. A., & Slattum, V., & Solomon, E. Effects of implied pressure toward commitment on ratings of choice alternatives. *Journal of Experimental Social Psychology,* 1970, *6,* 449–457.

Willis, J. A., & Goethals, G. R. Social responsibility and threat to behavioral freedom as determinants of altruistic behavior. *Journal of Personality,* 1973, *41,* 376–384.

Wolitzky, D. L. Cognitive control and cognitive dissonance. *Journal of Personality and Social Psychology,* 1967, *5,* 486–490.

Worchel, S. The effects of films on the importance of behavioral freedom. *Journal of Personality,* 1972, *40,* 417–435.

Worchel, S. The effect of three types of arbitrary thwarting on the instigation to aggression. *Journal of Personality,* 1974, *42,* 300–318.

Worchel, S., & Andreoli, V. A. Attribution of causality as a means of restoring behavioral freedom. *Journal of Personality and Social Psychology,* 1974, *29,* 237–245.

Worchel, S., & Brand, J. Role of responsibility and violated expectancy in the arousal of dissonance. *Journal of Personality and Social Psychology,* 1972, *22,* 87–97.

Worchel, S., & Brehm, J. W. Effect of threats to attitudinal freedom as a function of agreement with the communicator. *Journal of Personality and Social Psychology,* 1970, *14,* 18–22.

Worchel, S., & Brehm, J. W. Direct and implied social restoration of freedom. *Journal of Personality and Social Psychology,* 1971, *18,* 294–304.

Wortman, C. B., & Brehm, J. W. Responses to uncontrollable outcomes: An integration of reactance theory and the learned helplessness model. In L. Berkowitz (Ed.), *Advances in experimental social psychology*, (Vol. 8). New York: Academic Press, 1975.

Wortman, C. B., Costanzo, P., & Witt, T. Effect of anticipated performance on the attribution of causality to self and others. *Journal of Personality and Social Psychology*, 1973, *27*, 372–381.

Wylie, R. C. The present status of self theory. In E. Borgatta & W. Lambert (Eds.), *Handbook of personality theory and research.* Chicago: Rand McNally, 1968.

Yaryan, R. B., & Festinger, L. Preparatory action and belief in the probable occurrence of future events. *Journal of Abnormal and Social Psychology*, 1961, *63*, 603–606.

Zanna, M., & Cooper, J. Dissonance and the pill: An attribution approach to studying the arousal properties of dissonance. *Journal of Personality and Social Psychology*, 1974, *29*, 705–709.

Zanna, M., Lepper, M., & Abelson, R. Attentional mechanisms in children's devaluation of a forbidden activity in a forced compliance situation. *Journal of Personality and Social Psychology*, 1973, *28*, 355–359.

Zimbardo, P. G. Involvement and communication discrepancy as determinants of opinion conformity. *Journal of Abnormal and Social Psychology*, 1960, *60*, 89–94.

Zimbardo, P. G. The effect of effort and improvisation on self-persuasion produced by role-playing. *Journal of Experimental Social Psychology*, 1965, *1*, 103–120.

Zimbardo, P. G. *The cognitive control of motivation.* Glenview, Ill.: Scott, Foresman, 1969.

Zimbardo, P. G., & Ebbesen, E. B. Experimental modification of the relationship between effort, attitudes and behavior. *Journal of Personality and Social Psychology*, 1970, *16*, 207–213.

Zimbardo, P. G., Weisenberg, M., Firestone, I., & Levy, B. Communicator effectiveness in producing public conformity and private attitude change. *Journal of Personality*, 1965, *33*, 233–256.

AUTHOR INDEX

Urban, H. B., 145, 158, *246*

Valins, S., 160, 161, 162, 163, 166, 168, 170, 196, *245, 258*
Van Zante, A., 93, 101, *255*
Varella, J. A., *238*

Walster, E., 178, *258*
Walters, R. H., 79, *240*
Ward, L., 189, *250*
Ward, W., 139, *258*
Ware, R., 137, *249*
Waterman, A., 139, *258*
Watts, W. A., 99, 108, *247, 258*
Weiby, M., 188, *250*
Weik, K. E., 106, *258*
Weiner, B., 37, 188, 196, *255, 258*
Weisenberg, M., 96, *260*
Wheeler, L., 160, *256*
White, R. H., 199, *258*

Wicklund, R. A., 20, 37, 38, 39, 57, *63,* 75, 104, 105, 107, 121, 123, *142,* 204, 205, 206, 207, 208, 209, 210, *221, 242, 245, 249, 253, 259*
Wilson, G. T., 161, *251*
Witt, T., 189, 190, *260*
Worchel, S., 20, 22, 38, 56, 58, 59, 61, 98, 101, 104, 180, 210, *239, 244, 250, 253, 259*
Wortman, C. B., 57, 190, *222, 253, 260*
Wright, D. E., 129, *252*
Wright, J., 94, *258*
Wylie, R. C., 204, *260*

Yaryan, R. B., 105, *260*

Zanna, M., 94, 100, 107, 153, 165, 167, 172, *251, 252, 260*
Zimbardo, P. G., 96, 97, 104, 116, 117, 126, 136, 138, *142,* 164, 167, 169, *255, 260*

SUBJECT INDEX